A DICTIONARY OF ECONOMIC QUOTATIONS

A Dictionary of Economic Quotations

Compiled by Simon James

CROOM HELM LONDON

BARNES & NOBLE BOOKS
TOTOWA, NEW JERSEY

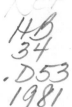

Croom Helm Ltd, 2–10 St John's Road, London SW11

British Library Cataloguing in Publication Data

James, Simon
    A dictionary of economic quotations.
    1. Quotations, English
    2. Economics - Quotations, maxims, etc.
    I. Title
    828'.02   PN6084.E/

    ISBN 0-85664-617-2

First published in the USA 1981 by
Barnes & Noble Books
81 Adams Drive,
Totowa, New Jersey, 07512
Library of Congress Cataloging in Publication Data
Main entry under title:

A Dictionary of economic quotations.

    Bibliography: p.
    Includes indexes.
    1. Economics - Quotations, maxims, etc. I. James,
Simon R.
HB34.D53   1981   330'.03'21   81-6632
ISBN 0-389-20230-4   (Barnes & Noble) AACR2

Printed and bound in Great Britain
by Billing and Sons Limited
Guildford, London, Oxford, Worcester

CONTENTS

There is no book so bad as not to
have something good in it.

Miguel De Cervantes (1547-1616)
Don Quixote, Ch. LIX

LIST OF TOPICS

PREFACE

This book began as a small personal collection of quotations which grew steadily over the years. As well as many topics on economics, defined in a fairly broad sense, there are also quotations from the related areas of economic history, law, mathematics, politics and statistics.

The quotations are arranged by topic, a list of which appears on p. ix. The allocation of quotations is sometimes rather arbitrary, since quotations often refer to more than one topic, but the index of key words should enable the reader to trace a particular quotation without too much difficulty.

The key word index gives a two figure reference for each quotation in which the key word plays an important part. The first figure refers to the topic and the second to the quotation itself. A part (or sometimes all) of the quotation is also given to indicate the context. For example, one entry under 'value' reads: 'market is the best judge of v. 83.2'. This refers to the second quotation appearing under the 83rd topic, which is Markets. Within each topic, the quotations are arranged alphabetically by author or source.

The index of authors and sources appears at the end of the book, not because it is in any sense less important than the word index, but to make it slightly easier to find.

Although consistency in the presentation of the quotations has an elegant simplicity, fuller references are given where it seemed appropriate, mainly where a frequently quoted work has appeared in a number of editions. In addition, while dates of birth and death have been given wherever possible for deceased authors, no attempt has been made to provide the dates of birth for living persons.

The collection has no pretensions about being complete — that would have taken a lifetime, even supposing it could have been done at all. However, there are some obvious gaps. One in particular is the relative scarcity of contributions from contemporary writers — perhaps partly because individuals tend to quote from established sources.

Nevertheless, suggestions for a later edition would be very welcome and are actively solicited. They should be sent to myself at the Department of Economics, University of Exeter, Exeter, EX4 4RJ, England.

So many people have helped in one way or another in the production of this volume that it is quite impractical to mention them all. Even so, particular thanks are due to quite a number of people. I am very grateful for the extensive assistance provided by the staff of the British Library of Political and Economic Science and the staff of the University of Exeter Library. Krystyna Grycuk gave a great deal of general help in collecting, sorting, checking and indexing the quotations. Mr S.L. Heasell and Professor R.H. Parker read through the whole collection and offered many valuable comments and suggestions. A number of useful suggestions were also made by Mr R. Bartlett, Mrs Jane Black, David Blake, Peter Dolton, Dr H.E.S. Fisher, Mrs A. Hardie, Mr F.M.M. Lewes, Dr R.A. Lewis, Dr F.V. Meyer, David de Meza, John Micklewright, Christopher Nobes, Dr F.R. Oliver, and Dr J.H. Porter. Marion Bradford cheerfully converted piles of index cards into typescript, assisted occasionally by Vi Palfrey and Melanie Hall, and Fiona Charlton checked some of the quotations. To everyone who helped, many thanks.

Finally, in checking quotations, it soon becomes clear that errors can creep in with alarming ease. I hope there are very few in the following pages.

Simon James
University of Exeter

1. ADVERTISING

1. Advertising is a necessary consequence of sale by description.
   - Anonymous

2. The advertisements in a newspaper are more full of knowledge in respect to what is going
   on in a state or community than
   the editorial columns are.
   - Henry Ward Beecher
     (1813-87)
     *Proverbs from Plymouth
     Pulpit*

3. Doing business without advertising is like winking at a girl in the
   dark. You know what you are
   doing, but nobody else does.
   - Steuart Henderson Britt
     Attributed

4. It is not necessary to advertise
   food to hungry people, fuel to
   cold people, or houses to the
   homeless.
   - J.K. Galbraith
     American Capitalism, 1957,
     Ch. 8

5. Puffing [advertising] is of
   various sorts; the principal are,
   the puff direct, the puff preliminary, the puff collateral, the
   puff collusive, and the puff
   oblique, or puff by implication.
   - Richard Brinsley Sheridan
     (1751-1816)
     The Critic, Act I

2. AGRICULTURE

1. The agricultural class is the least
   of all disposed to innovation,

and the most peculiarly attached
to ancient customs and routine.
- J.R. McCulloch (1789-1864)
  *Principles of Political
  Economy*, new ed., Pt. III,
  Ch. VI, p. 463.

2. American farm leaders are
   correct in arguing that our
   agriculture still must look
   forward to a definite 'surplus'
   problem. What they tend to
   overlook, however, is of what
   our 'surplus' consists. Funda-
   mentally America's long-term
   agricultural problem is not one
   of 'surplus' cotton, wheat or
   grapefruit. Rather it is one of
   'surplus' farmers.
   - William H. Nicholls
     Quoted in P.A. Samuelson,
     Economics, 8th ed.

3. He, [the farmer] more than any
   other class of the community is
   benefited by the depreciation of
   money, and injured by the
   increase of its value.
   - David Ricardo (1772-1823)
     Works, ed. Sraffa, Vol. III,
     pp. 136-7.

4. While agriculture prospers all
   other arts alike are vigorous and
   strong, but where the land is
   forced to remain desert, the
   spring that feeds the other arts
   is dried up.
   - Xenophon (c.440-c.355 B.C.)
     The Economist, trans.
     Dakyns, Ch. V

3. ALTRUISM

1. The desire of power in excess

15

caused the angels to fall; the desire of knowledge in excess caused man to fall; but in charity there is no excess; neither angel nor man come in danger by it.
- Francis Bacon (1561-1626)
  Essays, XIII, *Of Goodness and Goodness of Nature*

2. It is more blessed to give than to receive.
   - *Bible*, Authorised Version *Acts*, Ch. 20, v. 35

3. Philanthropist, *n*. A rich (and usually bald) old gentleman who has trained himself to grin while his conscience is picking his pocket.
   - Ambrose Bierce (1842-1914?)
     The Devil's Dictionary

4. The selection of presents for children is never easy, because in order to extract real pleasure from the purchase, it is necessary to find something that excites the donor as much as it is likely to excite the recipient.
   - Sir Compton Mackenzie (1883-1972)
     Poor Relations, 3

5. Do not do unto others as you would that they should do unto you. Their tastes may not be the same.
   - George Bernard Shaw (1856-1950)
     Maxims for Revolutionists

6. He who gives money he has not earned is generous with other people's labour.

- George Bernard Shaw (1856-1950)
  Ibid.

7. No benevolent man ever lost altogether the fruits of his benevolence.
   - Adam Smith (1723-90)
     The Theory of Moral Sentiments, 1759, Pt. VI, Sec. II, Ch. I

8. Our charity begins at home, And mostly ends where it begins.
   - Horace Smith (1779-1849)
     Horace in London, Bk. II, Ode 15

4. AVARICE

1. The avarice of mankind is insatiable.
   - Aristotle (384-322 B.C.)
     Politics, trans. B. Jowett, Bk. II, Ch. 7, 1267a

2. Nothing satisfies the man who is not satisfied with a little.
   - Epicurus (341-270 B.C.)
     The Extant Remains, trans. C. Bailey, p. 137

3. The world has enough for everyone's need, but not enough for everyone's greed.
   - Mahatma Gandhi (1869-1948)
     Attributed

4. None of the most furious excesses of love and ambition are, in any respect, to be compared to the extremes of avarice.
   - David Hume (1711-76)
     Essays, Of Avarice

5. The retainers of Avarice shall
   bury and conceal their riches,
   and thereby restore to the earth
   what they take from her.
   — David Hume (1711-76)
   Ibid.

6. Avarice, the spur of industry.
   — David Hume (1711-76)
   Ibid., *Of Civil Liberty. See
   also* 4.9

7. Nothing but the impossibility of
   general combination protects
   the public wealth against the
   rapacity of private avarice.
   — James Maitland (1759-1839)
   *An Inquiry Into the Nature
   and Origin of Public Wealth*,
   1804, Ch. II, p. 54.

8. The root of Evil, Avarice,
   That damn'd ill-natur'd, baneful
       Vice,
   Was Slave to Prodigality,
   That noble Sin; whilst Luxury
   Employed a Million of the Poor,
   And odious Pride a Million
       more:
   Envy itself, and Vanity,
   Were Ministers of Industry;
   Their darling Folly, Fickleness,
   In Diet, Furniture, and Dress
   That strange ridic'lous Vice, was
       made
   That very Wheel that turned the
       Trade
   — Bernard de Mandeville
   (1670-1733)
   The Fable of the Bees or
   *Private Vices, Publick
   Benefits*, 2nd ed., 1723, p. 10

9. The main spur to trade, or
   rather to industry and ingenuity,
   is the exorbitant appetites of

men, which they will take pains
to gratifie, and so be disposed to
work, when nothing else will
incline them to it; for did men
content themselves with bare
necessaries, we should have a
poor world.
   — Sir Dudley North (1641-91)
   Discourses upon Trade,
   1691, p. 14

10. Poverty wants much; but avarice,
    everything.
    — Publilius Syrus (*fl.* 1st
    century, B.C.)
    Attributed

5. BANKING

1. A banker is a man who lends
   you an umbrella when the
   weather is fair, and takes it
   away from you when it rains.
   — Anonymous

2. Banking is the smelting of
   capital.
   — Anonymous

3. If you can pay me, I don't want
   it; but if you can't, I do.
   — Anonymous, bank customer

4. A large bank always tends to
   become larger and a small bank
   to become smaller.
   — Walter Bagehot (1826-77)
   Quoted in J.A. Hobson,
   *The Evolution of Modern
   Capitalism*

5. The Old Lady of Threadneedle
   Street.
   — James Gilray (1757-1815)
   Title of a cartoon, 1797

6. A 'sound' banker, alas! is not one who foresees danger and avoids it, but one who, when he is ruined, is ruined in a conventional and orthodox way along with his fellows, so that no one can really blame him.
   - John Maynard Keynes (1883-1946)
   'The Consequences to the Banks of the Collapse of Money Values', in *Essays in Persuasion*, 1933, Pt. II, p. 176

7. One rule which woe betides the banker who fails to heed it, . . . Never lend money to anybody unless they don't need it.
   - Ogden Nash (1902-71)
   Attributed

8. There have been three great inventions since the beginning of time: fire, the wheel, and central banking.
   - Will Rogers (1879-1935)
   Quoted in P.A. Samuelson, *Economics*

9. Whereas in Russia the coercive machinery is represented by the GPU with its rifles and dungeons, in capitalism it is represented by the banking system with its cheques and overdrafts.
   - Wilhelm Röpke (1899-1966)
   Crises and Cycles, 1936, p. 107

10. The judicious operations of banking, by substituting paper in the room of a great part of this gold and silver, enables the country to convert a great part of this dead stock into active and productive stock.
    - Adam Smith (1723-90)
    Wealth of Nations, ed. Cannan, Vol. I, Bk. II, Ch. II, p. 304

6. BARGAINS

1. The theory of the modern bargain appears to be that of the mediaeval judicial combat: let each do his worst, and God will protect the right.
   - John Bates Clark (1847-1938)
   Philosophy of Wealth, 1887, Ch. IX, p. 159

2. What is ordinarily termed a good bargain is, morally, a bad bargain.
   - John Bates Clark (1847-1938)
   Ibid., p. 162

3. Here's the rule for bargains 'Do other men, for they would do you'.
   - Charles Dickens (1812-70)
   Martin Chuzzlewit, Ch. 11

4. Necessity never made a good bargain.
   - Benjamin Franklin (1706-90)
   Poor Richard's Almanac, 1735

5. Good bargains are pick-pockets.
   - Proverb, in Thomas Fuller
   Gnomologia, 1732, 1701

6. Make every bargain clear and plain, That none may afterward complain.
   - Proverb, in John Ray, *English Proverbs*, 1670

7. I'll give thrice so much land To any well-deserving friend; But in the way of a bargain,

mark ye me,
I'll cavil on the ninth part of a
    hair.
– William Shakespeare
    (1564-1616)
    King Henry IV, Pt. I, Act III

7. BORROWING

1. If you would know the value of
    money, go and try to borrow
    some; for he that goes
    a-borrowing goes a-sorrowing.
    – Benjamin Franklin
        (1706-90)
        Poor Richard's Almanac,
        1754

2. There can be no doubt that it is
    a rule of borrowing and lending
    that *to him that hath shall be
    lent*.
    – J.R. Hicks
        The Social Framework,
        1942, Pt. III, Ch. IX.

3. The human species, according to
    the best theory I can form of it,
    is composed of two distinct
    races, *the men who borrow*, and
    the men who lend.
    – Charles Lamb (1775-1834)
        *Essays of Elia, The Two Races
        of Men*

4. Neither a borrower nor a lender
    be;
    For loan oft loses both itself
        and friend,
    And borrowing dulls the edge of
        husbandry.
    – William Shakespeare
        (1564-1616)
        Hamlet, Act I, Sc. III

5. Who goeth a borrowing
    Goeth a sorrowing.
    Few lend (but fools)
    Their working tools.
    – Thomas Tusser (1524?-80)
        *Five Hundred Points of
        Good Husbandry*, 'September's Abstract'

6. Let us all be happy, and live
    within our means, even if we
    have to borrer the money to do
    it with.
    – Artemus Ward (1834-67)
        Science and Natural History

8. BUREAUCRACY

1. Life is full of special cases.
    – Anonymous

2. This island is almost made of
    coal and surrounded by fish.
    Only an organizing genius could
    produce a shortage of coal and fish
    in Great Britain at the same time.
    – Aneurin Bevan (1897-1960)
        Quoted in V. Brome,
        Aneurin Bevan, Ch. 12,
        p. 178

3. It is an undoubted truth, that
    the less one has to do, the less
    time one finds to do it in. One
    yawns, one procrastinates, one
    can do it when one will, and
    therefore one seldom does it
    at all.
    – Philip Dormer Stanhope,
        Earl of Chesterfield
        (1694-1773)
        Quoted by *Collins Gem
        Dictionary of Quotations*

4. It is not easy nowadays to

remember anything so contrary to all appearances as that officials are the servants of the public; and the official must try not to foster the illusion that it is the other way round.
— Sir Ernest Gowers
(1880-1966)
The Complete Plain Words,
Ch. 3

5. Substitute a functionary for an independent trader, and he finds himself precluded from doing anything which he cannot explain and defend, if called upon, to his official superior . . . There is a tendency for any official hierarchy to be limited to those decisions that can be readily communicated in language from one functionary to another.
— R.G. Hawtrey (1879-1971)
The Economic Problem,
1926, Ch. XXVIII,
pp. 339-40

6. Where distinction and rank is achieved almost exclusively by becoming a civil servant of the state . . . it is too much to expect that many will long prefer freedom to security.
— F.A. Hayek
The Road to Serfdom, 1944,
Ch. IX

7. You can cut any public expenditure except the Civil Service, those lads spent a hundred years learning to look after themselves.
— Sir Richard Marsh
Observer, Sayings of the Week, 19 September 1976

8. Work expands so as to fill the time available for its completion.
— C. Northcote Parkinson
Parkinson's Law

9. For this real or imagined overwork there are, broadly speaking, three possible remedies. He (A) may resign; he may ask to halve the work with a colleague called B; he may demand the assistance of two subordinates, to be called C and D. There is probably no instance, however, in history of A choosing any but the third alternative.
— C. Northcote Parkinson
Ibid.

10. The Law of Triviality. Briefly stated, it means that the time spent on any item of the agenda will be in inverse proportion to the sum involved.
— C. Northcote Parkinson
Ibid., 'High Finance'

11. *The Peter Principle*; In a hierarchy every employee tends to rise to his level of incompetence.
— Laurence J. Peter and
Raymond Hull
The Peter Principle, 1969,
Ch. I

12. In time, every post tends to be occupied by an employee who is incompetent to carry out its duties . . . Work is accomplished by those employees who have not yet reached their level of incompetence.
— Laurence J. Peter and
Raymond Hull
Ibid.

13. Bureaucracy is not an obstacle to democracy but an inevitable complement to it.
    - Joseph A. Schumpeter (1883-1950) *Capitalism, Socialism and Democracy*, Ch. XVIII, p. 206

14. The largest determining factor of the size and content of this year's budget is last year's budget.
    - Aaron Wildavsky *The Politics of the Budgetary Process*, 1964

9. BUSINESS

1. It is generally better to deal by speech than by letter; and by the mediation of a third man than by a man's self.
   - Francis Bacon (1561-1626) *Essays*, XLVII, *of Negotiating*

2. No man ever manages a legitimate business in this life without doing indirectly far more for other men than he is trying to do for himself.
   - Henry Ward Beecher (1813-87) *Proverbs from Plymouth Pulpit*

3. The maxim of the British people is 'Business as usual'.
   - Winston Churchill (1874-1965) Speech, 1914

4. Business repays men not only for their labours, but their fears.
   - John Bates Clark (1847-1938)

Quoted by F.Y. Edgeworth, *Papers relating to Political Economy*, 1925, Vol. I, p. 24

5. The business of America is business.
   - Calvin Coolidge (1872-1933) Address before the Society of American Newspaper Editors, Washington, 17 January 1925

6. The uncertainty of life itself casts a shadow on every business transaction into which time enters.
   - Irving Fisher (1867-1947) *The Theory of Interest*, 1930, Ch. IX, p. 216

7. It is difficult but not impossible to conduct strictly honest business.
   - Mahatma Gandhi (1869-1948) *Non-violence in Peace and War*, 1948

8. To find men capable of managing business efficiently and secure to them the positions of responsible control is perhaps the most important single problem of economic organisation on the efficiency scale.
   - Frank H. Knight *Risk, Uncertainty and Profit*, 1921, p. 283

9. Boldness in business is the first, second and third thing.
   - Proverb, in Thomas Fuller, *Gnomologia*, 1732, 1006

10. Business is business.

— Proverb, 18th century

11. Business before pleasure.
    — Proverb, 19th century

12. Great businesses turn on a little pin.
    — Proverb, in George Herbert,
    Outlandish Proverbs, 1640

13. A dinner lubricates business.
    — William Scott (1745-1836)
    Quoted in *Boswell's Life of
    Johnson,* 1781

14. Wise business management, and
    more particularly what is spoken
    of as safe and sane business
    management. . .reduces itself in
    the main to a sagacious use of
    sabotage.
    — Thorstein Veblen (1857-1929)
    The Nature of Peace, 1919,
    Ch. VII, p. 325

15. Business is a game, the greatest
    game in the world if you know
    how to play it.
    — Thomas J. Watson, Sr.
    Attributed

16. What is good for the country is
    good for General Motors, and
    vice versa.
    — Charles E. Wilson (1890-1961)
    Statement to US Congression-
    al Committee, 1953

10 BUSINESS CYCLE

1. The modern world regards
   business cycles much as the
   ancient Egyptians regarded the
   overflowing of the Nile. The
   phenomenon recurs at intervals;
   it is of great importance to

everyone, and natural causes of
it are not in sight.
— John Bates Clark (1847-1938)
'Introduction' to K. Rodbertus
Overproduction and Crises,
1898, p.1

2. The trade cycle is a *purely*
   monetary phenomenon.
   — R.G. Hawtrey (1879-1971)
   Monetary Reconstruction,
   1923, Ch. VI, p. 141

3. [The cause of the] great commercial fluctuations. . .seems to
   lie in the varying proportion
   which the capital devoted to
   permanent and remote investment bears to that which is but
   temporarily invested soon to
   reproduce itself.
   — W. Stanley Jevons (1835-82)
   *Investigations in Currency
   and Finance,* 1884, II, Ch. I,
   pp. 27-8

4. I am perfectly convinced that
   these decennial crises do depend
   upon meteorological variations
   of like period, which again
   depend, in all probability, upon
   cosmic variations of which we
   have evidence in the frequency
   of sun-spots, auroras, and
   magnetic perturbations.
   — W. Stanley Jevons (1835-82)
   Ibid., VIII, pp. 235-6

5. Booms and slumps are simply the
   expression of the results of an
   oscillation of the terms of credit
   about their equilibrium position.
   — John Maynard Keynes
   (1883-1946)
   A Treatise on Money, 1930
   Vol. I, Bk. III, Ch. 12, p. 184

6. The frequent recurrence of
economic crises and depressions,
is evidence that the automatic
functioning of our business
system is defective.
    - Wesley Clair Mitchell
(1874-1948)
*The Backward Art of Spend-
ing Money,* 1937, p. 91

7. If a policy of prices stabilisation
were successfully carried through,
the amplitude of industrial
fluctuations would be substantially
reduced — it might be cut down
to half what it is at present — but
considerable fluctuations would
still remain.
    - A.C. Pigou (1877-1959)
Industrial Fluctuations,
1927, p. 198

8. The answer to the problem of
the trade cycle is government
intervention to stop the laws of
economics working.
    - Student essay

11. BUSINESSMEN

1. Men of business have a solid
judgement — a wonderful
guessing power of what is going
to happen — each in his own
trade; but they have never
practised themselves in reasoning
out their judgement and in supporting their guesses by argument:
probably if they did so some of
the finer and correcter parts of
their anticipations would vanish.
    - Walter Bagehot (1826-77)
Economic Studies, ed.
Hutton, I, p. 9

2. Captains of Industry
    - Thomas Carlyle (1795-1881)
Past and Present, 1843,
Bk. IV, Ch. IV, title

3. Regarded as a means [the
business man] is tolerable;
regarded as an end he is not so
satisfactory.
    - John Maynard Keynes
(1883-1946)
'A Short View of Russia', in
Essays in Persuasion, 1933,
Pt. IV, p. 307

4. The businessman has the same
fundamental psychology as the
artist, inventor, or statesman.
He has set himself at a certain
work and the work absorbs and
becomes himself. It is the
expression of his personality; he
lives in its growth and perfection
according to his plans.
    - Frank H. Knight
Risk, Uncertainty and Profit,
1921, p. 163, footnote

5. So far, indeed, are men in
business from knowing the
conditions on which future
prices and profits depend, that
they are often ignorant, after
the event, of the causes of their
own past profits and losses.
    - Thomas Edward Cliffe Leslie
(1826-82)
*Essays in Political and Moral
Philosophy,* 1879, XII, p. 187

6. He [the businessman] is the only
man who is for ever apologizing
for his occupation.
    - H.L. Mencken (1880-1956)
Attributed

12. BUYING

1. *It is* naught, *it is* naught, saith the buyer: but when he is gone his way, then he boasteth.
   - *Bible*, Authorised Version *Proverbs*, Ch. 20, v. 14

2. Let the buyer beware (*caveat emptor*).
   - Legal Maxim

3. Buyers want a thousand eyes, sellers none.
   - Proverb, in Thomas Fuller, *Gnomologia*, 1732, 1035

4. He who findeth fault, meaneth to buy.
   - Proverb, ibid., 2383

5. When you go to buy, use your eyes, not your ears.
   - Czech proverb

13. CAPITAL

1. Capital is simply a book-keeping term.
   - Anonymous

2. Capital is nothing but the sum total of intermediate products which come into existence at the individual stages of the roundabout course of progression.
   - Eugen von Böhm-Bawerk (1851-1914) *Capital and Interest*, trans. Huncke, Vol. II, p. 14

3. Capital, in the sense of capital *value*, is simply future income discounted or, in other words, capitalised.
   - Irving Fisher (1867-1947) *The Theory of Interest*, 1930, Ch. I, p. 12

4. Man is the most versatile of all forms of capital.
   - Irving Fisher (1867-1947) Ibid., Ch. VIII, p. 200

5. Capital is a result of labour, and is used by labour to assist it in further production. Labour is the active and initial force, and labour is therefore the employer of capital.
   - Henry George (1839-97) *Progress and Poverty*, Bk.III, Ch. I.

6. Labour and capital are but different forms of the same thing – human exertion. Capital is produced by labour; it is, in fact, but labour impressed upon matter – labour stored up in matter, to be released again as needed, as the heat of the sun stored up in coal is released in the furnace.
   - Henry George (1839-97) Ibid., Ch. V

7. Fixed capital does not derive its utility from previous, but present labour; and does not bring its owner a profit because it has been stored up, but because it is a means of obtaining a command over labour.
   - Thomas Hodgskin (1787-1869) Quoted by H.S. Foxwell in A. Menger, *The Right to the Whole Produce of Labour*

8. Capital . . . is nothing but maintenance of labourers.
   - W. Stanley Jevons (1835-82) *Theory of Political Economy*, 4th ed., Appendix III, p. 312

9. The capital of a country consists of those portions of the produce of industry existing in it, which are *directly* available, either for the support of human beings, or the facilitating of production.
   - J.R. McCulloch (1789-1864) *Principles of Political Economy*, new ed., Pt. I, Ch. II, p. 96

10. Capital consists in a great part of knowledge and organisation: and of this some part is private property and other part is not.
    - Alfred Marshall (1842-1924) *Principles of Economics*, 8th ed., Bk. IV, Ch. II, p. 138

11. The value of the capital already invested in improving land or erecting a building; in making a railway or a machine is the aggregate discounted value of its estimated future net income.
    - Alfred Marshall (1842-1924) Ibid., Bk. VI, Ch. VI, 6, p. 593

12. Capital is commodities.
    - James Mill (1773-1836) *Elements of Political Economy*, 3rd ed., Ch. III, Sec. II

13. Capital is saved from profits.
    - David Ricardo (1772-1823) *Notes on Malthus*, in *Works*, ed. Sraffa, Vol. II, p. 19

14. To say that I have a very abundant capital is to say that I have a great demand for labour. To say that there is a great abundance of labour, is to say that there is not an adequate capital to employ it.
    - David Ricardo (1772-1823) Ibid., p. 241

15. *Owning* capital is not a productive activity.
    - Joan Robinson *An Essay on Marxian Economics*, 1947, Ch. III, p. 18

16. The term Capital . . . signifies an article of wealth, the result of human exertion, employed in the production or distribution of wealth.
    - Nassau W. Senior (1790-1864) *Outline of the Science of Political Economy*, 'Abstinence', p. 59

17. Capital is simply spare subsistence.
    - George Bernard Shaw (1856-1950) 'The Economic Basis of Socialism', in *Fabian Essays*, 1889

18. Capitals are increased by parsimony, and diminished by prodigality and misconduct.
    - Adam Smith (1723-90) *Wealth of Nations*, ed. Cannan, Vol. I, Bk. II, Ch. III, p. 320

19. Parsimony, and not industry, is the immediate cause of the

increase of capital. Industry, indeed, provides the subject which parsimony accumulates. But whatever industry might acquire, if parsimony did not save and store up, the capital would never be the greater.
— Adam Smith (1723-90)
Ibid.

20. In the first stone which he [the savage] flings at the wild animals he pursues, in the first stick that he seizes to strike down the fruit which hangs above his reach, we see the appropriation of one article for the purpose of aiding in the acquisition of another, and thus discover the origin of capital.
— Robert Torrens (1780-1864)
An Essay on the Production of Wealth, 1821, Ch. II, pp. 70-1

21. Invested capital yields income because it enjoys the usufruct of the community's technological knowledge; it has an effectual monopoly of this usufruct because . . . machine technology requires large material appliances with which to do its work.
— Thorstein Veblen (1857-1929)
The Nature of Peace, 1919, Ch. VII, p. 322

22. Every additional quantity of capital laid out produces a less proportionate return, and consequently, the larger the capital expended, the less the ratio of the profit to that capital.
— Sir Edward West (1782-1828)
Essay on the Application of Capital to Land, 1815, p. 2

23. Capital is saved-up labour and saved-up land. Interest is the difference between the marginal productivity of saved-up labour and land and of current labour and land.
— Knut Wicksell (1851-1926)
Lectures on Political Economy, trans. E. Classen, Vol. I, p. 154

14. CAPITALISM

1. The basic law of capitalism is you or I, not both you and I.
— Anonymous

2. Since human nature has been trained to be contrary to any other system than individualism, any other system appears to be 'contrary to human nature', whereas it may be merely contrary to human nurture.
— John Maurice Clark (1884-1963)
Social Control of Business, 1926, p. 82

3. The modern corporate or joint-venture capitalism has largely replaced tycoon capitalism. The one-man-band owner-manager is fast being replaced by a new class of professional managers, dedicated more to the advancement of the company than to the enrichment of a few owners.
— Henry Ford II
Speech, 1955

4. The unpleasant and unacceptable

face of capitalism.
- Edward Heath
  Speech, House of Commons,
  15 May 1973

5. The defence of capitalism
   consists mainly in ignoring
   positive attacks and in concen-
   trating upon the errors, follies,
   and divided counsels of its
   assailants.
   - J.A. Hobson (1858-1940)
     *Confessions of an Economic
     Heretic*, 1938, Ch. XIV

6. The fundamentals of capitalist
   ethics require that 'You shall
   earn your bread in sweat' –
   unless you happen to have
   private means.
   - M. Kalecki (1899-1970)
     'Political Aspects of Full
     Employment', 1943, in
     *Selected Essays on the
     Dynamics of the Capitalist
     Economy*, p. 140

7. The capitalist system is not a
   'harmonious' regime, whose
   purpose is the satisfaction of the
   needs of its citizens but an
   'antagonistic' regime which is to
   secure profits for capitalists.
   - M. Kalecki (1899-1970)
     'The Problem of Effective
     Demand, with Tugan-
     Baronovski and Rosa
     Luxemburg', 1967, in
     *Selected Essays on the
     Dynamics of the Capitalist
     Economy*, p. 147

8. Under the old type of capitalism,
   when free competition prevailed,
   the export of commodities was
   the most typical feature. Under

modern capitalism, when
monopolies prevail, the export
of *capital* has become the
typical feature.
- V.I. Lenin (1870-1924)
  *Imperialism: The Highest
  Stage of Capitalism*, Ch. 4

9. The transformation of numerous
   intermediaries into a handful of
   monopolists represents one of
   the fundamental processes in
   the transformation of capitalism
   into capitalist imperialism.
   - V.I. Lenin (1870-1924)
     Selected Works, Vol. 5, p. 27

10. Uneven economic and political
    development is an absolute law
    of capitalism. Hence, the victory
    of socialism is possible, first in a
    few or even in one single
    country.
    - V.I. Lenin (1870-1924)
      Ibid., p. 141

11. To believe that there is no way
    out of the present crisis for
    capitalism is an error. No situa-
    tion is ever absolutely hopeless.
    - V.I. Lenin (1870-1924)
      Speech, March 1919. Quoted
      by William C. White, *Lenin*,
      1936, p. 45

12. There is a serious tendency
    towards capitalism among the
    well-to-do peasants.
    - Mao Tse-tung (1893-1976)
      *Quotations from Chairman
      Mao Tse-tung*, 1976, p. 32

13. The production of surplus-value,
    or the extraction of surplus
    labour, is the specific end and
    aim, the sum and substance, of

capitalist production.
- Karl Marx (1818-83)
  Capital, Vol. I, Pt. III,
  Ch. X, 7

14. Along with the constantly
diminishing number of the
magnates of capital, who usurp
and monopolise all advantages
of this process of transformation, grows the mass of misery,
oppression, slavery, degradation,
exploitation; but with this too
grows the revolt of the working-
class, a class always increasing in
numbers, and disciplined, united,
organised by the very mechanism of the process of capitalist
production itself. The monopoly of capital becomes a fetter
upon the mode of production,
which has sprung up and
flourished along with, and under
it. Centralisation of the means
of production and socialisation
of labour at last reach a point
where they become incom-
patible with their capitalist
integument. This integument is
burst asunder. The knell of
capitalist private property
sounds. The expropriators are
expropriated.
- Karl Marx (1818-83)
  Ibid., Pt. VIII, Ch. XXXII

15. The industrial economy which
divides society absolutely into
two portions, the payers of
wages and the receivers of them,
the first counted by thousands
and the last by millions, is
neither fit for, nor capable of,
indefinite duration.
- John Stuart Mill (1806-73)
  Principles of Political

Economy, ed. Ashley, Bk. V,
Ch. IX, 5, p. 898

16. Capitalist society, is the realisa-
tion of what we should call
economic democracy . . . the
power which belongs to the
entrepreneurs and capitalists,
can only be acquired by means
of the consumers' ballot, held
daily in the market place.
- Ludwig von Mises
  (1881-1973)
  Socialism, English ed., 1936,
  p. 21

17. Any government which had
both the power and the will to
remedy the major defects of the
capitalist system would have the
will and the power to abolish it
altogether.
- Joan Robinson
  Review of R.F. Harrod's
  'The Trade Cycle', *Economic
  Journal*, Dec. 1936

18. Capitalism with near-full
employment was an impressive
spectacle
- Joan Robinson
  'The Second Crisis of
  Economic Theory',
  American Economic Review,
  May 1972, p. 7

19. Capitalism . . . is by nature a
form or method of economic
change and not only never is but
never can be stationary.
- Joseph A. Schumpeter
  (1883-1950)
  *Capitalism, Socialism and
  Democracy*, Ch. VII, p. 82

20. Modern pacificism and modern

international morality are . . . products of capitalism . . . As a matter of fact, the more completely capitalist the structure and attitude of a nation, the more pacifist — and the more prone to count the costs of war — we observe it to be.
- Joseph A. Schumpeter (1883-1950)
Ibid., Ch. XI, pp. 128-9.
See also 18.13

21. Capitalism creates a critical frame of mind which, after having destroyed the moral authority of so many other institutions, in the end turns against its own.
- Joseph A. Schumpeter (1883-1950)
Ibid., Ch. XIII, p. 143

22. Industrial crisis, unemployment, waste, widespread poverty, these are the incurable diseases of capitalism.
- Joseph Stalin (1879-1953)
Speech, 1931

23. The basic economic law of contemporary capitalism could be formulated as follows: Assurance of maximum capitalist profits . . . by means of enslavement and systematic plundering of the peoples of other countries, especially backward countries.
- Joseph Stalin (1879-1953)
Attributed

24. The Protestant Ethic and the Spirit of Capitalism
- Max Weber (1864-1920)
Title of Essay

15. CAPITALISTS

1. Capitalists and proprietors do no more than give the working man, for his labour of one week, a part of the wealth they obtained. from him the week before.
- John Francis Bray (1809-95)
Labour's Wrongs and Labour's Remedy, 1839

2. While the miser is merely a capitalist gone mad, the capitalist is a rational miser.
- Karl Marx (1818-83)
Capital, Vol. I, Pt. II, Ch. IV

3. The money-owner, now strides in front as capitalist; the possessor of labour-power follows as his labourer. The one with an air of importance, smirking, intent on business; the other, timid and holding back, like one who is bringing his own hide to market and has nothing to expect but a hiding.
- Karl Marx (1818-83)
Ibid., Ch. VI

4. Capitalists can do nothing without labourers, nor the labourers without capital.
- John Stuart Mill (1806-73)
Principles of Political Economy, ed. Ashley, Bk. II, Ch. II, 1, p. 219

16. CHOICE

1. A decision is always a choice among alternative perceived images of the future.
- Kenneth E. Boulding
'The Economics of

Knowledge and the Knowledge of Economics',
American Economic Review,
May 1966, p. 7

2. The strongest principle of growth lies in human choice.
   - George Eliot (1819-80)
     Daniel Deronda, 1876,
     Bk. VI, Ch. XLII

3. The difficulty in life is the choice.
   - George Moore (1852-1933)
     The Bending of the Bough,
     Act IV

4. Beggars cannot be choosers.
   - Proverb, in John Heywood,
     Proverbs, 1546

5. Hobson's choice.
   - English proverb, 17th century

6. You can't eat your cake and have it.
   - Proverb, 16th century

7. You pays your money and you takes your choice.
   - *Punch*, 1846, Vol. X, p. 17

8. Even children learn in growing up that 'both' is not an admissible answer to a choice of 'Which one?'.
   - Paul A. Samuelson
     Economics, 8th ed.,
     pp. 16-17

17. CLASS

1. The rich man in his castle,
   The poor man at his gate,
   God made them, high or lowly,
   And order'd their estate.
   - Cecil Frances Alexander
     (1818-95)
     All Things Bright and Beautiful

2. Our dangerous class is not at the bottom, it is near the top of society. Riches without law are more dangerous than is poverty without law.
   - Henry Ward Beecher
     (1813-87)
     Proverbs from Plymouth Pulpit

3. The poor is hated even of his own neighbour: but the rich *hath* many friends.
   - *Bible*, Authorised Version
     Proverbs, Ch. 14, v. 20

4. No artificial class distinctions can long prevail in a society like ours, of which it is truly said to be often but three generations 'from shirt-sleeves to shirt-sleeves'.
   - Nicholas Murray Butler
     (1867-1947)
     True and Fake Democracy,
     1940, p. 48

5. The oligarchic character of the modern English commonwealth does not rest, like many oligarchies, on the cruelty of the rich to the poor. It does not even rest on the kindness of the rich to the poor. It rests on the perennial and unfailing kindness of the poor to the rich.
   - G.K. Chesterton
     (1874-1936)
     Heretics, Ch. XV

6. What a social class gets is, under
   natural law, what it contributes
   to the general output of
   industry.
   — John Bates Clark
   (1847-1938)
   'Distribution as Determined
   by a Law of Rent', *Quarterly
   Journal of Economics*,
   April 1891, p. 313

7. The English proletariat is
   becoming more and more
   bourgeois so that this most
   bourgeois of all nations is
   apparently aiming ultimately
   at the possession of a bourgeois
   aristocracy and a bourgeois
   proletariat *as well* as a
   bourgeoisie.
   — Frederich Engels (1820-95)
   Attributed

8. Of the three classes it is the
   middle that saves the country.
   — Euripides (341-270 B.C.)
   Quoted in W.R. Inge, *The
   End of an Age*, 1948

9. F. Scott Fitzgerald: You know,
   Ernest, the rich are different
   from us.
   Ernest Hemingway: Yes I know.
   They have more money than
   we do.
   Attributed

10. There are only two classes in
    society; those who get more
    than they earn, and those who
    earn more than they get.
    — Holbrook Jackson
    (1874-1948)
    Quoted in Esar and Bentley,
    *The Treasury of Humorous
    Quotations*

11. No one can feel much com-
    miseration for the richer classes
    of the community even when
    their expenditure presses
    inconveniently close upon their
    income.
    — W. Stanley Jevons (1835-82)
    *Investigations in Currency
    and Finance*, 1884, II,
    Ch. V, p. 92

12. Bourgeois means an owner of
    property. The bourgeoisie are all
    the owners of property taken
    together. A big bourgeois is the
    owner of big property. A petty
    bourgeois is the owner of small
    property.
    — V.I. Lenin (1870-1924)
    Selected Works, Vol. 2,
    p. 254

13. The proletarians have nothing to
    lose but their chains. They have
    a world to win.
    Working men of all countries,
    unite!
    — Karl Marx (1818-83) and
    Friedrich Engels (1820-95)
    The Communist Manifesto,
    closing words

14. All privileged and powerful
    classes, as such, have used their
    power in the interest of their
    own selfishness, and have
    indulged their self-importance in
    despising, and not in lovingly
    caring for, those who were, in
    their estimation, degraded, by
    being under the necessity of
    working for their benefit.
    — John Stuart Mill (1806-73)
    *Principles of Political
    Economy*, ed. Ashley,
    Bk. IV, Ch. VII, 1, p. 754

15. If the rich regard the poor, as by a kind of natural law, their servants and dependants, the rich in their turn are regarded as a mere prey and pasture for the poor.
    — John Stuart Mill (1806-73)
    Ibid., 4, p. 761

16. The rich would have to eat money, but luckily the poor provide food.
    — Russian proverb

17. What is the matter with the poor is Poverty: what is the matter with the rich is Uselessness.
    — George Bernard Shaw (1856-1950)
    Maxims for Revolutionists

18. There is only one class in the community that thinks more about money than the rich, and that is the poor.
    — Oscar Wilde (1854-1900)
    The Soul of Man Under Socialism, 1912, p. 27

18. COMMERCE

1. Men who have been very stingy and very grasping are usually men who have very strong commercial instincts.
   — Henry Ward Beecher (1813-87)
   Proverbs from Plymouth Pulpit

2. The commerce of the world is conducted by the strong; and usually it operates against the weak.
   — Henry Ward Beecher (1813-87)
   Ibid.

3. Merchant, *n*. One engaged in a commercial pursuit. A commercial pursuit is one in which the thing pursued is a dollar.
   — Ambrose Bierce (1842-1914?)
   The Devil's Dictionary

4. Commerce . . . is apt to decay in absolute governments, not because it is there less *secure*, but because it is less *honourable*.
   — David Hume (1711-76)
   Essays, Of Civil Liberty

5. The public becomes powerful in proportion to the opulence and extensive commerce of private men.
   — David Hume (1711-76)
   Ibid., *Of Commerce*

6. The increase of riches and commerce in any one nation, instead of hurting, commonly promotes the riches and commerce of all its neighbours.
   — David Hume (1711-76)
   Ibid., *Of the Jealousy of Trade*

7. Not only as a man, but as a British subject, I pray for the flourishing commerce of Germany, Spain, Italy and even France itself.
   — David Hume (1711-76)
   Ibid.

8. The selfish spirit of commerce knows no country, and feels no passion or principle but that of

gain.
— Thomas Jefferson
(1743-1826)
Letter, 1809

9. Labour once spent has no
influence on the future value of
any article: it is gone and lost
for ever. In commerce bygones
are for ever bygones.
— W. Stanley Jevons (1835-82)
Theory of Political Economy,
4th ed., Ch. IV, p. 164

10. Wealth depends upon commerce,
and commerce depends upon
circulation.
— John Law (1671-1729)
*Money and Trade Con-
sidered*, 1705

11. Commerce is virtually a mode of
cheapening production; and in
all such cases the consumer is the
person ultimately benefited.
— John Stuart Mill (1806-73)
*Principles of Political
Economy*, ed. Ashley,
Bk. III, Ch. XVII, 4, p. 580

12. Commerce is the purpose of the
far greater part of the communication which takes place
between civilized nations. Such
communication has always
been, and is peculiarly in the
present age, one of the primary
sources of progress.
— John Stuart Mill (1806-73)
Ibid., 5, p. 581

13. It is commerce which is rapidly
rendering war obsolete, by
strengthening and multiplying
the personal interests which are
in natural opposition to it.

— John Stuart Mill (1806-73)
Ibid., p. 582
See also 14.20

14. Commerce is the agency by
which the power of choice is
obtained.
— John Ruskin (1819-1900)
Munera Pulveris, IV

15. As in true commerce there is no
'profit', so in true commerce
there is no 'sale'.
— John Ruskin (1819-1900)
Ibid.

16. He's a man. I know him: his
principles are thoroughly
commercial.
— George Bernard Shaw
(1856-1950)
Man and Superman, Act IV

17. Commerce has set the mark of
selfishness,
The signet of its all-enslaving
power
Upon a shining ore, and called
it gold.
— Percy Bysshe Shelley
(1792-1822)
Queen Mab, V

19. COMMUNISM

1. What is a communist? One who
hath yearnings
For equal division of unequal
earnings.
Idler or bungler, or both, he is
willing,
To fork out his copper and
pocket your shilling.
— Ebenezer Elliot (1781-1849)
Epigram

2. Communism will pass away from Russia, but it will have lighted a torch for the world of workers not readily to be extinguished.
   - Maxim Gorky (1868-1936)
     Observer, Sayings of the Week, 9 October 1921

3. The Communist is a Socialist in a violent hurry.
   - G.W. Gough
     The Economic Consequences of Socialism, 1926, I

4. Leninism is a combination of two things which Europeans have kept for some centuries in different compartments of the soul – religion and business.
   - John Maynard Keynes (1883-1946)
     'A short view of Russia', in *Essays in Persuasion*, 1933, Pt. IV, p. 297

5. Communism . . . is the name we apply to a system under which people become accustomed to the performance of public duties without any specific machinery of compulsion, when unpaid work for the common good becomes the general phenomenon.
   - V.I. Lenin (1870-1924)
     Selected Works, Vol. 8, p. 239

6. Communism is the Soviet power plus the electrification of the whole country.
   - V.I. Lenin (1870-1924)
     Ibid., p. 276

7. Communists who believed we could completely alter the economic form of society in three years were visionaries. I say it will take at least a century.
   - V.I. Lenin (1870-1924)
     Observer, Sayings of the Week, 7 April 1921

8. Communists should set an example in study; at all times they should be pupils of the masses as well as their teachers.
   - Mao Tse-tung (1893-1976)
     Quotations from Chairman Mao Tse-tung, 1976, p. 272

9. A spectre is haunting Europe – the spectre of Communism.
   - Karl Marx (1818-83) and Friedrich Engels (1820-95)
     The Communist Manifesto, Opening Sentence

10. The theory of the Communists may be summed up in the single sentence: Abolition of private property.
    - Karl Marx (1818-83) and Friedrich Engels (1820-95)
      Ibid., Ch. 2

11. Communism deprives no man of the power to appropriate the products of society: all that it does is to deprive him of the power to subjugate the labour of others by means of such appropriation.
    - Karl Marx (1818-83) and Friedrich Engels (1820-95)
      Ibid.

12. A factory operative has less personal interest in his work than a member of a Communist association, since he is not, like

him, working for a partnership
of which he is himself a member.
— John Stuart Mills (1806-73)
*Principles of Political
Economy*, ed. Ashley, Bk. II,
Ch. I, 3, pp. 204-5.

13. In communism, inequality
springs from placing mediocrity
on a level with excellence.
— Pierre-Joseph Proudhon
(1809-65)
What is Property?, trans.
Tucker, Ch. V, Pt. II

14. Communism is inequality, but
not as property is. Property is
the exploitation of the weak by
the strong. Communism is the
exploitation of the strong by
the weak.
— Pierre-Joseph Proudhon
(1809-65)
Ibid.

15. Communism is the religion of
poverty.
— Pierre-Joseph Proudhon
(1809-65)
Attributed

20. COMPETITION

1. Free competition is equivalent
to a reward granted to those
who furnish the best goods at
the lowest price.
— Jeremy Bentham
(1748-1832)
Principles of Penal Law,
Part 3, Ch. 1. In J. Bowring
(ed.), *Works of Jeremy
Bentham*, Vol. 1, p. 534

2. Two-sided competition.

— Eugen von Böhm-Bawerk
(1851-1914)
Quoted by F.Y. Edgeworth,
*Papers relating to Political
Economy*, 1925, Vol. I,
p. 51

3. Economic competition is not
war, but rivalry in mutual
service.
— Edwin Cannan (1861-1935)
*A Review of Economic
Theory*, 1929, Ch. IV, $5,
p. 91

4. Free competition tends to give
to labour what labour creates,
to capitalists what capital
creates, and to entrepreneurs
what the co-ordinating function
creates.
— John Bates Clark
(1847-1938)
The Distribution of Wealth,
1899, p. 3

5. Strife is increasing in our times
because true competition is
diminishing.
— John Bates Clark
(1847-1938)
The Philosophy of Wealth,
1886, Ch. IV, p. 65

6. Competition without moral
restraints is a monster as
completely antiquated as the
saurians of which the geologists
tell us.
— John Bates Clark
(1847-1938)
Ibid., Ch. IX, p. 151

7. Competition is no longer
adequate to account for the
phenomena of social industry.

What was once assumed as a universal law is now but partial in its operation.
- John Bates Clark (1847-1938)
Ibid., Ch XI, p. 203

8. The essential nature of *competition* is to harness the predatory interest, perverting it, if you will, to a rivalry in attracting voluntary patronage by methods which necessarily centre largely in service.
- John Maurice Clark (1884-1963)
Social Control of Business, 1926, p. 39

9. Competitors are free – except to combine.
[under 'free competition']
- John Maurice Clark (1884-1963)
Ibid., p. 146

10. Competition is the completest expression of the battle of all against all which rules in a modern civil society. This battle . . . is fought not between the different classes of society only, but also between the individual members of these classes.
- Frederick Engels (1820-95)
The Condition of the Working Class in England in 1844, 1892, Ch. III, p. 75

11. Merchants are occupied solely with crushing each other: such is the effect of free competition.
- Charles Fourier (1772-1837)
Selections, ed. Franklin, Ch. XI, p. 131

12. UNFAIR COMPETITION: selling cheaper than someone else.
- Ralph Harris
'Everyman's Guide to Contemporary Economic Jargon', *Growth, Advertising and the Consumer*, 1964, p. 24

13. One of the main arguments in favour of competition is that it dispenses with the need for 'conscious social control' and that it gives the individuals a chance to decide whether the prospects of a particular occupation are sufficient to compensate for the disadvantages and risks connected with it.
- F.A. Hayek
The Road to Serfdom, 1944, Ch. III

14. An ideal system of perfect competition . . . is inherently self-defeating and could not exist in the real world.
- Frank H. Knight
Risk, Uncertainty and Profit, 1921, p. 193

15. The system of free competition is rather a peculiar one. Its mechanism is one of *fooling* entrepreneurs. It requires the pursuit of maximum profit in order to function, but it destroys profits when they are actually pursued by a larger number of people.
- Oskar Lange (1904-65)
On the Economic Theory of Socialism, 1938, p. 117

16. The work I have set before me is this — how to get rid of the evils of competition while retaining its advantages.
    — Alfred Marshall (1842-1924)
    Farewell address, Bristol, 29 Sept. 1881. Quoted in A.C. Pigou, *Memorials of Alfred Marshall*, p. 16

17. Competition rages in direct proportion to the number, and in inverse proportion to the magnitudes, of the antagonistic capitals. It always ends in the ruin of many small capitalists, whose capitals partly pass into the hands of their conquerors, partly vanish.
    — Karl Marx (1818-83)
    Capital, Vol. I, Pt. VII, Ch. XXV, 2

18. If competition has its evils, it prevents greater evils. . .It is the common error of Socialist to overlook the natural indolence of mankind; their tendency to be passive, to be the slaves of habit, to persist indefinitely in a course once chosen. Let them once attain any state of existence which they consider tolerable, and the danger to be apprehended is that they will thenceforth stagnate.
    — John Stuart Mill (1806-73)
    Principles of Political Economy, ed. Ashley, Bk. IV, Ch. VII, 7, p. 793

19. The imperfection of competition is simply a form of friction, producing, for the most part, a negligible variation from the standards that prevail in a regime of perfect competition.

    — H.L. Moore
    'Paradoxes of Competition', *Quarterly Journal of Economics*, February 1906, p. 212

20. Monopolies, trade unions, political parties, arise out of the very process of competition and prevent it from being effective as a mechanism for ensuring the general good.
    — Joan Robinson
    Marx, Marshall and Keynes, 1955

21. By perfect competition I propose to mean a state of affairs in which the demand for the output of an individual seller is perfectly elastic.
    — Joan Robinson
    'What is Perfect Competition?', *Quarterly Journal of Economics*, Nov. 1934, p. 104

22. Competition can only be absolutely perfect, given rising marginal costs, if the number of firms is infinite. Absolute perfection of competition is therefore an impossibility.
    — Joan Robinson
    Ibid., p. 119

23. From the time of the physiocrats and Adam Smith there has never been absent from the main body of economic literature the feeling that in some sense perfect competition represented the optimum solution.
    — Paul A. Samuelson
    Foundations of Economic Analysis, 1947, p. 203

24. All professions are conspiracies against the laity.
    - George Bernard Shaw
      (1856-1950)
      The Doctor's Dilemma,
      Act I

25. The natural price, or the price of free competition . . . is the lowest which can be taken, not upon every occasion indeed, but for any considerable time together . . . [It] is the lowest which the sellers can commonly afford to take, and at the same time continue their business.
    - Adam Smith (1723-90)
      Wealth of Nations, ed.
      Cannan, Vol. I, Bk. I,
      Ch. VII, p. 63

26. Competition, perfect competition, affords the ideal condition for the distribution of wealth.
    - Francis A. Walker (1840-97)
      Political Economy, 1892,
      para. 466.

21. COMPUTERS

1. The 'gigo principle' – garbage in, garbage out.
   - Anonymous

2. The very power of the computer to simulate complex systems by very high-speed arithmetic may prevent search for those simplified formulations which are the essence of progress in theory.
   - Kenneth E. Boulding
     'The Economics of Knowledge and the Knowledge of Economics' *American Economic Review*,

May 1966, p. 10

22. CONSUMERS

1. Consumer's delusions result in producer's blunders.
   - John Bates Clark
     (1847-1938)
     'Introduction' to K. Rodbertus, *Overproduction and Crises*, 1898, p. 5

2. The diffuse and inchoate consumer interest has been no match for the sharply focused, articulate and well-financed efforts of producer groups.
   - Walter W. Heller
     'What's Right With Economics?', *American Economic Review*, March 1975, p. 5

3. The Concept of Consumers' Sovereignty.
   - W.H. Hutt
     Title of article, *Economic Journal*, March 1940

4. The supposed conflict of labour with capital is a delusion. The real conflict is between producers and consumers.
   - W. Stanley Jevons (1835-82)
     Attributed

5. The publick is an acute, as well as merciless beast, which neither over-sees a failing, nor forgives it – but stamps judgment and execution immediately, tho' upon a member of itself.
   - Sir Dudley North (1641-91)
     Discourses upon Trade,
     1691, Preface

6. The consumer, so it is said, is the king . . . each is a voter who uses his money as votes to get the things done that he wants done.
   - Paul A. Samuelson
     Economics, 8th ed., p. 55

7. Economists know a lot about what makes producers tick, while they know almost nothing about the motivation of consumers.
   - Tibor Scitovsky
     The Joyless Economy, 1977, Ch. 1, p. 6

8. Consumers are often far from happy – always wanting more of what they can't get and having too much of what they don't want.
   - Student essay

23. CONSUMPTION

1. In an economy, such as that of the United States of America, where leisure is barely moral, the problem of creating sufficient wants (i.e. competing ends) to absorb productive capacity may become chronic in the not too distant future. In such a situation the economist begins to lead a furtive existence.
   - W. Beckerman
     'The Economist as a Modern Missionary', *Economic Journal*, March 1956, p. 112

2. We take it as a fundamental psychological rule of any modern community that, when its real income is increased, it will not increase its consumption by an equal *absolute* amount.
   - John Maynard Keynes (1883-1946)
     The General Theory of Employment Interest and Money, Bk. III, Ch. 8, p. 97

3. Consumption, in the sense in which the word is used in this science, is synonymous with use; and is, in fact, the great end and object of industry.
   - J.R. McCulloch (1789-1864)
     Principles of Political Economy, new ed., Pt. IV, p. 523

4. [Everything is a luxury which is not] immediately necessary to make man subsist as he is, a living creature.
   - Bernard de Mandeville (1670-1733)
     The Fable of the Bees or *Private Vices, Publick Benefits*, 2nd ed., 1723

5. *Consumption* may be regarded as negative production.
   - Alfred Marshall (1842-1924)
     Principles of Economics, 8th ed., Bk. II, Ch. III, 1, p. 64

6. The price which a person pays for a thing can never exceed, and seldom comes up to that which he would be willing to pay rather than go without it so that the satisfaction which he gets from its purchase generally exceeds that which he gives up in paying away its price; and he

thus derives from the purchase a surplus of satisfaction . . . It may be called *consumer's surplus*.
- Alfred Marshal (1842-1924)
  Ibid., Bk. III, Ch. VI, 1,
  p. 124

7. [Consumption is] a quantity always indefinite, for there is no end to the desire of enjoyment, the grand concern is to increase the supply.
   - James Mill (1773-1836)
     Elements of Political Economy, 3rd ed.,
     Introduction

8. Consumption never needs encouragement.
   - John Stuart Mill (1806-73)
     Essays on some Unsettled Questions of Political Economy, 1844, p. 48

9. Everything which is produced is consumed; both what is saved and what is said to be spent; and the former quite as rapidly as the latter.
   - John Stuart Mill (1806-73)
     Principles of Political Economy, ed. Ashley, Bk. I, Ch. V, 6, p. 73 *See also* 108.3

10. Consumption is the sudden or gradual destruction of a valuable article obtained from a retail trader or other final producer.
    - A.F. Mummery (1855-95) and J.A. Hobson (1858-1940)
      The Physiology of Industry, 1889, 'Definitions'

11. If men ceased to consume, they would cease to produce.
    - David Ricardo (1772-1823)
      Principles of Political Economy and Taxation, ed. Sraffa, Ch. XXI, p. 293

12. It would be an improvement in the language of political economy if the expression 'to use' could be substituted for that 'to consume'.
    - Nassau William Senior (1790-1864)
      Political Economy, 6th ed., p. 54

13. Consumption is the sole end and purpose of all production; and the interest of the producer ought to be attended to, only so far as it may be necessary for promoting that of the consumer.
    - Adam Smith (1723-90)
      Wealth of Nations, ed. Cannan, Vol. II, Bk. IV, Ch. VIII, p. 159

14. Conspicuous consumption of valuable goods is a means of reputability to the gentleman of leisure.
    - Thorstein Veblen (1857-1929)
      The Theory of the Leisure Class, Ch. IV

15. With the exception of the instinct of self-preservation, the propensity for emulation is probably the strongest and most alert and persistent of the economic motives proper.
    - Thorstein Veblen (1857-1929)
      Ibid., Ch. V

24. CORPORATIONS

1. Corporation, *n*. An ingenious
device for obtaining individual
profit without individual
responsibility.
   - Ambrose Bierce
(1842-1914?)
The Devil's Dictionary

2. Did you ever expect a corporation to have a conscience, when
it has no soul to be damned and
no body to be kicked.
   - Lord Thurlow (1731-1806)
Attributed

25. COST(S)

1. Cost means sacrifice, and
cannot, without risk of hope-
lessly confusing ideas, be
identified with anything that is
not sacrifice.
   - J.E. Cairnes (1824-75)
*Some Leading Principles
of Political Economy*, 1874,
Part I, Ch. III, p. 60

2. If cost accounting sets out,
determined to discover what the
cost of everything is and
convinced in advance that there
is one figure which can be found
and which will furnish exactly
the information which is desired
for every possible purpose, it
will necessarily fail, because
there is no such figure. If it
finds a figure which is right for
some purposes it must
necessarily be wrong for others.
   - J. Maurice Clark (1884-1963)
*Studies in the Economics of
Overhead Costs*, 1923, p. 14

3. If the choice lies between the
production or purchase of two
commodities, the value of one is
measured by the sacrifice of
going without the other.
   - H.J. Davenport (1861-1931)
'The Formula of Sacrifice',
*Journal of Political
Economy*, 1893-4, pp. 567-8

4. Costs merely register competing
attractions.
   - Frank H. Knight
Risk, Uncertainty and Profit,
1921, p. 159

5. From the economic point of
view it is most advantageous if
freight is only charged in
accordance with running costs
(*Betriebskosten*). This proposition holds whatever the form of
the demand equation. This
proves most emphatically that
railways are a concern which
should never be left to private
enterprise.
   - Wilhelm Launhardt
(1832-1918)
*Mathematische Begründung
der Volkswirtschafslehre*,
1885, p. 203

6. Persons whose capital is already
embarked, and cannot be easily
extricated, will persevere for a
considerable time without
profit, and have been known to
persevere even at a loss, in hope
of better times.
   - John Stuart Mill (1806-73)
*Principles of Political
Economy*, ed. Ashley,
Bk. III, Ch. III, 1, p. 451

7. As a general rule . . . things tend
to exchange for one another at

41

such values as will enable each producer to be repaid the cost of production with the ordinary profit.
  — John Stuart Mill (1806-73)
    Ibid., p. 452

8. By *Cost of Production*, ... we mean the sum of labour and abstinence necessary to production.
  — Nassau W. Senior
    (1790-1864)
    Outline of the Science of Political Economy, 'Cost of Production', p. 101

9. Cost [is] of two kinds, either (1) the endurance of pain, discomfort, or something else undesirable, or (2) the sacrifice of something desirable, either as an end or a means.
  — Henry Sidgwick (1838-1900)
    Principles of Political Economy, 3rd ed., 1901, Bk. III, Ch. I, p. 396.

10. Cost of production ... in the sense of the historical and irrevocable fact that resources have been devoted to this or that special purpose, has no influence on the value of the thing produced, and therefore does not affect its price.
  — Philip H. Wicksteed
    (1844-1927)
    The Common Sense of Political Economy, ed. Robbins, Vol. I, Bk. I, Ch. IX, p. 380

26. *CREDIT*

1. Credit, like a looking glass, Broken once, is gone, alas!
  — Anonymous

2. IN GOD WE TRUST All others pay cash
  — Anonymous

3. Of all things that have existence only in the minds of men, nothing is more fantastical and nice than Credit; it is never to be forced; it hangs upon opinion; it depends upon our passions of hope and fear; it comes many times unsought for, and often goes away without reason; and when once lost, is hardly to be quite recovered.
  — Charles d'Avenant
    (1656-1714)
    Discourses on the Public Revenues and on the Trade of England, 1698, in *Works*, ed. Whitworth, republished 1967, Vol. I, p. 151

4. No man's credit is as good as his money.
  — Edgar Watson Howe
    (1853-1937)
    Sinner Sermons, 1926

5. Credit has a great, but not, as many people seem to suppose, a magical power; it cannot make something out of nothing.
  — John Stuart Mill (1806-73)
    Principles of Political Economy, ed. Ashley, Bk. III, Ch. XI, 1, p. 511

6. Credit is but a transfer of capital from hand to hand, it is

generally, and naturally, a transfer to hands more competent to employ the capital efficiently in production.
- John Stuart Mill (1806-73) Ibid., 2, p. 512

7. Creditors have better memories than debtors.
- Proverb, in James Howell, *Proverbs*, 1659

8. Who tells a lie to save his credit wipes his nose on his sleeve to save his napkin.
- Proverb, ibid.

9. Take care you don't hurt your credit by offering too much security.
- Richard Brinsley Sheridan (1751-1816) *The Rivals*, Act II

10. Commercial credit may be defined to be that confidence which subsists among commercial men in respect to their mercantile affairs.
- Henry Thornton (1760-1815) *An Enquiry into the Nature and Effects of the Paper Credit of Great Britain*, 1802, Ch. I, p. 13

27. CRIME

1. Pecuniary punishments are highly economical, since all the evil felt by him who pays turns into an advantage for him who receives.
- Jeremy Bentham (1748-1832)

Attributed

2. 'Are you afraid of having your pockets picked?' 'Alas!' replied Mr Beveridge, 'it would take two men to do that.' 'Hugh!' snorted the Emperor, 'you are so d–d strong, are you?' 'I mean', answered his *vis-à-vis* . . . 'that it would take one man to put something in and another to take it out.'
- Storer Clouston (1870-1944) *The Lunatic at Large*, Pt. I, Ch. II

3. The State by killing, mutilating, or imprisoning their members, do withall punish themselves; wherefore such punishments ought (as much as possible) to be avoided and commuted for pecuniary mulcts, which will encrease labour and publick wealth.
- Sir William Petty (1623-87) 'A Treatise of Taxes and Contributions', 1662, in *The Economic Writings of Sir William Petty*, ed. Hull, Vol. I, p. 68

4. Mendoza. I am a brigand: I live by robbing the rich. Tanner. I am a gentleman: I live by robbing the poor.
- George Bernard Shaw (1856-1950) *Man and Superman*, Act III

28. CURRENCY

1. This currency, as we manage it, is a wonderful machine. It

43

performs its office when we issue it: it pays and clothes troops and provides victuals and ammunition; and when we are obliged to issue a quantity excessive, it pays itself off by depreciation.
— Benjamin Franklin (1706-90)
Letter to Samuel Cooper, 22 April 1779

2. The substitution of paper for metallic currency is a national gain; any further increase of paper beyond this is but a form of robbery.
— John Stuart Mill (1806-73)
Principles of Political Economy, ed. Ashley, Bk. III, Ch. XIII, 5, p. 551

3. A currency, to be perfect, should be absolutely invariable in value.
— David Ricardo (1772-1823)
Works, ed. Sraffa, Vol. IV, p. 58.

4. A circulation can never be so abundant as to overflow; for by diminishing its value, in the proportion you will increase its quantity, and by increasing its value, diminish its quantity.
— David Ricardo (1772-1823)
Principles of Political Economy and Taxation, ed. Sraffa, Ch. XXVII, p. 352

5. A currency is in its most perfect state when it consists wholly of paper money, but of paper money of an equal value with the gold it professes to represent.
— David Ricardo (1772-1823)

Ibid., p. 361

29. DEBT

1. Debt is an inexhaustible fountain of dishonesty.
— Henry Ward Beecher (1813-87)
Proverbs from Plymouth Pulpit

2. Women hate a debt as men a gift.
— Robert Browning (1812-89)
Robert Browning's Poetical Works, 1889, *In a Balcony*, p. 14

3. If the prodigal quits life in debt to others, the miser quits it, still deeper in debt to himself.
— Reverend C.C. Colton (1780-1832)
Lacon, Vol. II, CXXXI

4. A man in debt is so far a slave.
— Ralph Waldo Emerson (1803-82)
'Wealth', *The Conduct of Life*, 1860

5. An opulent knave, even though one could not force him to pay, is a preferable debtor to an honest bankrupt.
— David Hume (1711-76)
Essays, Of Public Credit

6. Small debts are like small shot; they are rattling on every side, and can scarcely be escaped without a wound: great debts are like cannon; of loud noise, but little danger.
— Samuel Johnson (1709-84)

Letter to Joseph Simpson,
1759

7. Debt is the worst poverty.
   — Proverb, in Thomas Fuller,
   Gnomologia, 1732, 1258

8. Debtors are liars.
   — Proverb, in George Herbert,
   Outlandish Proverbs, 1640

9. Speak not of my debts unless
   you mean to pay them.
   — Proverb, ibid.

10. He that dies pays all debts.
    — William Shakespeare
    (1564-1616)
    The Tempest, Act III, Sc. II

30. DEMAND

1. Each individual contains as it
   were within himself, a series of
   demands of successively increasing degrees of intensity; that the
   lowest degree of this series
   which at any time leads to a
   purchase is exactly the same for
   both rich and poor, and is that
   which regulates the market
   price.
   — Mountifort Longfield
   (1802-84)
   *Lectures on Political
   Economy*, 1834, VI

2. The *elasticity* (or responsive-
   ness) *of demand* in a market is
   great or small according as the
   amount demanded increases
   much or little for a given fall
   in price, and diminishes much or
   little for a given rise in price.
   — Alfred Marshall (1842-1924)

Principles of Economics, 8th
ed., Bk. III, Ch. IV, 1, p. 102

3. In the usual and ordinary course
   of things, the demand for all
   commodities precedes their
   supply.
   — David Ricardo (1772-1823)
   *Principles of Political
   Economy and Taxation*, ed.
   Sraffa, Ch. XXXII, p. 409

4. Can one desire too much of a
   good thing?
   — William Shakespeare
   (1564-1616)
   As You Like It, Act IV, Sc. I

5. A very poor man may be said in
   some sense to have a demand
   for a coach and six; he might
   like to have it; but his demand is
   not an effectual demand, as the
   commodity can never be
   brought to market in order to
   satisfy it.
   — Adam Smith (1723-90)
   Wealth of Nations, ed.
   Cannan, Vol. I, Bk. I,
   Ch. VII, p. 58

6. The desire of food is limited in
   every man by the narrow
   capacity of the human stomach;
   but the desire of the conveniences and ornaments of
   building, dress, equipage and
   household furniture, seems to
   have no limit or certain
   boundary.
   — Adam Smith (1723-90)
   Ibid., Ch. XI, Pt. II, p. 165

7. By necessaries I understand, not
   only the commodities which are
   indispensably necessary for the

support of life, but whatever the custom of the country renders it indecent for creditable people, even of the lowest order, to be without.
- Adam Smith (1723-90)
  Ibid., Vol. II, Bk. V, Ch. II, Pt. II, p. 354

8. Because I cannot 'afford to buy' a thing it does not follow that I have less need of it or less desire to have it than another man who can and does afford it.
   - Philip H. Wicksteed (1844-1927)
     Alphabet of Economic Science, 1888, p. 83

31. DEPRESSION

1. The root-evil of depressed trade is under-consumption.
   - J.A. Hobson (1858-1940)
     The Evolution of Modern Capitalism, revised edition, 1926, Ch. XI, p. 288

2. If the planets govern the sun, and the sun governs the vintages and harvests, and thus the prices of food and raw materials and the state of the money market, it follows that the configurations of the planets may prove to be the remote causes of the greatest commercial disasters.
   - W. Stanley Jevons (1835-82)
     Investigations in Currency and Finance, 1884, VI, p. 205

3. It is pauperism and a glutted market that lie at the root of

the economic distresses of the time.
- Karl Rodbertus (1805-75)
  Overproduction and Crises, trans. Franklin, 1898, p. 19

4. Our analysis leads us to believe that recovery is sound only if it does come of itself. For any revival which is merely due to artificial stimulus leaves part of the work of depressions undone and adds, to an undigested remnant of maladjustment, new maladjustments of its own.
   - Joseph A. Schumpeter (1883-1950)
     Essays, ed. Richard V. Clemence, 1951, p. 117

32. DEVALUATION

1. Britain was saved from fascism by the floating of the pound in 1931.
   - Harry G. Johnson (1923-77)
     Lecture at the London School of Economics, 1971

2. Devaluation, whether of sterling, or the dollar, or both, would be a lunatic, self-destroying operation.
   - Harold Wilson
     Speech, 1963

3. From now the Pound abroad is worth 14 per cent or so less in terms of other currencies. It does not mean, of course, that the Pound here in Britain, in your pocket or purse, or in your bank has been devalued.
   - Harold Wilson
     Speech, 1967

33. DIMINISHING RETURNS

1. Knowledge is the only instru-
   ment of production that is not
   subject to diminishing returns.
   — John Maurice Clark
   (1884-1963)
   Quoted by
   Paul A. Samuelson,
   Economics, 8th ed.

2. While the part which nature
   plays in production shows a
   tendency to diminishing return,
   the part which man plays shows
   a tendency to increasing return.
   — Alfred Marshall (1842-1924)
   Principles of Economics,
   8th ed., Bk. IV, Ch. XIII,
   2, p. 318

3. In agriculture, the state of the
   art being given, doubling the
   labour does not double the
   produce.
   — John Stuart Mill (1806-73)
   *Principles of Political
   Economy*, ed. Ashley,
   Bk. III, Ch. V, 1, p. 469

4. Each equal additional quantity
   of work bestowed on
   agriculture, yields an actually
   diminished return.
   — Sir Edward West
   (1782-1828)
   *Essay on the Application of
   Capital to Land*, 1815, p. 6

5. In the progress of improvement
   an equal quantity of work
   extracts from the soil a
   gradually diminishing return.
   — Sir Edward West
   (1782-1828)
   Ibid., pp. 11-12

34. DISTRIBUTION OF
INCOME AND WEALTH

1. The poor man's coin which goes
   to pay for the necessaries of life
   and the last coin that goes to fill
   the financier's purse are in the
   opinion of the mathematician
   two units of the same order, but
   to the moralist the one is worth
   a louis, the other not a cent.
   — Georges Louis Leclerc, Comte
   de Buffon (1707-88)
   Essai d'Arithmétique Morale

2. Where natural laws have their
   way, the share of income that
   attaches to any productive
   function is gauged by the
   actual product of it.
   — John Bates Clark
   (1847-1938)
   The Distribution of Wealth,
   1899, Ch. 1, p. 3

3. The adjustment of rates of
   exchange constitutes, in the
   aggregate, the process of
   distribution.
   — John Bates Clark
   (1847-1938)
   The Philosophy of Wealth,
   1886, Ch. IV, p. 64

4. Distribution is the species of
   Exchange by which produce is
   divided between the parties who
   have contributed to its
   production.
   — F.Y. Edgeworth
   (1845-1926)
   *Papers Relating to Political
   Economy*, 1925, Vol. I,
   p. 13

5. Every person, if possible, ought

to enjoy the fruits of his labour, in a full possession of all the necessaries, and many of the conveniences of life . . . Such an equality is most suitable to human nature, and diminishes much less from the *happiness* of the rich, than it adds to that of the poor.
- David Hume (1711-76)
Essays, Of Commerce

6. How much harder would it be if the same persons had both all the merit and all the prosperity. Would not this be a miserable distribution for the poor dunces.
- Samuel Johnson (1709-84)
Boswell's Life of Johnson, 23 March 1783

7. There is no question but that crises promote rather than diminish inequalities in the distribution of wealth, for in the extremity of the man of ordinary means lies the opportunity of men of very large wealth.
- Edward D. Jones (1870-1944)
Economic Crises, 1900, Ch. X, pp. 221-2

8. The relative share of gross capitalist income and salaries in the aggregate turnover is with great approximation equal to the average degree of monopoly.
- M. Kalecki (1899-1970)
Essays in the Theory of Economic Fluctuations, 1939, p. 22

9. From each according to his ability, to each according to his needs!
- Karl Marx (1818-83)
Critique of the Gotha Programme

10. The distribution of wealth . . . depends on the laws and customs of society. The rules by which it is determined are what the opinions and feelings of the ruling portion of the community make them, and are very different in different ages and countries; and might be still more different, if mankind so chose.
- John Stuart Mill (1806-73)
Principles of Political Economy, ed. Ashley, Bk. II, Ch. I, 1, p. 200

11. What is economically needed is a better distribution . . . Levelling institutions, either of a just or of an unjust kind, cannot alone accomplish it; they may lower the heights of society, but they cannot, of themselves, permanently raise the depths.
- John Stuart Mill (1806-73)
Ibid., Bk. IV, Ch. VI, 2, p. 749

12. Income distribution is from the very start the outcome of an intricate economic complex.
- Jan Pen
Income Distribution, 1971, Ch. I, 2

13. The produce of the earth . . . is divided among three classes of the community; namely, the proprietor of the land, the owner of the stock or capital

necessary for its cultivation,
and the labourers by whose
industry it is cultivated.
- David Ricardo (1772-1823)
  *Principles of Political
  Economy and Taxation*,
  ed. Sraffa, Preface, p. 5

14. The great metaphysical question
of the scientific comparability
of different individual
experiences.
   - Lionel Robbins
     *An Essay on the Nature and
     Significance of Economic
     Science*, 2nd ed., 1935,
     p. 137

15. In short, we have not got a
theory of distribution. We have
nothing to say on the subject
which above all others occupies
the minds of the people whom
economics is supposed to
enlighten.
   - Joan Robinson
     'The Second Crisis of
     Economic Theory',
     American Economic Review,
     May 1972, p. 9

16. The good of any one individual
is of no more importance, from
the point of view (if I may so
say) of the Universe, than the
good of any other; unless, that
is, there are special grounds for
believing that more good is
likely to be realized in the one
case than in the other.
   - Henry Sidgwick (1838-1900)
     The Methods of Ethics,
     4th ed., 1890, Bk. III,
     Ch. XIII, 3

17. A gardener who cultivates his

own garden with his own hands,
unites in his own person the
three different characters, of
landlord, farmer, and labourer.
His produce, therefore, should
pay him the rent of the first,
the profit of the second, and the
wages of the third.
   - Adam Smith (1723-90)
     Wealth of Nations, ed.
     Cannan, Vol. I, Bk. I,
     Ch. VI, p. 55

18. The whole annual produce of
the land and labour of every
country . . . naturally divides
itself . . . into three parts: the
rent of the land, the wages of
labour, and the profits of stock.
   - Adam Smith (1723-90)
     Ibid., Ch. XI, p. 248

19. Nobody who has wealth to
distribute ever omits himself.
   - Leon Trotsky (1879-1940)
     *Observer, Sayings of the
     Week*, 23 March 1937

20. Look at it how we will . . . it
is impossible to establish any
scientific comparison between
the wants and desires of two or
more separate individuals.
   - Philip H. Wicksteed
     (1844-1927)
     *Alphabet of Economic
     Science*, 1888, p. 69

21. We have no common measure
by which we can compare the
necessities, wants, or desires of
one man with those of another.
We cannot even say that 'a
shilling is worth more to a poor
man than to a rich one' if we
mean to enunciate a rule that

can be safely applied to individual cases. The most we can say is, that a shilling is worth more to a man *when he is poor* than (*cæteris paribus*) to *the same man* when he is rich.
- Philip H. Wicksteed (1844-1927)
  Ibid., p. 86

35. DIVISION OF LABOUR

1. Jack of all trades and master of none.
   - Maria Edgeworth (1767-1849)
     Attributed

2. Cloth must be cheaper made, when one cards, another spins, another weaves, another draws, another dresses, another presses and packs; than when all the operations above-mentioned, were clumsily performed by the same hand.
   - Sir William Petty (1623-87) 'Political Arithmetick', 1690, in *The Economic Writings of Sir William Petty*, ed. Hull, Vol. I, p. 260

3. The gain which is made by manufacturers, will be greater, as the manufacture itself is greater and better. For in so vast a city manufactures will beget one another, and each manufacture will be divided into as many parts as possible, whereby the work of each artisan will be simple and easie; as for example. In the making of a watch, if one man shall make the wheels, another the spring,

another shall engrave the dial-plate, and another shall make the cases, then the watch will be better and cheaper, than if the whole work be put upon any one man.
- Sir William Petty (1623-87) 'Another Essay in Political Arithmetick, Concerning the Growth of the City of London', 1682, ibid., Vol. II, p. 473

4. More things will be produced and the work be more easily and better done, when every man is set free from all other occupations to do, at the right time, the one thing for which he is naturally fitted.
   - Plato (c. 428-347 B.C.) *The Republic*, trans. Cornford, Bk. II, Ch. VI

5. We have laid down, as a universal principle, that everyone ought to perform the one function in the community for which his nature best suited him. Well, I believe that that principle, or some form of it is justice.
   - Plato (c. 428-347 B.C.) Ibid., Bk. IV, Ch. XII

6. Every man to his trade.
   - English proverb, 16th century

7. Communion or community of labour would be a better term than division of labour.
   - J.K. Robertus (1805-75) Attributed

8. The greatest improvement in the productive powers of labour,

and the greater part of the skill, dexterity and judgement with which it is any where directed, or applied, seem to have been the effects of the division of labour.
- Adam Smith (1723-90) *Wealth of Nations*, ed. Cannan, Vol. I, Bk. I, Ch. I, p. 5

9. The difference between the most dissimilar characters, between a philosopher and a common street porter, for example, seems to arise not so much from nature, as from habit, custom, and education.
   - Adam Smith (1723-90) Ibid., Ch. II, p. 17

10. As it is the power of exchanging that gives occasion to the division of labour, so the extent of this division must always be limited by the extent of that power, or, in other words, by the extent of the market.
    - Adam Smith (1723-90) Ibid., Ch. III, p. 19

11. Every member of the community who stands in economic relations with others alternately generalises his special resources and then specialises his general resources.
    - P.H. Wicksteed (1844-1927) 'The Scope and Method of Political Economy', *Economic Journal*, March 1914, p. 3

36. ECONOMETRICS

1. Experience has shown that each of these three view-points, that of statistics, economic theory, and mathematics, is a necessary, but not by itself a sufficient, condition for a real understanding of the quantitative relations in modern economic life. It is the *unification* of all three that is powerful. And it is this unification that constitutes econometrics.
   - Ragnar Frisch (1895-1973) 'Editorial', *Econometrica*, 1933, p. 2

2. The quantification of economic theory is not a mechanical task. In particular, it is not simply a matter of fitting curves to data, of 'measurement without theory'.
   - Arthur S. Goldberger *Econometric Theory*, Ch. 1, p. 4

3. The 'testing of hypotheses' is frequently merely a euphemism for obtaining plausible numbers to provide ceremonial adequacy for a theory chosen and defended on *a priori* grounds.
   - Harry G. Johnson (1923-77) 'The Keynesian Revolution and the Monetarist Counter-Revolution', *American Economic Review Papers and Proceedings*, 1971, p. 2

4. Incompatible data are useless data.
   - Wassily Leontief 'Theoretical Assumptions and Nonobserved Facts',

American Economic Review,
March 1971, p. 6

5. Let us remember the unfortunate
econometrician who, in one of
the major functions of his
system, had to use a proxy for
risk and a dummy for sex.
   — Fritz Machlup
   *Journal of Political
   Economy*, July/August
   1974, p. 892

6. Econometrics may be broadly
interpreted to include every
application of mathematics or
of statistical methods to the
study of economic phenomena.
   — E. Malinvaud
   *Statistical Methods of
   Econometrics*, trans. Silvey,
   p. vii

7. With optimistic expectations
I started on my explorations,
And swore to move without a
   swerve
Along my sinusoidal curve.
Alas! I knew how it would end;
I've mixed the cycle and the
   trend.
   — Sir Dennis H. Robertson
   (1890-1963)
   'The Non-econometrician's
   Lament', *Economic
   Commentaries*, 1956, p. 174

8. [Econometricians] are not, it
seems to me, engaged in forging
tools to arrange and measure
actual facts so much as making a
marvellous array of pretend-
tools which would perform
wonders if ever a set of facts
should turn up in the right
form.

   — G.D.N. Worswick
   'Is Progress in Economic
   Science Possible?', *Economic
   Journal*, March 1972, p. 79

37. ECONOMIC HISTORY

1. There is no finality in history.
   — T.S. Ashton (1923-77)
   Preface to P. Mantoux *The
   Industrial Revolution in the
   Eighteenth Century*, revised
   ed., 1961, p. 22

2. The use of the word 'revolution'
to describe a process of
economic change may come too
easily to the pen of the
economic historian.
   — J.D. Chambers and
   G.E. Mingay
   The Agricultural Revolution,
   Preface, p. v

3. Figures are invaluable; but the
statistician's world is not the
historian's.
   — J.H. Clapham (1873-1946)
   *An Economic History of
   Modern Britain*, 2nd ed.,
   Preface, p. viii

4. We might put the task of
economic history in a nutshell
by saying it is concerned, not
with tracing the rigid operation
of economic laws in the past,
but with understanding the
pressure of *economic* forces to
overcome the *social* obstacles
to change.
   — Ralph Davis
   'History and the Social
   Sciences', Inaugural lecture,
   University of Leicester

2 March 1965

5. All decisions in the field of economic policies are essentially decisions with regard to combinations of a number of relevant factors. And the historian's contribution consists in pointing at *potentially* relevant factors and at potentially significant combinations among them which could not be easily perceived within a more limited sphere of experience.
    − Alexander Gerschenkron
       Economic Backwardness,
       1965, Ch. 1, p. 6

6. What experience and history teach is this − that people and governments never have learned anything from history, or acted on principles deduced from it.
    − G.W.F. Hegel (1770-1831)
       Philosophy of History,
       Introduction

7. A major function of economic history, as I see it, is to be a forum where economists and political scientists, lawyers, sociologists, and historians . . . can meet and talk to one another.
    − John Hicks
       A Theory of Economic History, 1969, Ch. 1, p. 2

8. The Industrial Revolution was not indeed an episode with a beginning and an end . . . It is still going on.
    − E.J. Hobsbawm
       The Age of Revolution, 1789-1848, 1962, Ch. 2, p. 46

9. Relevance in economics depends on its being integrally tied up with the fundamentals of institutional history.
    − Frank H. Knight
       'Preface to the Re-Issue',
       Risk, Uncertainty and Profit,
       1933, p. xxviii

10. Since we can only properly understand ourselves and our world, here and now, if we have something to contrast it with, the historian must provide that something.
    − Peter Laslett
       The World We Have Lost,
       1965, Ch. 10, p. 229

11. Economists and historians generally do not seem to understand the nature of causal explanation, the nature of counterfactual speculation, the problems associated with both, and the relationship between the two.
    − Peter D. McClelland
       Causal Explanation and Model Building in History, Economics, and the New Economic History, 1975, p. 17

12. Only the rare scholars in economic history can escape the condescension of economists or historians.
    − Peter Mathias
       'Living with the Neighbours: The Role of Economic History', Inaugural lecture, Oxford, 24 Nov. 1970

13. It has long been agreed that the economist is not trained who is

not numerate; but neither is he
trained if he is not historiate.
  − E.H. Phelps Brown
    'The Underdevelopment of
    Economics', *Economic
    Journal*, March 1972, p. 9

14. I don't see that anyone save a
sap-head can now think he
knows any history until he
understands economics.
  − Ezra Pound (1885-1972)
    Attributed

15. The economic interpretation of
history does *not* mean that men
are, consciously or unconcious-
ly, wholly or primarily, actuated
by economic motives.
  − Joseph A. Schumpeter
    (1883-1950)
    *Capitalism, Socialism and
    Democracy*, Ch. II, p. 10

16. The Industrial Revelation.
  − W.C. Sellar (1898-1951) and
    R.J. Yeatman (1897-1968)
    1066 and All That, Ch. 49

17. Overcrowded conditions meant
that the rise in the birthrate was
accentuated with the sexes
virtually living on top of one
another.
  − Student essay

18. History, as I understand it, is
concerned with the study, not
of a series of past events, but of
the life of society, and with the
records of the past as a means
to that end.
  − R.H. Tawney (1880-1962)
    'The Study of Economic
    History', Inaugural lecture,
    London School of

Economics, 12 Oct. 1932

38. ECONOMIC THEORY

1. The 'theory of business' leads a
life of obstruction, because
theorists do not see the
business, and the men of
business will not reason out the
theories.
  − Walter Bagehot (1826-77)
    Economic Studies, ed.
    Hutton, I, pp. 9-10

2. The maxim of science is simply
that of common sense − simple
cases first; begin with seeing
how the main force acts when
there is as little as possible to
impede it, and when you
thoroughly comprehend that,
add to it in succession the
separate effects of each of the
encumbering and interfering
agencies.
  − Walter Bagehot (1826-77)
    Ibid., II, p. 98

3. Of Empty Economic Boxes
  − J.H. Clapham (1873-1946)
    Title of Article, *Economic
    Journal*, September 1922,
    pp. 305-14.

4. It is a capital mistake to theorise
before one has data. Insensibly
one begins to twist facts to suit
theories, instead of theories to
suit facts.
  − Sir Arthur Conan Doyle
    (1859-1930)
    'A Scandal in Bohemia',
    1891, in *The Complete
    Sherlock Holmes Short*

Stories, 1928

5. Knowing how to simplify one's description of reality without neglecting anything essential is the most important part of the economist's art.
   — James S. Duesenberry
   Business Cycles and Economic Growth, 1958, pp. 14-15

6. As the astronomer will proceed from a first approximation to a second, so economists should soften the hard outline of abstract theory by a regard to particular circumstances.
   — F.Y. Edgeworth (1845-1926)
   Papers Relating to Political Economy, 1925, Vol. I, p. 51

7. The only relevant test of the *validity* of a hypothesis is comparison of its predictions with experience.
   — Milton Friedman
   'The Methodology of Positive Economics' in *Essays in Positive Economics*, 1953, pp. 8-9

8. Truly important and significant hypotheses will be found to have 'assumptions' that are wildly inaccurate descriptive representations of reality, and, in general, the more significant the theory, the more unrealistic the assumptions (in this sense).
   — Milton Friedman
   Ibid., p. 14

9. It is not enough to construct an abstract model and provide an explanation of how it operates; it is just as important to demonstrate the explanatory effectiveness of such a model as applied to historical realities.
   — Celso Furtado
   Development and Underdevelopment, 1964, p. 1

10. Pure economics has a remarkable way of producing rabbits out of a hat — apparently *a priori* propositions which apparently refer to reality.
    — J.R. Hicks
    Value and Capital, 2nd ed., Pt. I, I, p. 23

11. The great tragedy of Science — the slaying of a beautiful hypothesis by an ugly fact.
    — Thomas Henry Huxley (1825-95)
    Biogenesis and Abiogenesis, 1870

12. The theory of economics must begin with a correct theory of consumption.
    — W. Stanley Jevons (1835-82)
    Theory of Political Economy, 4th ed., Ch. III, p. 40

13. In matters of philosophy and science authority has ever been the great opponent of truth. A despotic calm is usually the triumph of error. In the republic of the sciences sedition and even anarchy are beneficial in the long run to the greatest happiness of the greatest number.
    — W. Stanley Jevons (1835-82)
    Ibid., Ch. VIII, pp. 275-6

14. The theory of economics does not furnish a body of settled conclusions immediately applicable to policy. It is a method rather than a doctrine, an apparatus of the mind, which helps its possessor to draw correct conclusions.
    - John Maynard Keynes
      (1883-1946)
      Attributed
      See also 39.48

15. A *positive science* may be defined as a body of systematized knowledge concerning what is; a *normative* or *regulative science* a body of systematized knowledge relating to criteria of what ought to be, and concerned therefore with the ideal as distinguished from the actual.
    - John Neville Keynes
      (1852-1949)
      The Scope and Method of Political Economy, 4th ed., 1917, Ch. II, pp. 34-5

16. The attempt to combine theoretical and practical enquiries tends to confirm the popular confusion as to the nature of many economic truths. What are laid down as theorems of pure science are constantly interpreted as if they were maxims for practical guidance.
    - John Neville Keynes
      (1852-1949)
      Ibid., p. 50

17. In economic analysis, the business firm is a postulate in a web of logical connections.
    - Sherman R. Krupp
      'Theoretical Explanation and the Nature of the Firm', *Western Economic Journal*, Summer 1963, p. 196

18. Unfortunately, any one capable of learning elementary, or preferably advanced calculus and algebra, and acquiring acquaintance with the specialised terminology of economics can set himself up as a theorist.
    - Wassily Leontief
      'Theoretical Assumptions and Nonobserved Facts', *American Economic Review*, March 1971, p. 1

19. The weak and all too slowly growing empirical foundation clearly cannot support the proliferating superstructure of pure, or should I say, speculative economic theory.
    - Wassily Leontief
      Ibid.

20. Familiarity with the classical models has become a kind of hallmark of the education of an economic theorist, even if it helps him more in the comprehension of the traditional lingo than in the analysis of current economic problems.
    - Fritz Machlup
      The Economics of Sellers' Competition, 1952, p. 369

21. Marginal analysis of the firm should not be understood to imply anything but subjective estimates, guesses and hunches.
    - Fritz Machlup
      'Marginal Analysis and

Empirical Research',
American Economic Review,
September 1946, p. 522

22. The choice of theory has to
depend on the problem we have
to solve.
   — Fritz Machlup
     'Theories of the Firm',
     American Economic Review,
     March 1967, p. 31

23. Facts by themselves are silent.
   — Alfred Marshall (1842-1924)
     *The Present Position of
     Economics*, 1885, p. 41

24. The most reckless and treacher-
ous of all theorists is he who
professes to let facts and figures
speak for themselves, who keeps
in the background the part he
has played, perhaps uncon-
sciously, in selecting and
grouping them, and in
suggesting the argument *post
hoc ergo propter hoc*.
   — Alfred Marshall (1842-1924)
     Ibid., p. 44

25. Economic theory is, in my
opinion, as mischievous an
imposter when it claims to be
economics *proper* as is mere
crude unanalysed history.
   — Alfred Marshall (1842-1924)
     Letter to F.Y. Edgeworth,
     28 Aug. 1902. Quoted in
     A.C. Pigou, *Memorials of
     Alfred Marshall*, p. 437

26. Happily, there is nothing in the laws
of value which remains [1848]
for the present or any future
writer to clear up; the theory of
the subject is complete.

   — John Stuart Mill (1806-73)
     *Principles of Political
     Economy*, ed. Ashley,
     Bk. III, Ch. I, 1, p. 436
     See also 39.89

27. [An economic law] . . . a statement of economic tendencies.
   — John Stuart Mill (1806-73)
     Attributed

28. Following the money-making
pattern, economic theory
became, not an account of
actual behaviour such as
historians attempt to provide,
but an analysis of what it is to
the interest of men to do
under a variety of imagined
conditions.
   — Wesley Clair Mitchell
     (1874-1948)
     'The Role of Money in
     Economic History', *Journal
     of Economic History*,
     Supplement, December
     1944, p. 65

29. Economic theory became a
fascinating subject — the
orthodox types particularly —
when one began to take the
mental operations of the
theorists as the problem.
   — Wesley Clair Mitchell
     (1874-1948)
     Quoted in Guy Roth, *The
     Origin of Economic Ideas*

30. The economist . . . who in
commending a law takes into
consideration its economic
effects alone, is not very much
of a theorist. He is not
theoretical enough because he is
neglecting other theories which

he should combine with his own in order to make a judgement in this practical case.
- Vilfredo Pareto (1848-1923) *Manual of Political Economy*, trans. Schwier, Ch. 1, p. 14

31. Let us look at these awkward questions squarely in the face and pass rapidly on.
    - Sir Dennis Robertson (1890-1963) Attributed

32. The isolation of the theory of Political Economy is peculiar to our own day. In more remote times, we find this study confounded with the other moral sciences, of which it was an integral part. When the genius of Adam Smith gave it a distinct character, he did not desire to separate it from those branches of knowledge without which it could only remain a bleached plant from the absence of the sunlight of ethics.
    - W. Roscher (1817-94) *Principles of Political Economy*, trans. Lalor, Vol. I, 'Preliminary Essay', p. 23

33. The abstraction according to which all men are by nature the same, different only in consequence of a difference of education, position in life, etc., all equally well equipped, skilful, and free in the matter of economic production and consumption, is one which . . . must pass as an indispensable stage in the preparatory labours of political economists . . . But

it never should be lost sight of, that such a one is only an abstraction after all, from which, not only in the transition to practice, but even in finished theory, we must turn to the infinite variety of real life.
- W. Roscher (1817-94) Ibid., Ch. III, Sec. XXII, pp. 104-5

34. A body of propositions, such as those of pure mathematics or theoretical physics, can be deduced from a certain apparatus of initial assumptions concerning initial undefined terms. Any reduction in the number of undefined terms and unproved premises is an improvement since it diminishes the range of possible error and provides a smaller assemblage of hostages for the truth of the whole system.
    - Bertrand Russell (1872-1970) 'Philosophical Analysis', *Hibbert Journal*, July 1956, p. 321

35. Good theory is usually trying to tell you something, even if it is not the literal truth.
    - Robert M. Solow 'The Economics of Resources or the Resources of Economics', *American Economic Review*, May 1974, p. 10

36. It is notorious, that many positions are true in the abstract, which are utterly false when applied to particular cases and circumstances.

— William Spence (1783-1860)
Tracts on Political Economy,
1822, p. xxvii

37. Pareto optimentality.
  — Student essay

38. It is a fascinating paradox that
the received theory of the firm,
by and large, assumes that the
firm does not exist.
  — Hans B. Thorelli
  'The Political Economy of
  the Firm', *Schweiz. Zeitschr.
  Volkswirtschaft und Stat.*,
  1965, p. 249

39. There now exist whole branches
of abstract economic theory
which have no links with
concrete facts and are almost
indistinguishable from pure
mathematics.
  — G.D.N. Worswick
  'Is Progress in Economic
  Science Possible?', *Economic
  Journal*, March 1972,
  p. 78

39. ECONOMICS

1. Economics isn't fair.
  — Anonymous

2. In economics, everything
depends on everything else —
and in more than one way.
  — Anonymous

3. In economics the basic
questions do not change — it is
the answers that change from
time to time.
  — Anonymous

4. You cannot understand anything in economics until you
have already understood it all.
  — Anonymous

5. Who put the con in economics?
  — Anonymous

6. The science of Political Economy
as we have it in England may be
defined as the science of
business, such as business is in
large productive and trading
communities.
  — Walter Bagehot (1826-77)
  Economic Studies, ed.
  Hutton, I, p. 6

7. Nothing but unreality can come
of [political economy] till we
know when and how far its first
assertions are true in matter of
fact, and when and how far they
are not.
  — Walter Bagehot (1826-77)
  Ibid., p. 94

8. Wants, Efforts, Satisfaction —
this is the circle of Political
Economy.
  — Frédéric Bastiat (1801-50)
  *Harmonies of Political
  Economy*, trans. P.J. Stirling,
  1860, p. 65

9. Like other sciences, economics
has two sides: the theories and
the facts.
  — Wilfred Beckerman
  *In Defence of Economic
  Growth*, 1976, Ch. I, p. 21

10. [Economics is] the study of the
general methods by which men
co-operate to meet their
material needs.

- Sir William Beveridge
(1879-1963)
'Economics as a Liberal
Education', *Economica*,
January 1921, p. 2

11. It is always depressing to go
back to Adam Smith, especially
on economic development, as
one realises how little we have
learned in nearly two hundred
years.
    - Kenneth E. Boulding
    'The Economics of Know-
    ledge and the Knowledge of
    Economics', *American
    Economic Review*, May
    1966, p. 6

12. Political Economy offers no
opinion, pronounces no judgement, thus . . . standing neutral
between competing social
schemes; neutral, as the science
of Mechanics stands neutral
between competing plans of
railway construction, in which
expense for instance, as well as
mechanical efficiency, is to be
considered; neutral, as
Chemistry stands neutral
between competing plans of
sanitary improvement, . . . it
supplies the means, or, more
correctly, a portion of the
means for estimating all; it
refuses to identify itself with
any.
    - J.E. Cairnes (1824-75)
    *The Character and Logical
    Mind of Political Economy*,
    2nd ed., 1875, p. 21

13. The really fundamental
questions of economics are why
all of us, taken together, are as

well off — or as ill off, if that
way of putting it be preferred —
as we are, and why some of us
are much better off and others
much worse off than the average.
    - Edwin Cannan (1861-1935)
    Wealth, Preface to the
    1st ed., 1914

14. There is no precise line between
economic and non-economic
satisfactions, and therefore the
province of economics cannot
be marked out by a row of posts
or a fence like a political
territory or a landed property.
    - Edwin Cannan (1861-1935)
    Ibid., 3rd ed., Ch. 1, p. 4

15. Social science . . . which finds
the secret of this Universe in
'supply and demand', and
reduces the duty of human
governors to that of letting men
alone . . . Not a gay science . . .
no, a dreary, desolate, and
indeed quite abject and
distressing one; what we might
call, by way of eminence, the
dismal science.
    - Thomas Carlyle (1795-1881)
    'The Nigger Question' in
    *Critical and Miscellaneous
    Essays*, 1872, Vol. VII, p. 84

16. [Economics is] the science that
treats phenomena from the
standpoint of price.
    - H.J. Davenport (1861-1931)
    The Economics of Enterprise,
    1925, p. 25

17. Political economy is, in the last
analysis, applied psychology —
the study of human activities in
certain classes of phenomena.

      — H.J. Davenport (1861-1931)
      'The Formula of Sacrifice',
      *Journal of Political
      Economy*, 1893-4, p. 561

18. Economic forces are tendencies
to conformity with a moving
equilibrium whose energy is the
expression of human demands.
      — H.J. Davenport (1861-1931)
      Ibid., p. 573

19. Economic policy affects the
well-being of the people, and its
success or failure in meeting
social objectives is, in the last
analysis, the only thing that
matters.
      — J.C.R. Dow
      *The Management of the
      British Economy 1945-60*,
      Ch. XIV, p. 364

20. Economics investigates the
arrangements between agents
each tending to his own
maximum utility.
      — F.Y. Edgeworth
      (1845-1926)
      Mathematical Psychics,
      1881, p. 6

21. The first principle of Economics
is that every agent is actuated
only by self-interest.
      — F.Y. Edgeworth
      (1845-1926)
      Ibid., p. 16

22. It is utterly indifferent to the
English bourgeois whether his
working-men starve or not, if
only he makes money. All the
conditions of life are measured
by money, and what brings no
money is non-sense, unpractical,
idealistic bosh. Hence Political
Economy, the science of Wealth,
is the favourite study of these
bartering Jews. Every one of
them is a Political Economist.
      — Frederick Engels (1820-95)
      *The Condition of the
      Working Class in England in
      1844*, 1892, Ch. XI, p. 277

23. If there ever is another great
synthetic statement to cover
economics and its current
problems of growth, then that
new statement or theory will
not be a general theory of
economics alone, it will instead
be a general theory of social
affairs.
      — M.J. Fores
      'No More General Theories?',
      Economic Journal, March
      1969, p. 19

24. The first problem for the
economist to solve is to discover
some way of transforming the
wage-earner into a co-operative
owner.
      — Charles Fourier (1772-1837)
      Association Domestique,
      Vol. I, p. 466, quoted in
      Gide and Rist *A History of
      Economic Doctrines*, 1913

25. In politics, equality; in
economics, subordination. One
man, one vote; why not also one
man, one wage?
      — H.S. Foxwell (1849-1936)
      Introduction to A. Menger,
      *The Right to the Whole
      Produce of Labour*

26. The economist's value judgements doubtless influence the

subjects he works on and perhaps also at times the conclusions he reaches . . . Yet this does not alter the fundamental point that, in principle there are no value judgements in economics.
- Milton Friedman
'Value Judgements in Economics', in Sidney Hook (ed.), *Human Values and Economic Policy*, 1967, p. 86

27. The name of political economy has been constantly invoked against every effort of the working classes to increase their wages or decrease their hours of labour.
- Henry George (1839-97)
Lecture at the University of California, 9 March 1877, in *Works*, 1904, Vol. VIII, p. 139

28. For the study of political economy you need no special knowledge, no extensive library, no costly laboratory. You do not even need text-books nor teachers, if you will but think for yourselves.
- Henry George (1839-97)
Ibid., p. 148

29. The origin of economic thought is lost in the past. In its simplest form it must have always existed wherever thinking beings sought to gain a living.
- Lewis H. Haney
History of Economic Thought, revised ed., 1920, Ch. II, p. 24

30. The most basic law of economics . . . that one cannot get something for nothing.
- Sir Roy Harrod
Towards a Dynamic Economics, 1948, p. 36

31. Economics is indubitably a study of the functions exercised by individuals working in combination for personal ends.
- Frederick Barnard Hawley (1843-1929)
Enterprise and the Productive Process, 1907, Ch. IX, p. 272

32. Economic solutions create their own problems and move the economist relentlessly from one new frontier to another.
- Walter W. Heller
'What's Right With Economics?', *American Economic Review*, March 1975, p. 22

33. Economic life is an organisation of producers to satisfy the wants of consumers.
- J.R. Hicks
The Social Framework, 1942, Pt. I, Ch. I

34. The nature of Wealth and Value is explained by the consideration of indefinitely small amounts of pleasure and pain, just as the Theory of Statics is made to rest upon the equality of indefinitely small amounts of energy.
- W. Stanley Jevons (1835-82)
Theory of Political Economy, Preface to the 1st ed.

35. I have attempted to treat Economy as a Calculus of Pleasure and Pain.
    - W. Stanley Jevons (1835-82) Ibid.

36. [Economics is] the mechanics of utility and self-interest.
    - W. Stanley Jevons (1835-82) Ibid., 4th ed., Introduction, p. 21

37. Economics, if it is to be a science at all, must be a mathematical science.
    - W. Stanley Jevons (1835-82) Ibid., Ch. I, p. 3

38. Pleasure and pain are undoubtedly the ultimate objects of the Calculus of Economics. To satisfy our wants to the utmost with the least effort — to procure the greatest amount of what is desirable at the expense of the least that is undesirable — in other words, *to maximise pleasure*, is the problem of Economics.
    - W. Stanley Jevons (1835-82) Ibid., Ch. III, p. 37

39. The methodology of positive economics was an ideal methodology for justifying work that produced apparently surprising results without feeling obliged to explain just why they occurred.
    - Harry G. Johnson (1923-77) 'The Keynesian Revolution and the Monetarist Counter-Revolution', *American Economic Review, Papers and Proceedings*, 1971, p. 13

40. For the social sciences man is his own environment.
    - Harry G. Johnson (1923-77) 'Mercantilism: Past, Present and Future', *Manchester School*, March 1974, p. 2

41. If we wish to make ourselves acquainted with the economy and arrangements by which the different nations of the earth produce or distribute their revenues, I really know of but one way to obtain our object, and that is to look and see.
    - Richard Jones (1790-1855) Introductory Lecture at King's College, *Literary Remains*, p. 569

42. There is no need for the economist to prove — as indeed he never could prove — that as a result of the adoption of a certain measure nobody in the community is going to suffer. In order to establish his case, it is quite sufficient for him to show that even if all those who suffer as a result are fully compensated for their loss, the rest of the community will still be better off than before.
    - Nicholas Kaldor 'Welfare Propositions of Economics', *Economic Journal*, September 1939

43. Economic policy should not be a matter of tearing up by the roots but of slowly training a plant to grow in a different direction.
    - John Maynard Keynes (1883-1946) Quoted by Margaret

Thatcher, Speech, 1975

44. There is no more important prerequisite to clear thinking in regard to economics itself than is recognition of its limited place among human interests at large.
    - Frank H. Knight
    The Economic Organisation, 1951, p. 3

45. *Das Kapital* instead of being the prologue to the communal critique, is simply the epilogue of *bourgeois* economics.
    - Antonio Labriola (1843-1904)
    Conception Matérialiste, p. 91

46. It's called political economy because it has nothing to do with either politics or economy.
    - Stephen Leacock (1869-1944)
    Quoted in Esar and Bentley, *The Treasury of Humorous Quotations*

47. Political Economy is not a body of natural laws in the true sense, or of universal and immutable truths, but an assemblage of speculations and doctrines which are the result of a particular history.
    - Thomas Edward Cliffe Leslie (1826-82)
    Essays in Political and Moral Philosophy, 1879, X, p. 148

48. While attributing . . . high and transcendent universality to the central scheme of economic reasoning; I do not assign any universality to economic dogmas . . . It is not a body of concrete truth, but an engine for the discovery of concrete truth.
    - Alfred Marshall (1842-1924)
    The Present Position of Economics, 1885, p. 25
    See also 38.14

49. Economics is a study of mankind in the ordinary business of life.
    - Alfred Marshall (1842-1924)
    Principles of Economics, 8th ed., Bk. I, Ch. I, 1, p. 1

50. The laws of economics are to be compared with the laws of the tides, rather than with the simple and exact law of gravitation. For the actions of men are so various and uncertain, that the best statement of tendencies, which we can make in a science of human conduct, must needs be inexact and faulty.
    - Alfred Marshall (1842-1924)
    Ibid., Ch. III, 3, p. 32

51. Economic science is but the working of common sense aided by appliances of organised analysis and general reasoning.
    - Alfred Marshall (1842-1924)
    Ibid., Ch. IV, 1, p. 38

52. The 'principles' of economics must aim at affording guidance to an entry on problems of life, without making claim to be a substitute for independent study and thought.
    - Alfred Marshall (1842-1924)

Ibid., Bk. V, Ch. XII, 3,
p. 459, footnote

53. The function then of analysis
and deduction in economics is
not to forge a few long chains of
reasoning, but to forge rightly
many short chains and single
connecting links.
   − Alfred Marshall (1842-1924)
   Ibid., Appendix C, p. 773

54. If I had to live my life over
again I should have devoted it
to psychology. Economics has
too little to do with ideals.
   − Alfred Marshall (1842-1924)
   Quoted in A.C. Pigou,
   Memorials of Alfred Marshall,
   p. 37

55. Though a simple book can be
written on selected topics, the
central doctrines of Economics
are not simple and cannot be
made so.
   − Alfred Marshall (1842-1924)
   Ibid., p. 38

56. Memory is quite as often a curse
as a blessing to the student of
economics, because it tempts
him to recollect particulars, and
there never was a memory that
could retain a hundredth part of
the particulars needful for
solving a very small problem.
   − Alfred Marshall (1842-1924)
   Letter to A.L. Bowley,
   3 March 1901, ibid., p. 412

57. My favourite *dictum* is: Every
statement in regard to economic
affairs which is short is a
misleading fragment, a fallacy or
a truism. I think this dictum of

mine is an exception to the
general rule: but I am not bold
enough to say that it *certainly*
is.
   − Alfred Marshall (1842-1924)
   Letter to L. Fry, 7 November
   1914, ibid., p. 484

58. But the more I studied
economic science, the smaller
appeared the knowledge which I
had of it, in proportion to the
knowledge that I needed; and
now, at the end of nearly half
a century of almost exclusive
study of it, I am conscious of
more ignorance of it than I was
at the beginning of the study.
   − Alfred Marshall (1842-1924)
   Quoted in J.M. Keynes,
   Essays in Biography, Royal
   Economic Society ed.,
   p. 171

59. In the domain of Political
Economy, free scientific inquiry
meets not merely the same
enemies as in all other domains.
The peculiar nature of the
material it deals with, summons
as foes into the field of battle
the most violent, mean and
malignant passions of the
human breast, the Furies of
private interest.
   − Karl Marx (1818-83)
   Capital, Preface to the 1st
   German ed., 25 July 1867

60. It is not the articles made, but
how they are made, and by
what instruments, that enables
us to distinguish different
economical epochs.
   − Karl Marx (1818-83)
   Ibid., Vol. I, Pt. III, Ch. VII, 2

61. Economics is the science of
    greed.
    – F.V. Meyer
    Attributed

62. Political Economy is to the
    State, what domestic economy
    is to the family.
    – James Mill (1773-1836)
    *Elements of Political
    Economy*, 3rd ed.,
    Introduction

63. If Political Economy be a
    science, it cannot be a collection
    of practical rules; though,
    unless it be altogether a useless
    science, practical rules must
    be capable of being founded
    upon it.
    – John Stuart Mill (1806-73)
    *Essays on some Unsettled
    Questions of Political
    Economy*, 1844, p. 124

64. For practical purposes, Political
    Economy is inseparably inter-
    twined with many other
    branches of Social Philosophy.
    Except on matters of mere
    detail, there are perhaps no
    practical questions, even among
    those which approach nearest
    to the character of purely
    economical questions, which
    admit of being decided on
    economical premises alone.
    – John Stuart Mill (1806-73)
    *Principles of Political
    Economy*, ed. Ashley,
    Preface, pp. xxvii-xxviii

65. Economic activity is rational
    activity . . . it consists firstly in
    valuation of ends, and then in
    the valuation of the means

leading to these ends.
    – Ludwig Von Mises
    (1881-1973)
    Socialism, English ed.,
    1936, p. 22

66. We ought to value powers of
    observation more highly than
    powers of abstraction, and the
    insight of the historian more
    than the rigour of the
    mathematician.
    – E.H. Phelps Brown
    'The Underdevelopment of
    Economics', *Economic
    Journal*, March 1972, p. 9

67. The main motive of economic
    study is to help social
    improvement.
    – A.C. Pigou (1877-1959)
    Economics of Welfare,
    4th ed., p. ix

68. Economic welfare may be
    defined roughly as that part of
    welfare that can be brought into
    relation with the measuring rod
    of money.
    – A.C. Pigou (1877-1959)
    Ibid.

69. Contrasted with . . . pure
    science stands realistic
    economics, the interest of which
    is concentrated upon the world
    known in experience, and in
    nowise extends to the
    commercial doings of a
    community of angels.
    – A.C. Pigou (1877-1959)
    Ibid., Pt. I, Ch. I, p. 6

70. Our subject in popular versions
    of it, sometimes even in the
    hands of distinguished writers,

has furnished forth for the ungodly blunt instruments with which to bludgeon at birth useful projects of social betterment.
  − A.C. Pigou (1877-1959)
    Quoted in Guy Roth, *The Origin of Economic Ideas*

71. Economic perfection lies in the absolute independence of the workers, just as political perfection consists in the absolute independence of the citizens.
  − Pierre-Joseph Proudhon (1809-65)
    La Révolution démontrée par le Coup d'État, p. 54

72. To secure the greatest amount of pleasure with the least possible outlay should be the aim of all economic effort.
  − François Quesnay (1694-1774)
    Dialogues sur les Artisans, quoted in Gide and Rist, *A History of Economic Doctrines*, 1913, pp. 10-11

73. The laws which regulate this distribution [of rent, profits and labour], is the principle problem in Political Economy.
  − David Ricardo (1772-1823)
    Principles of Political Economy and Taxation, ed. Sraffa, Preface, p. 5

74. Political Economy you think is an inquiry into the nature and causes of wealth − I think it should rather be called an inquiry into the laws which determine the division of the produce of industry amongst the classes who concur in its formation.
  − David Ricardo (1772-1823)
    Letter to Malthus, 9 Oct. 1820, in *Works*, ed. Sraffa, Vol. VIII, p. 278

75. Economics is a science which studies human behaviour as a relationship between ends and scarce means which have alternative uses.
  − Lionel Robbins
    An Essay on the Nature and Significance of Economic Science, 2nd ed., 1935, p. 16

76. Economics is not concerned at all with any ends *as such* ... It takes the ends as given in scales of relative valuation, and enquires what consequences follow in regard to certain aspects of behaviour.
  − Lionel Robbins
    Ibid., p. 30

77. The purpose of studying economics is not to acquire a set of ready-made answers to economic questions, but to learn how to avoid being deceived by economists.
  − Joan Robinson
    Marx, Marshall and Keynes, 1955

78. Normality is a fiction of economic textbooks.
  − Joan Robinson
    'The Second Crisis of Economic Theory', *American Economic Review*, May 1972, p. 2

79. In economics, arguments are largely devoted, as in theology, to supporting doctrines rather than testing hypotheses.
    - Joan Robinson
      'What Are The Questions?',
      Journal of Economic Literature, 1977, p. 1318

80. There is no human relation, not even the highest and the sweetest, but has its economic interests.
    - W. Roscher (1817-94)
      Principles of Political Economy, trans. Lalor, Vol. I, Ch. II, Sec. XVI, p. 88

81. Political Economy does not deal with particular facts but with general tendencies, and when we assign to cost of production the power of regulating price in cases of equal competition, we mean to describe it not as a point to which price is attached, but as a centre of oscillation which it is always endeavouring to approach.
    - Nassau W. Senior
      (1790-1864)
      Outline of the Science of Political Economy, 'Cost of Production, p. 102

82. Economics for Pleasure.
    - G.L.S. Shackle
      Title of book

83. Economic man deals with the 'real world' in all its complexity.
    - Herbert Simon
      Administrative Behaviour, 2nd ed., 1957, p. xxv

84. Economics, whether normative or positive, has not simply been the study of the allocation of scarce resources, it has been the study of the *rational* allocation of scarce resources.
    - Herbert Simon
      'Rationality as Process and as Product of Thought',
      American Economic Review, May 1978, p. 2

85. The great object of the political economy of every country, is to increase the riches and power of that country.
    - Adam Smith (1723-90)
      Wealth of Nations, ed. Cannan, Vol. I, Bk. II, Ch. V, p. 351

86. Less than a century ago a treatise on economics began with a sentence such as, 'Economics is a study of mankind in the ordinary business of life.' Today it will often begin, 'This unavoidably lengthy treatise is devoted to an examination of an economy in which the second derivatives of the utility function possess a finite number of discontinuities. To keep the problem manageable, I assume that each individual consumes only two goods, and dies after one Robertsonian week. Only elementary mathematical tools such as topology will be employed, incessantly.'
    - George J. Stigler
      The Intellectual and the Market Place, 1963, p. 94
      See also 39.49

87. The most difficult issues of
    political economy are those
    where goals of efficiency,
    freedom of choice, and equality
    conflict.
    – James Tobin
      'On Limiting the Domain of
      Inequality', *Journal of Law
      and Economics*, October
      1970, p. 263

88. The labouring classes compose
    the great bulk of any
    community: and a country is
    happy or miserable, as they are
    well or ill supplied with the
    necessaries, comforts and
    enjoyments of life. The study of
    Political Economy, if it did not
    teach the way in which labour
    may obtain an adequate reward,
    might serve to gratify a merely
    speculative curiosity, but could
    scarcely conduce to any
    purposes of practical utility.
    – Robert Torrens (1780-1864)
      *Colonel Torrens on Wages
      and on the Means of Improv-
      ing the Conditions of the
      Labouring Classes*, 1832

89. With respect to Political
    Economy the period of
    controversy is passing away, and
    that of unanimity rapidly
    approaching. Twenty years
    hence there will scarcely exist a
    doubt respecting any of its
    fundamental principles.
    – Robert Torrens (1780-1864)
      *An Essay on the Production
      of Wealth*, 1821, Preface,
      p. xiii

90. The hedonistic conception of
    man is that of a lightning

calculator of pleasures and
pains, who oscillates like a
homogeneous globule of desire
of happiness under the impulse
of stimuli that shift him about
the area, but leave him intact.
He has neither antecedent nor
consequent. He is an isolated,
definitive human datum, in
stable equilibrium except for
the buffets of the impinging
forces that displace him in one
direction or another. Self-
imposed in elemental space,
he spins symmetrically about his
own spiritual axis until the
parallelogram of forces bears
down upon him, whereupon he
follows the line of the resultant.
When the force of impact is
spent, he comes to rest, a self-
contained globule of desire
as before.
– Thorstein Veblen
  (1857-1929)
  'Why is Economics Not an
  Evolutionary Science?', in
  *The Place of Science in
  Modern Civilisation*, 1961,
  pp. 73-4

91. I have maintained from first to
    last that the laws of Economics
    are the laws of life.
    – Philip H. Wicksteed
      (1844-1927)
      *The Common Sense of
      Political Economy*, ed.
      Robbins, Vol. II, Bk. II,
      Ch. I, p. 404

92. MISS PRISM: Cecily, you will
    read your political economy in
    my absence. The chapter on the
    fall of the rupee you may omit.
    It is somewhat too sensational.

Even these metallic problems
have their melodramatic side.
 — Oscar Wilde (1854-1900)
   *The Importance of Being
   Earnest*, 1895, Act II

93. Very much of the literature of
economics strikes me as
rationalisation after the event.
 — John H. Williams
   'An Economist's Con-
   fessions', *American
   Economic Review*, March
   1952, p. 2

94. Those who have never seen the
inhabitants of a nineteenth-
century London slum can have
no idea of the state to which
dirt, drink and economics can
reduce human beings.
 — Leonard Woolf (1880-1969)
   Sowing, 1960

95. What is lacking [in econo-
mics] is any effective means
of communication between
abstract theory and concrete
application.
 — Barbara Wootton
   Lament for Economics,
   1938, p. 64

40. ECONOMISTS

1. Economists are technological
radicals. They assume every-
thing can be done.
 — Anonymous
   Quoted by Tjalling C.
   Koopmans, 'Economics
   Among the Sciences',
   American Economic Review,
   March 1979, p. 12

2. I will not go so far as to say that
English economists have lived
by taking in one another's
washing, but it is certainly true
that they have spent a vast
amount of time mangling one
another's theories.
 — Anonymous

3. When two or three economists
are gathered together, there are
four or five opinions.
 — Anonymous

4. You can make even a parrot
into a learned political
economist — all he must learn
are the two words 'supply' and
'demand'.
 — Anonymous

5. English political economists are
not speaking of real men, but of
imaginary ones; not of men as
we see them, but of men as it is
convenient to us to suppose
they are.
 — Walter Bagehot (1826-77)
   Economic Studies, ed.
   Hutton, I, p. 7

6. But the age of chivalry is gone.
That of sophisters, economists,
and calculators, has succeeded;
and the glory of Europe is
extinguished for ever.
 — Edmund Burke (1729-97)
   *Reflections on the Revolu-
   tion in France*, Everyman
   ed., p. 73

7. The almost complete absorption
of the younger teachers in
making what they rightly or
wrongly believe to be important
advances in the higher branches

of theory is leaving the public at the mercy of quacks.
- Edwin Cannan (1861-1935) 'The Need for Simpler Economics', *Economic Journal*, September 1933, p. 367

8. Most of the simplest things in economics have never been put in such a way as to carry conviction to the mind of the sort of person who is in the great majority of every public, and the blame is not altogether to be put on his feeble mind, but in large measure on the unnecessarily complicated expositions offered by the economists.
- Edwin Cannan (1861-1935) Ibid., p. 368

9. Economists, indeed, seem never in danger of unemployment, because, while new problems are constantly arising, old ones are never settled.
- Warren B. Catlin *The Progress of Economics*, Ch. 26, p. 557

10. Economists do not grow bitter gracefully. Many of them came to the subject hoping to do good and to be useful and find that they can do far less than they had expected.
- F.H. Hahn 'The Winter of our Discontent', *Economica*, August 1973, p. 322

11. What Do Economists Know?
- Benjamin Higgins Title of book, 1951

12. But ... do not let us overestimate the importance of the economic problem, or sacrifice to its supposed necessities other matters of greater and more permanent significance. It should be a matter for specialists – like dentistry. If economists could manage to get themselves thought of as humble, competent people, on a level with dentists, that would be splendid!
- John Maynard Keynes (1883-1946) 'Economic Possibilities for our Grandchildren', in *Essays in Persuasion*, 1933, Pt. V, p. 373 *See also 73.4*

13. The ideas of economists and political philosophers, both when they are right and when they are wrong, are more powerful than is commonly understood. Indeed the world is ruled by little else. Practical men, who believe themselves to be quite exempt from any intellectual influences, are usually the slaves of some defunct economist.
- John Maynard Keynes (1883-1946) *The General Theory of Employment Interest and Money*, Bk. VI, Ch. 24, p. 383

14. The dominant feature, which makes status relations among the Econ of unique interest to the serious student, is the way that status is tied to the manufacture of certain types of

implements, called 'modls'. The status of the adult male is determined by his skill at making the 'modl' of his 'field'. The facts (a) that the Econ are highly status-motivated, (b) that status is only to be achieved by making 'modls', and (c) that most of these 'modls' seem to be of little or no practical use, probably accounts for the backwardness and abject cultural poverty of the tribe . . .
— Axel Leijonhufvud
'Life Among the Econ',
Western Economic Journal,
1973, pp. 328 and 330

15. The bane of political economy has been the haste of its students to possess themselves of a complete and symmetrical system, solving all the problems before it with mathematical certainty and exactness. The very attempt shows an entire misconception of the nature of those problems, and of the means available for their solution.
— Thomas Edward Cliffe Leslie (1826-82)
Essays in Political and Moral Philosophy, 1879, XIV, p. 241

16. One of the principle causes [of the notorious differences of opinion among political economists] may be traced to the different meanings in which the same terms have been used by different writers.
— Thomas Robert Malthus (1766-1834)

Definitions in Political Economy, 1827, Preface

17. Nowadays, in most of the world's capitals, nearly every official fancies himself as an economist, and, particularly in this country [the UK], nearly every economist fancies himself as something of an administrator.
— R.L. Marris
'The Position of Economics and Economists in the Government Machine',
Economic Journal,
December 1954, p. 759

18. Among the bad results of the narrowness of the work of English economists early in the century perhaps the most unfortunate was the opportunity which it gave to sciolists to quote and misapply economic dogmas.
[A sciolist is a person who uses superficial knowledge to impress others]
— Alfred Marshall (1842-1924)
The Present Position of Economics, 1885, p. 18

19. An economist as such cannot say which is the best course to pursue, any more than an engineer as such can decide which is the best route for the Panama canal.
— Alfred Marshall (1842-1924)
Ibid., p. 38

20. The vulgar economists.
— Karl Marx (1818-83)
Capital, Vol. I, Pt. I, Ch. I
4

21. Political economists . . . are apt
to express themselves as if they
thought that competition
actually does, in all cases,
whatever it can be shown to be
the tendency of competition
to do.
   – John Stuart Mill (1806-73)
   *Principles of Political
   Economy*, ed. Ashley, Bk. II,
   Ch. IV, 1, p. 242

22. I find it a common experience
that when graduates in
economics first assume practical
responsibilities they have
something to unlearn.
   – E.H. Phelps Brown
   'The Underdevelopment of
   Economics', *Economic
   Journal*, March 1972, p. 2

23. Among persons interested in
economic analysis, there are
tool-makers and tool-users.
   – A.C. Pigou (1877-1959)
   'The Function of Economic
   Analysis', Sidney Ball
   Lecture, 1929, reprinted in
   *Economic Essays and
   Addresses*, p. 3

24. My objection to the counsel of
economists is not that it is
wholly and always wrong, but
that it is so often insufficient.
   – M.M. Postan
   'The Uses and Abuses of
   Economics' in *Fact and
   Relevance*, 1971, p. 93

25. It has been well said by M. Say
that it is not the province of the
Political Economist to advise: –
he is there to tell you how you
may become rich, but he is not

to advise you to prefer riches to
indolence, or indolence to
riches.
   – David Ricardo (1772-1823)
   Notes on Malthus, in *Works*,
   ed. Sraffa, Vol. II, p. 338

26. It is only by using their tools
upon observed facts that
economists can build up that
working model of the actual
world which it is their aim to
construct.
   – Joan Robinson
   *The Economics of Imperfect
   Competition*, 1934, p. 1

27. The purpose of this book has
been to provide a box of tools
for the analytical economist.
   – Joan Robinson
   Ibid., p. 327

28. The orthodox economists have
been much preoccupied with
elegant elaborations of minor
problems.
   – Joan Robinson
   *An Essay on Marxian
   Economics*, 1947, Ch. I,
   p. 2

29. Economists have been and
remain largely a teaching order;
when they enter government or
business or field research in the
UDCs, their tools become an
encumbrance and are soon
thrown away.
   – Guy Routh
   *The Origin of Economic
   Ideas*, 1975, Ch. 6, p. 295

30. I am struck by the fact that
economists – both inside and
outside government – will

support their views by reference to non-economic considerations without subjecting their allegations to the same rigorous tests they would apply to the most humble equation.
— George P. Schultz
'Reflections on Political Economy', *Journal of Finance*, 1974, p. 324

31. His conclusions, whatever be their generality and their truth, do not authorize him in adding a single syllable of advice . . . The business of a Political Economist is neither to recommend nor to dissuade, but to state general principles, which it is fatal to neglect, but neither advisable, nor perhaps practicable, to use as the sole, or even the principal, guides in the actual conduct of affairs.
— Nassau W. Senior (1790-1864)
Outline of the Science of Political Economy, Introduction, p. 3

32. If all economists were laid end to end, they would not reach a conclusion.
— George Bernard Shaw (1856-1950)
Attributed

33. If the proper study of mankind is man, then the proper study of market economists is surely the market for economists. In decrying the imperfections of other product and labor markets, we would be delinquent without an occasional look at our own.

— G.S. Somers
'The Functioning of the Market for Economists', *American Economic Review*, Papers and Proceedings, May 1962, p. 509

34. Unhappily the lay disciples of the economists have a tendency to adopt their conclusions and then discard their definitions.
— Philip H. Wicksteed (1844-1927)
Alphabet of Economic Science, 1888, p. 84

35. Even if positive economics were an exact science, the idea that the generation of policy would be exclusively decided by the layman or the politician, who would then simply ask the economist to explain the consequences of alternative policies, has never been wholly convincing.
— G.D.N. Worswick
'Is Progress in Economic Science Possible?', *Economic Journal*, March 1972, p. 86

41. ECONOMY

1. Economy, *n.* Purchasing the barrel of whiskey that you do not need for the price of the cow that you cannot afford.
— Ambrose Bierce (1842-1914?)
The Devil's Dictionary

2. Everybody is always in favour of general economy and particular expenditure.
— Sir Anthony Eden

(1897-1977)
Quoted in *The Observer*,
17 June 1956

3. Economy is going without
    something you do want in case
    you should, some day, want
    something you probably won't
    want.
    — Anthony Hope (1863-1933)
    The Dolly Dialogues, 12

4. The mixed-up economy.
    — Harry G. Johnson (1923-77)
    Attributed

5. The truth is, that the whole
    economy of every nation, as
    regards the occupations and
    pursuits of both sexes, the
    nature, amount, distribution
    and consumption of wealth, is
    the result of a long evolution in
    which there has been both
    continuity and change, and of
    which the economical side is
    only a particular aspect or
    phase.
    — Thomas Edward Cliffe Leslie
    (1826-82)
    *Essays in Political and Moral
    Philosophy*, 1879, XIV,
    p. 227

6. The principle of economy is one
    of the basic principles of
    socialist economies.
    — Mao Tse-tung (1893-1976)
    *Quotations from Chairman
    Mao Tse-tung*, 1976, p. 187

7. Human economy and property
    have a joint economic origin
    since both have, as the ultimate
    reason for their existence, the
    fact that goods exist whose

available quantities are smaller
than the requirements of men.
— Carl Menger (1840-1921)
Principles of Economics,
trans. Dingwall and Hozelitz,
Ch. II, 3, p. 97

8. I would rather have my people
    laugh at my economies than
    weep for my extravagance.
    — King Oscar II of Sweden
    (1829-1907)
    Attributed

9. It is not economical to go to
    bed early to save candles if the
    results are twins.
    — Chinese proverb

10. Economy is the art of making
    the most of life.
    — George Bernard Shaw
    (1856-1950)
    Maxims for Revolutionists

11. The love of economy is the root
    of all virtue.
    — George Bernard Shaw
    (1856-1950)
    Ibid.

12. Economy: the art or method of
    attaining the greatest possible
    amount of some desirable result
    for a given cost, or a given result
    for the least possible cost.
    — Henry Sidgwick (1838-1900)
    *Principles of Political
    Economy*, 3rd ed., 1901,
    Bk. III. Ch. I, p. 396

42. EDUCATION

1. Lecturer, *n.* One with his hand
    in your pocket, his tongue in

your ear and his faith in your patience.
– Ambrose Bierce (1842-1914?)
The Devil's Dictionary

2. All that is spent during many years in opening the means of higher education to the masses would be well paid for if it called out one more Newton or Darwin, Shakespeare or Beethoven.
   – Alfred Marshall (1842-1924)
   Principles of Economics, 8th ed., Bk. IV, Ch. VI, 7, p. 216

3. Give a man a fish and you feed him for a day. Teach a man to fish and you feed him for a lifetime.
   – Chinese proverb

43. EFFICIENCY

1. Economic efficiency consists of making things that are worth more than they cost.
   – J. Maurice Clark (1884-1963)
   Studies in the Economics of Overhead Costs, 1923, Ch. II, Sec. 1, p. 17

2. This Modern Efficiency you are hearing about is the same old Hard Work your grandfather dreaded.
   – E.W. Howe (1853-1937)
   Sinner Sermons, 1926, p. 30

3. X-efficiency.
   – Harvey Liebenstein
   'Allocative Efficiency Vs "X-Efficiency" ', *American Economic Review*, 1966, pp. 392-415

4. There are only two qualities in the world: efficiency and inefficiency, and only two sorts of people: the efficient and the inefficient.
   – George Bernard Shaw (1856-1950)
   John Bull's Other Island, Act IV

44. EMPLOYMENT

1. Lord Finchley tried to mend the 'lectric light himself; it struck him dead and serve him right; it is the business of the wealthy man to give employment to the artisan.
   – Hilaire Belloc (1870-1953)
   Quoted in *The Times*, 25 Oct. 1975

2. *They only* are productive members of society who apply *their own hands* either to the cultivation of the earth itself, or to the preparing or appropriating the produce of the earth to the uses of life, . . . every individual not so employed, is a direct tax upon those who are so employed.
   – John Gray (1799-1883)
   Lecture on Human Happiness, 1825

3. One of the important functions of fascism, as typified by the Nazi system, was to remove the capitalist objections to full employment.

— M. Kalecki (1899-1970)
'Political Aspects of Full
Employment', 1943, in
*Selected Essays on the
Dynamics of the Capitalist
Economy*, p. 141

4. The behaviour of each
individual firm in deciding its
daily output will be determined
by its *short-term expectations* ...
It is upon these various
expectations that the amount of
employment which the firms
offer will depend.
— John Maynard Keynes
(1882-1946)
*The General Theory of
Employment Interest and
Money*, Bk. II, Ch. 4, p. 47

5. The social hygiene of full
employment.
— Abba P. Lerner
'Employment Theory and
Employment Policy',
American Economic Review,
1967, p. 17

6. If we are to enjoy very high
levels of full employment
without inflation, it must be
necessary to give up the
determination of wages by
collective bargaining.
— Abba P. Lerner
'Rising Prices', *Review of
Economics and Statistics*,
1948, p. 26

7. Better to burn a thousand mens
labours for a time, than to let
those thousand men by non-
employment lose their faculty
of labouring.
— Sir William Petty (1623-87)

'A Treatise of Taxes and
Contributions', 1662, in *The
Economic Writings of Sir
William Petty*, ed. Hull,
Vol. I, p. 60

45. ENTERPRISE

1. Whatever may be thought as to
the respective merits of private
and public ownership, it cannot
be denied that private enterprise
does take more risk than any
government is likely to do
except under pressure of
military necessities.
— Sir George Gibb
(1850-1925)
Railway Nationalisation, p. 9

2. Most, probably, of our decisions
to do something positive, the
full consequences of which will
be drawn out over many days to
come, can only be taken as a
result of animal spirits — of a
spontaneous urge to action
rather than inaction, and not
as the outcome of a weighted
average of quantitative benefits
multiplied by quantitative
probabilities.
— John Maynard Keynes
(1883-1946)
*The General Theory of
Employment Interest and
Money*, Bk. IV, Ch. 12,
p. 161

3. If Enterprise is afoot, wealth
accumulates whatever may be
happening to Thrift; and if
Enterprise is asleep, wealth
decays whatever Thrift may
be doing.

    — John Maynard Keynes
(1883-1946)
A Treatise on Money, 1930,
Vol. II, Bk. VI, Ch. 30,
p. 149

4. Our free enterprise system has
rightly been compared to a
gigantic computing machine
capable of solving its own
problems automatically. But
any one who has had some
practical experience with large
computers knows that they do
break down and can't operate
unattended.
    — Wassily Leontief
'Theoretical Assumptions
and Nonobserved Facts',
American Economic Review,
March 1971, p. 6

5. Private enterprise and public
enterprise are both useful
instruments for serving the
public welfare, and . . . the issue
between them is best resolved in
each particular instance by the
pragmatic economic test of
which is able to operate more
efficiently.
    — A.P. Lerner
'Foreign Economic Relations
of the United States', in
Saving American Capitalism,
ed. S.E. Harris, 1948, p. 279

6. The successful conduct of an
industrial enterprise requires
two quite distinct qualifications:
fidelity and zeal.
    — John Stuart Mill (1806-73)
*Principles of Political
Economy*, ed. Ashley, Bk. I,
Ch. IX, 2, p. 139

7. Enterprise does not have to be
private in order to be enterprise.
    — Herbert Morrison
(1888-1965)
*Observer, Sayings of the
Week*, 27 December 1942

8. The nature of accumulation
under private enterprise
necessarily generates inequality
and is therefore condemned to
meeting the trivial wants of a
few before the urgent needs of
the many.
    — Joan Robinson
'What Are the Questions?',
*Journal of Economic
Literature*, 1977, p. 1337

46. ENTREPRENEURS

1. The most important prerequisite
for becoming an entrepreneur is
the *ownership* of capital.
    — M. Kalecki (1899-1970)
'Entrepreneurial Capital and
Investment', 1954, in
*Selected Essays on the
Dynamics of the Capitalist
Economy*, p. 109

2. The typical entrepreneur is no
longer the bold and tireless
business man of Marshall, or the
sly rapacious Moneybags of
Marx, but a mass of inert
shareholders, indistinguishable
from *rentiers*, who employ
salaried managers to run their
concerns.
    — Joan Robinson
*An Essay on Marxian
Economics*, 1947, Ch. III,
p. 18

47. EQUALITY

1. When quarrels and complaints
   arise, it is when people who are
   equal have not got equal shares,
   or *vice versa*.
   - Aristotle (384-322 B.C.)
     Nicomachean Ethics,
     Book 5, Ch. 3

2. It is not the possessions but the
   desires of mankind which
   require to be equalized.
   - Aristotle (384-322 B.C.)
     Politics, trans. B. Jowett,
     Bk. II, Ch. 7, 1266b

3. The democrats think that as
   they are equal they ought to
   be equal in all things.
   - Aristotle (384-322 B.C.)
     Ibid., Bk.V, Ch. 1, 1301a

4. Equality consists in the same
   treatment of similar persons.
   - Aristotle (384-322 B.C.)
     Ibid., Bk. VII, Ch. 14,
     1332b

5. It is still imagined by many that
   inequalities of income coincide
   broadly with inequalities of
   merit.
   - Hugh Dalton (1887-1962)
     The Inequality of Incomes,
     2nd ed., 1925, Pt. IV, Ch. I,
     p. 240

6. Just as the modern mass production requires the standardization
   of commodities, so the social
   process requires standardization
   of man, and this standardization
   is called 'equality'.
   - Erich Fromm
     The Art of Loving, 1957,

Ch. II, p. 16

7. There is not ordinarily a greater
   sign of the equal distribution of
   any thing, than that every man
   is contented with his share.
   - Thomas Hobbes
     (1588-1679)
     Leviathan, 1651, Pt. I,
     Ch. XIII

8. It is better that some should be
   unhappy, than that none should
   be happy, which would be the
   case in a general state of
   equality.
   - Samuel Johnson (1709-84)
     Boswell's Life of Johnson,
     7 April 1776

9. All of us do not have equal
   talent, but all of us should have
   an equal opportunity to develop
   our talents.
   - John F. Kennedy (1917-63)
     Speech, 1963

10. We pass easily over great
    inequalities, and smaller shock
    us.
    - Walter Savage Landor
      (1775-1864)
      'Aeschines and Phocion',
      Imaginary Conversations

11. In general great inequality of
    fortune, by impoverishing the
    lower orders, has everywhere
    been the principle impediment
    to the increase of public
    wealth.
    - James Maitland (1759-1839)
      *A New View of Society and
      Other Writings*

12. There is no real necessity, and

therefore no moral justification for extreme poverty side by side with great wealth. The inequalities of wealth though less than they are often represented to be, are a serious flaw in our economic organization.
  — Alfred Marshall (1842-1924)
    Principles of Economics,
    8th ed., Bk. VI, Ch. XIII,
    11, pp. 713-14

13. It is an abuse of the principle of equality to demand that no individual be permitted to be better off than the rest if his being so makes none of the others worse off than they otherwise would be.
    — John Stuart Mill (1806-73)
      Quoted in M.H. Cadman
      (ed.), *Taxation Economics*

14. All animals are equal, but some animals are more equal than others.
    — George Orwell (1903-50)
      Animal Farm, Ch. 10

15. Every capacity for labour being, like every instrument of labour, an accumulated capital, and a collective property, inequality of wages and fortunes (on the ground of inequality of capacities) is, therefore, injustice and robbery.
    — Pierre-Joseph Proudhon
      (1809-65)
      What is Property?, trans.
      Tucker, Ch. V, Pt. II

16. The idea of inequality is both very simple and very complex.
    — Amartya Sen

On Economic Inequality,
Preface

17. Who made your millions for you? Me and my like. Whats kep us poor? Keepin you rich.
    — George Bernard Shaw
      (1856-1950)
      Major Barbara, Act II

18. Inequality, again, leads to the misdirection of production. For, since the demand of one income of £50,000 is as powerful a magnet as the demand of 500 incomes of £100, it diverts energy from the creation of wealth to the multiplication of luxuries.
    — R.H. Tawney (1880-1962)
      The Acquisitive Society,
      1921, Ch. IV

19. Those who dread a dead-level of income or wealth . . . do not dread, it seems, a dead-level of law and order, and of security of life and property. They do not complain that persons endowed by nature with unusual qualities of strength, audacity, or cunning are prevented from reaping the full fruits of these powers.
    — R.H. Tawney (1880-1962)
      Equality, 4th ed., p. 85

48. EQUILIBRIUM

1. The point of equilibrium will be known by the criterion, that an infinitely small amount of commodity exchanged in addition, at the same rate, will bring neither gain nor loss of utility.

— W. Stanley Jevons (1835-82)
*Theory of Political
Economy*, 4th ed., Ch. IV,
p. 96

2. A crisis is certainly a disturbance
of the equilibrium between
demand and supply.
   — Edward D. Jones
   (1870-1944)
   Economic Crises, 1900,
   Ch. X, p. 219

3. In economics we are chiefly
concerned with equilibrium not
as a state of rest but as a *process*
in equilibrium, with a slower
process forming the 'given
condition' within which a more
rapid one takes place and tends
toward a moving equilibrium.
   — Frank H. Knight
   *On the History and Method
   of Economics*, 1956, p. 187

4. In the earlier stages of
economics, we think of demand
and supply as crude forces
pressing against one another,
and tending towards a
mechanical equilibrium; but in
the later stages, the balance or
equilibrium is conceived not as
between crude mechanical
forces, but as between the
organic forces of life and decay.
   — Alfred Marshall (1842-1924)
   'Distribution and Exchange',
   Economic Journal, March
   1898, p. 43

5. Economic problems are
imperfectly presented when
they are treated as problems of
statical equilibrium, and not of
organic growth.

— Alfred Marshall (1842-1924)
Principles of Economics,
8th ed., Bk. V, Ch. XII,
3, p. 461

6. Equilibrium is just equilibrium.
   — Lionel Robbins
   Quoted by B. Wooton,
   Lament for Economics,
   1938

7. Let us beware of this dangerous
theory of equilibrium which is
supposed to be automatically
established. A certain kind of
equilibrium, it is true, is
re-established in the long run,
but it is only after a frightful
amount of suffering.
   — Simonde de Sismondi
   (1773-1842)
   *Nouveaux Principes
   d'Economie politique*, 2nd
   ed., 1827, Vol. I, p. 221,
   quoted in Gide and Rist,
   *A History of Economic
   Doctrines*

8. A great many economic
theorists give the impression
that disequilibrium is a pretty
bad state to be in.
   — G.D.N. Worswick
   'Is Progress in Economic
   Science Possible?', *Economic
   Journal*, March 1972, p. 78

49. EXCHANGE

1. Nothing is to be had for nothing.
   — Epictetus (*fl.* A.D. 100)
   Discourses, trans. E. Carter,
   Bk. IV, Ch. 10

2. Exchange can . . . bring about

co-ordination without coercion.
- Milton Friedman
Capitalism and Freedom,
1962, Ch. I, p. 13

3. The practical application of the principle of individualism is entirely dependent on the practice of exchange.
   - R.G. Hawtrey (1879-1971)
   The Economic Problem,
   1926, Ch. III, p. 13

4. Perfect freedom of exchange . . . tends to the maximising of utility.
   - W. Stanley Jevons (1835-82)
   Theory of Political Economy,
   4th ed., Ch. IV, p. 145

5. A partner to an exchange is very much like a field that needs tilling or a mine that requires exploiting.
   - Maffeo Pantaleoni
   (1857-1924)
   Des Différences d'Opinion entre Économistes, 1897,
   quoted in Gide and Rist, *A History of Economic Doctrines*

6. A fair exchange is no robbery.
   - English proverb, 16th century

7. Man might be defined as 'An animal that makes exchanges'.
   - Richard Whately
   (1787-1863)
   Attributed

8. Each of us puts in what he has at one point of the circle of exchange and takes out what he wants at another.

- P.H. Wicksteed (1844-1927)
'The Scope and Method of Political Economy',
Economic Journal, March 1914, p. 3

50. EXTERNAL EFFECTS

1. External effects may be said to arise when relevant effects on production and welfare go wholly or partially unpriced.
   - Edward Joshua Mishan
   'Reflections on Recent Developments in the Concept of External Effects'
   in *Essays in Welfare Economics*, 2nd ed., p. 184

2. We have . . . to distinguish precisely between the two varieties of marginal net product which I have named respectively *social* and *private*.
   - A.C. Pigou (1877-1959)
   Economics of Welfare,
   4th ed., Pt. II, Ch. II, p. 134

51. FINANCE

1. Rags make Paper
   Paper makes Money
   Money makes Banks
   Banks make Loans
   Loans make Beggars
   Beggars make Rags
   - Anonymous, 18th century

2. I would rather see Finance less proud and Industry more content.
   - Sir Winston Churchill
   (1874-1965)
   Quoted in D.E. Moggridge,

The Return to Gold, 1925,
p. 54

3. Financial sense is knowing that certain men will promise to do certain things and fail.
   - E.W. Howe (1853-1937)
     Sinner Sermons, 1926, p. 44

4. Finance must determine expenditure, not expenditure finance.
   - Sir Geoffrey Howe
     Budget Speech, House of Commons, 12 June 1979

5. A financier is a pawnbroker with imagination.
   - Sir Arthur Wing Pinero (1855-1934)
     The Second Mrs Tanqueray, 1893

52. FORECASTING

1. Forecasting is very difficult, especially if it is about the future.
   - Anonymous

2. A trend is a trend is a trend
   But the question is, will it bend?
   Will it alter its course
   Through some unforeseen force
   And come to a premature end?
                    Stein Age Forecaster
   - Alec Cairncross
     'Economic Forecasting',
     Economic Journal, Dec.
     1969, p. 796

3. FORECAST: A pretence of knowing what would have happened if what does happen hadn't.

- Ralph Harris
  'Everyman's Guide to Contemporary Economic Jargon', *Growth, Advertising and the Consumer*, 1964, p. 22

4. The best forecast(s) which the Treasury can make of expenditure, imports and gross domestic product . . . give a spurious impression of certainty. But their origin lies in the extrapolation from a partially known past, through an unknown present, to an unknowable future according to theories about the causal relationships between certain economic variables which are hotly disputed by academic economists, and may well in fact change from country to country or from decade to decade.
   - Denis Healey
     Budget Speech, House of Commons, 12 Nov. 1974

5. The economists are generally right in their predictions, but generally a good deal out in their dates.
   - Sidney Webb (1859-1947)
     Observer, Sayings of the Week, 25 February 1924

53. FREE TRADE

1. If we take care of our imports, our exports will take care of themselves.
   - Anonymous

2. We are suffering from the

intolerable competition of a
foreign rival, who is placed . . .
in a condition so infinitely
superior to ours for the
production of light, that he
inundates our *national market*
at a marvellously reduced
price . . . This rival . . . is no
other than the sun . . . We pray
that you will be pleased to make
a law ordering that all windows,
skylights, inside and outside
shutters, curtains, fan-lights,
bulls'-eyes, carriage-blinds, in
short that all openings, holes,
chinks, and crevices should be
closed, by which the light of the
sun can penetrate into houses,
to the injury of the flourishing
trade with which we have
endowed our country.
  − Frédéric Bastiat (1801-50)
    Sophismes Economiques,
    trans. G.R. Porter, Ch. VII,
    pp. 79-80

3. As a matter of history, the
   assertion that the advantages of
   Free Trade depend upon its
   being mutual, has always been
   made by people who were
   attacking Free Trade. It has
   never been made or admitted by
   any of the principal advocates
   of Free Trade. For this there is
   a simple reason. It represents a
   complete misunderstanding of
   the nature of international
   trade and the working of tariffs.
   − Sir William Beveridge
     (1879-1963) *et al.*
     Tariffs, The Case Examined,
     1931, pp. 108-9

4. The call for free trade is as
   unavailing as the cry of a spoiled

child for the moon. It never has
existed; it never will exist.
  − Henry Clay (1777-1852)
    Speech, 1832

5. If we will not buy we cannot
   sell.
   − William McKinley
     (1843-1901)
     Quoted by Ludwell Denny,
     America Conquers Britain,
     1930, p. 73

6. There are many things which
   free-trade does passably. There
   are none which it does absolutely
   well; for competition is as rife in
   the career of fraudulent practice
   as in that of real excellence.
   − John Stuart Mill (1806-73)
     'Endowments', *Dissertations
     and Discussions,* Vol. IV,
     pp. 12-13

7. It is evidently, the common
   interest of all nations that each
   of them should abstain from
   every measure by which the
   aggregate wealth of the
   commercial world would be
   diminished, although of this
   smaller sum total it might
   thereby be enabled to attract
   to itself a larger share.
   − John Stuart Mill (1806-73)
     *Essays on some Unsettled
     Questions of Political
     Economy,* 1844, p. 31

8. Cost of carriage is a natural
   protecting duty, which free
   trade has no power to abrogate.
   − John Stuart Mill (1806-73)
     *Principles of Political
     Economy,* ed. Ashley, Bk. V,
     Ch. X, 1, p. 923

9. It is the maxim of every prudent master of a family, never to attempt to make at home what it will cost him more to make than to buy ... What is prudence in the conduct of every private family, can scarce be folly in that of a great kingdom. If a foreign country can supply us with a commodity cheaper than we ourselves can make it, better buy it of them with some part of the produce of our own industry, employed in a way in which we have some advantage.
   — Adam Smith (1723-90)
   Wealth of Nations, ed. Cannan, Vol. I, Bk. IV, Ch. II, p. 422

10. To expect, indeed, that the freedom of trade should ever be entirely restored in Great Britain, is as absurd as to expect that an Oceana or Utopia should ever be established in it. Not only the prejudices of the public, but what is much more unconquerable, the private interests of many individuals, irresistibly oppose it.
    — Adam Smith (1723-90)
    Ibid., p. 435

54. FUTURE

1. We generally prefer a present pleasure or enjoyment to a distant one, not superior to it in other respects.
   — Samuel Bailey (1791-1870)
   A Critical Dissertation on the Nature, Measures and Causes of Value, 1825, p. 218

2. The Man who lives only from day to day, is precisely the man in a state of nature.
   — Jeremy Bentham (1748-1832)
   Principles of the Civil Code, Part I, Ch. 9. In J. Bowring (ed.), *Works of Jeremy Bentham*, Vol. 1, p. 309

3. Future, *n.* That period of time in which our affairs prosper, our friends are true and our happiness is assured.
   — Ambrose Bierce (1842-1914?)
   The Devil's Dictionary

4. Improvidence, *n.* Provision for the needs of today from the revenues of tomorrow.
   — Ambrose Bierce (1842-1914?)
   Ibid.

5. Other things being equal, the smaller the income, the higher the preference for present over future income; that is, the greater the impatience to acquire income as early as possible.
   — Irving Fisher (1867-1947)
   The Theory of Interest, 1930, Ch. IV, p. 72

6. This *long run* is a misleading guide to current affairs. *In the long run* we are all dead. Economists set themselves too easy, too useless a task if in tempestuous seasons they can only tell us that when the storm is long past the ocean is flat again.
   — John Maynard Keynes (1883-1946)

*A Tract on Monetary
Reform*, 1924, Ch. III,
p. 80

7. Human nature is so constituted
that in estimating the 'present
value' of a future benefit most
people generally make a second
deduction from its future value,
in the form of what we may call
a 'discount', that increases with
the period for which the benefit
is deferred.
   – Alfred Marshall (1842-1924)
     Principles of Economics,
     8th ed., Bk. III, Ch. V,
     3, p. 120

8. It is an excellent maxim to
make present resources suffice
for present wants: the future
will have its own wants to
provide for.
   – John Stuart Mill (1806-73)
     *Principles of Political
     Economy*, ed. Ashley, Bk. V,
     Ch. VII, 1, p. 876

9. It follows that the aggregate
amount of economic satisfaction
which people in fact enjoy is
much less than it would be if
their telescopic faculty were
not perverted.
   – A.C. Pigou (1877-1959)
     Economics of Welfare,
     4th ed., Pt. I, Ch. II, p. 26

10. To abstain from the enjoyment
which is in our power, or to
seek distant rather than
immediate results, are among
the most painful exertions of
the human will.
    – Nassau W. Senior
      (1790-1864)

*Outline of the Science of
Political Economy*,
'Abstinence', p. 60

11. If the hangover came the night
before, and the elation the
morning after, brewers would be
out of business. The principle
that a lesser but early benefit
will offset a substantial but post-
poned liability is one which
rules human life; indeed it is the
principle on which the human
race reproduces itself.
    – *The Times*, Leading article,
      13 Sept. 1977

55. GAMBLING

1. The gambling known as business
looks with austere disfavour
upon the business known as
gambling.
   – Ambrose Bierce
     (1842-1914?)
     The Devil's Dictionary

2. Man is a gaming animal.
   – Charles Lamb (1775-1834)
     *Essays of Elia, Mrs Battle's
     Opinions on Whist*

3. Now in the way of lottery men
do also tax themselves in the
general, though out of hopes of
advantage in particular: a
lottery therefore is properly a
tax upon unfortunate self-
conceited fools; men that have
good opinion of their own
luckiness.
   – Sir William Petty (1623-87)
     'A Treatise of Taxes and
     Contributions', 1662, in
     The Economic Writings of

Sir William Petty, ed. Hull, Vol. I, p. 64

4. In gambling the many must lose in order that the few may win.
   – George Bernard Shaw (1856-1950)
   'The Economic Basis of Socialism', in *Fabian Essays*, 1889

5. Adventure upon all the tickets in the lottery, and you lose for certain; and the greater the number of your tickets the nearer you approach to this certainty.
   – Adam Smith (1723-90)
   Wealth of Nations, ed. Cannan, Vol. I, Bk. I, Ch. X, Pt. I, p. 110

6. [Gambling] is the child of avarice, the brother of iniquity, and the father of mischief.
   – George Washington (1732-99)
   Letter, 1783

56. GNP (GROSS NATIONAL PRODUCT)

1. As every economist knows, calculations of GNP, especially in the poor countries, are largely exercises in the statistical imagination, and even if they were accurate, the GNP itself can be a very poor measure of welfare.
   – Kenneth E. Boulding
   'The Economics of Knowledge and the Knowledge of Economics', *American Economic Review*, May 1966, p. 11

2. The values included in incomes are valued in exchange, which are dependent not only on the goods or services in question, but also on the whole complex of a society . . . the numerical measurement of total national income is thus dependent on the distribution of income and would alter with it.
   – A.L. Bowley (1869-1957)
   The Nature and Purpose of the Measurement of Social Phenomena, 2nd ed., 1923, p. 208

3. I believe in materialism. I believe in all the proceeds of a healthy materialism, – good cooking, dry houses, dry feet, sewers, drain pipes, hot water, baths, electric lights, automobiles, good roads, bright streets, long vacations away from the village pump, new ideas, fast horses, swift conversation, theatres, operas, orchestras, bands, – I believe in them all for everybody. The man who dies without knowing these things may be as exquisite as a saint, and as rich as a poet; but it is in spite of, not because of, his deprivation.
   – Francis Hackett (1883-1962)
   Quoted in P.A. Samuelson, *Economics*

4. GNP: gross naive 'proximation.
   – Ralph Harris
   'Everyman's Guide to Contemporary Economic Jargon', *Growth, Advertising and the Consumer*, 1964, p.23

87

5. If a man marries his house-
keeper or his cook, the national
dividend is diminished.
   - A.C. Pigou (1877-1959)
   Economics of Welfare,
   4th ed., Pt. I, Ch. III, p. 33

6. Man does not live by GNP
alone.
   - Paul A. Samuelson
   Economics, 8th ed., Ch. 39,
   p. 762

7. Indifference to the aesthetic will
in the long run lessen the
economic product ... attention
to the aesthetic will increase
economic welfare.
   - Sir Josiah Stamp
   (1880-1941)
   *Some Economic Factors in
   Modern Life*, 1929, Ch. I, p. 4

57. GOLD

1. You shall not press down upon
the brow of labor this crown of
thorns, you shall not crucify
mankind upon a cross of gold.
   - William Jennings Bryan
   (1860-1925)
   Speech at the National
   Democratic Convention,
   Chicago, 1896

2. Almighty gold.
   - George Farquhar
   (1678-1707)
   The Recruiting Officer,
   Act III, Sc. 2

3. [Gold] which does not change
its nature, which has no
nationality, which is eternally
and universally accepted as the
unalterable fiduciary value par
excellence.
   - General Charles de Gaulle
   (1890-1970)
   Press conference, 1965,
   quoted in *The Economist*,
   22 March 1975, 'Survey',
   p. 4

4. The end is easily foretold,
   When every blessed thing you
   hold
   Is made of silver, or of gold,
   You long for simple pewter.

   When you have nothing else to
   wear
   But cloth of gold and satins
   rare,
   For cloth of gold you cease to
   care —
   Up goes the price of shoddy.
   - W.S. Gilbert (1836-1911)
   The Gondoliers, II

5. In itself gold-digging has ever
seemed to me almost a dead loss
of labour as regards the world in
general — a wrong against the
human race, just such as is that
of a Government against its
people, in over-issuing and
depreciating its own currency.
   - W. Stanley Jevons (1835-82)
   *Investigations in Currency
   and Finance*, 1884, II,
   Ch. V, p. 104

6. Dr Freud relates that there are
peculiar reasons deep in our
subconsciousness why gold in
particular should satisfy strong
instincts and serve as a symbol.
   - John Maynard Keynes
   (1883-1946)
   'The Return to Gold', in

Essays in Persuasion, 1933, Pt. III, p. 182

7. Gold and silver, like all other commodities, are valuable only in proportion to the quantity of labour necessary to produce them, and bring them to market.
   — David Ricardo (1772-1823)
   Principles of Political Economy and Taxation, ed. Sraffa, Ch. XXVII, p. 352

8. Saint-seducing gold.
   — William Shakespeare (1564-1616)
   Romeo and Juliet, Act I, Sc. I

58. GOVERNMENT

1. If you want to show that crime doesn't pay, put it in the hands of the government.
   — Anonymous
   Quoted in Michael Z. Hepker, *A Modern Approach to Tax Law*, 2nd ed., 1975, p. 7

2. All Governments like to interfere; it elevates their position to make out that they can cure the evils of mankind.
   — Walter Bagehot (1826-77)
   Economic Studies, ed. Hutton, I, p. 5

3. Faith in the manipulative omnipotence of the State has all but displaced analysis of its social structure and understanding of its political and economic functions.
   — Paul A. Baran (?-1964)
   'On the Political Economy

of Backwardness', *Manchester School*, January 1952, p. 78

4. Government is the great fiction, through which everybody endeavours to live at the expense of everybody else.
   — Frédéric Bastiat (1801-50)
   Essays on Political Economy, People's ed., 1872, Part III, 'Government', p. 8

5. Parliamentary government is being asked to solve the problem which so far it has failed to solve: that is how to reconcile parliamentary popularity with sound economic planning . . . how to persuade the people to forgo immediate satisfactions in order to build up the economic resources of the country.
   — Aneurin Bevan (1897-1960)
   Quoted by Denis Healey, *The Times*, 17 April 1975

6. What the proletarian lacks is capital, and the duty of the State is to see that he gets it. Were I to define the State, I should prefer to think of it as the poor man's bank.
   — Louis Blanc (1813-82)
   Organisation du Travail, p. 14

7. All government, indeed every human benefit and enjoyment, every virtue, and every prudent act, is founded on compromise and barter.
   — Edmund Burke (1729-97)
   Speech, 22 March 1775

8. Government is a contrivance of human wisdom to provide for human wants. Men have a right that these wants should be provided for by this wisdom.
   — Edmund Burke (1729-97)
   Reflections on the Revolution in France, 1790

9. The government is, in a sense, a super firm (but of a very special kind) since it is able to influence the use of factors of production by administrative decision.
   — R.H. Coase
   'The Problem of Social Cost', *Journal of Law and Economics*, October 1960, p. 17

10. The point to remember is that what the government gives it must first take away.
    — John S. Coleman
    (1897-1958)
    Quoted in *The International Thesaurus of Quotations*

11. It is mostly by accident that for most of the time most Chancellors have been successful.
    — J.C.R. Dow
    The Management of the British Economy 1945-60, p. 65

12. Under all forms of government the ultimate power lies with the masses. It is not kings nor aristocracies, nor landowners nor capitalists, that anywhere really enslave the people. It is their own ignorance.
    — Henry George (1839-97)
    Protection or Free Trade, Ch. I

13. The government that is big enough to give you all you want is big enough to take it all away.
    — Barry Goldwater
    Speech, 1964

14. There is the fundamental paradox of the welfare state: that it is not built for the desperate, but for those who are already capable of helping themselves.
    — Michael Harrington
    The Other America, Ch. 9

15. The more the state 'plans' the more difficult planning becomes for the individual.
    — F.A. Hayek
    The Road to Serfdom, 1944, Ch. VI

16. Frankly, I'd like to see the government get out of war altogether and leave the whole field to private industry.
    — Joseph Heller
    Catch-22, Ch. 24

17. Democratic governments, by their nature, are pressure-responders rather than problem anticipators.
    — Walter W. Heller
    'What's Right With Economics?', *American Economic Review*, March 1975, p. 18

18. My experience in government is that when things are non-controversial, beautifully co-ordinated and all the rest, it must be that there is not much going on.
    — John F. Kennedy (1917-63)

The Kennedy Wit, ed. Adler

19. We must aim at separating those services which are *technically social* from those which are *technically individual* . . . The important thing for Government is not to do things which individuals are doing already, and to do them a little better or a little worse; but to do those things which at present are not done at all.
    — John Maynard Keynes (1883-1946)
    The End of Laissez-Faire, 1926, Pt. IV, pp. 46-7

20. The State is a machine for the oppression of one class by another.
    — V.I. Lenin (1870-1924)
    Selected Works, Vol. 11, p. 649

21. Government creates scarcely anything . . . A Government could print a good edition of Shakespeare's works, but it could not get them written.
    — Alfred Marshall (1842-1924)
    'The Social Possibilities of Economic Chivalry',
    Economic Journal, March 1907, pp. 21-2

22. The executive of the modern state is but a committee for managing the common affairs of the whole bourgeoisie.
    — Karl Marx (1818-83) and Friedrich Engels (1820-95)
    The Communist Manifesto, Ch. 1

23. In all the more advanced communities the great majority of things are worse done by the intervention of government, than the individuals most interested in the matter would do them, or cause them to be done, if left to themselves.
    — John Stuart Mill (1806-73)
    Principles of Political Economy, ed. Ashley, Bk. V, Ch. XI, 5, p. 947

24. Government management is, indeed, proverbially jobbing, careless, and ineffective, but so likewise has generally been joint-stock management. The directors of a joint-stock company, it is true, are always shareholders; but also the members of a government are invariably taxpayers.
    — John Stuart Mill (1806-73)
    Ibid., 11, pp. 960-1

25. Government even in its best state is but a necessary evil; in its worst state an intolerable one.
    — Thomas Paine (1737-1809)
    'Of the Origin and Design of Government in General',
    Common Sense, 1776

26. Society is produced by our wants, and government by our wickedness; the former promotes our happiness *positively* by uniting our affections, the latter *negatively* by restraining our vices.
    — Thomas Paine (1737-1809)
    Ibid.

27. It is not sufficient to contrast the imperfect adjustments of

unfettered private enterprise with the best adjustment that economists in their studies can imagine. For we cannot expect that any public authority will attain, or will even whole-heartedly seek, that ideal. Such authorities are liable alike to ignorance, to sectional pressure and to personal corruption by private interest.
- A.C. Pigou (1877-1959)
  Economics of Welfare,
  4th ed., Pt. II, Ch. XX,
  p. 332

28. A state comes into existence because no individual is self-sufficing, we all have many needs.
    - Plato (c. 428-347 B.C.)
      The Republic, trans.
      Cornford, Bk. II, Ch. VI

29. If it were not for the necessity of taxation, the business of Government regarding Agriculture, Commerce and Manufactures would be very easy indeed, – all that would be required of them would be to avoid all interference.
    - David Ricardo (1772-1823)
      Letter to James Brown,
      13 Oct. 1919, in *Works*,
      ed. Sraffa, Vol. VIII, p. 101

30. The very best of all plans of finance is to spend little, and the best of all taxes is that which is the least in amount.
    - Jean Baptiste Say
      (1767-1832)
      Traité d'Économie politique,
      2nd ed., 1814, Vol. II,
      p. 298

31. Englishmen never will be slaves: they are free to do whatever the Government and public opinion allow them to do.
    - George Bernard Shaw
      (1856-1950)
      Man and Superman, Act III

32. The uniform, constant and uninterrupted effort of every man to better his condition, the principle from which public and national, as well as private opulence is originally derived, is frequently powerful enough to maintain the natural progress of things toward improvement, in spite both of the extravagance of government, and of the greatest errors of administration. Like the unknown principle of animal life, it frequently restores health and vigour to the constitution, in spite, not only of the disease, but of the absurd prescriptions of the doctor.
    - Adam Smith (1723-90)
      Wealth of Nations, ed.
      Cannan, Vol. I, Bk. II,
      Ch. III, p. 325

33. Though the profusion of govern-ment must, undoubtedly, have retarded the natural progress of England towards wealth and improvement, it has not been able to stop it.
    - Adam Smith (1723-90)
      Ibid., p. 327

34. To found a great empire for the sole purpose of raising up a people of customers may at first sight appear a project fit only for a nation of shopkeepers. It

is, however, a project altogether
unfit for a nation of shopkeepers; but extremely fit for a
nation whose government is
influenced by shopkeepers.
- Adam Smith (1723-90)
  Ibid., Vol. II, Bk. IV,
  Ch. VII, Pt. III, p. 114

35. Civil government, so far as it is
instituted for the security of
property, is in reality instituted
for the defence of the rich
against the poor, or of those
who have some property against
those who have none at all.
- Adam Smith (1723-90)
  Ibid., Bk. V, Ch. I, Pt. II,
  p. 207

36. It is not till it is discovered that
high individual incomes will not
purchase the mass of mankind
immunity from cholera, typhus,
and ignorance, still less secure
them the positive advantages of
educational opportunity and
economic security, that slowly
and reluctantly, amid prophecies
of moral degeneration and
economic disaster, society
begins to make collective
provision for needs which no
ordinary individual, even if he
works overtime all his life, can
provide himself.
- R.H. Tawney (1880-1962)
  Equality, 4th ed., pp. 134-5

37. In a country where the sole
employer is the State, opposition
means death by slow starvation.
The old principle: who does not
work shall not eat, has been
replaced by a new one: who
does not obey shall not eat.

- Leon Trotsky (1879-1940)
  Quoted in F.A. Hayek,
  The Road to Serfdom

38. There is nothing as unsound as
hoary doctrines that have
acquired the support of
authority simply because they
are traditional and have stood
for so long without genuinely
critical examination. One of
these mouldy fallacies is that
regardless of the circumstances
the government must balance its
budget in each year. Why not in
each month or week or hour?
- Jacob Viner (1892-1970)
  'Inflation as a Remedy for
  Depression', *Proceedings of
  the Institute of Public
  Affairs*, 1933

39. It seems ideally conceivable that
the state . . . should undertake
public works, that must be
executed some time, in the slack
periods when they can be
executed at least expense, and
will, at the same time, have a
tendency to counteract a
serious evil.
- Philip H. Wicksteed
  (1844-1927)
  *The Common Sense of
  Political Economy*, ed.
  Robbins, Vol. II, Bk. III,
  Ch. I, p. 640

59. GROWTH

1. The anti-growth movement and
its accompanying excessive
concern with the environment
not merely leads to a regressive
change in the distribution of

resources in the community, it also distracts attention from the real issues of choice that society has to face.
- Wilfred Beckerman
  In Defence of Economic Growth, 1976, Ch. 9, p. 245

2. Economic advance is not the same thing as human progress.
   - Sir John Clapham (1873-1946)
     A Concise Economic History of Britain, 1957, 'Introduction'

3. We can move away from the recent sterile argument of growth versus anti-growth, and resume the real argument. How do we use and direct our growth?
   - Anthony Crosland (1918-77)
     'Pollution – or Poverty', *The Sunday Times*, 26 June 1972

4. Growth in the productive capacity of a developed economy is inevitable.
   W.A. Eltis
   Economic Growth, 1966, Ch. I, p. 9

5. The rate of growth at a given time is a phenomenon rooted in past economic, social and technological developments rather than determined fully by the coefficients of our equations.
   - M. Kalecki (1899-1970)
     'Trend and the Business Cycle', 1968, in *Selected Essays on the Dynamics of the Capitalist Economy*, p. 183

6. The chief sources of social welfare are not to be found in economic growth *per se*, but in a far more selective form of development which must include a radical reshaping of our physical environment with the needs of pleasant living, and not the needs of traffic or industry, foremost in mind.
   - E.J. Mishan
     The Costs of Economic Growth, 1969, Ch. 1, p. 32

60. HAPPINESS

1. The excess of happiness on the part of the most wealthy will not be so great as the excess of his wealth . . . the more nearly the actual proportion approaches to equality, the greater will be the total mass of happiness.
   - Jeremy Bentham (1748-1832)
     Principles of the Civil Code, Part 1, Ch. 6. In J. Bowring (ed.), *Works of Jeremy Bentham*, Vol. 1, p. 305

2. It's pretty hard to tell what does bring happiness; poverty and wealth have both failed.
   - Frank McKinney Hubbard (1868-1930)
     Quoted in Esar and Bentley, *The Treasury of Humorous Quotations*

3. We have no more right to consume happiness without producing it than to consume wealth without producing it.
   - George Bernard Shaw (1856-1950)

Candida, Act I

61. HONESTY

1. It is not true that honesty, as far as material gain is concerned, profits individuals. A clever and cruel knave will in a mixed society always be richer than an honest person can be.
   - John Ruskin (1819-1900)
     Munera Pulveris, IV

2. To be honest, as this world goes, is to be one man pick'd out of ten thousand.
   - William Shakespeare (1564-1616)
     Hamlet, Act II, Sc. II

3. Honesty is the best policy, but he who acts on that principle is not an honest man.
   - Richard Whately (1787-1863)
     Apothegms

62. INCENTIVES

1. The mere necessarties of life may, in favourable seasons and situations, be obtained with comparatively little labour; and those uncivilized tribes who have no desire to possess its comforts, are proverbially indolent and poor, and are exposed in bad years to the greatest privations. To make men industrious – to make them shake off that lethargy which benumbs their faculties when in a rude or degraded condition, they must be inspired with a taste for comforts, luxuries, and enjoyments.
   - J.R. McCulloch (1789-1864)
     Principles of Political Economy, new ed., Pt. IV, p. 528

2. The only thing then that can render the labouring man industrious, is a moderate quantity of money; for as too little will, according to his temper is, either dispirite or make him desperate, so too much will make him insolent and lazy.
   - Bernard de Mandeville (1670-1733)
     The Fable of the Bees or *Private Vices, Publick Benefits*, 2nd ed., 1723

3. Individuals, or nations, do not differ so much in the efforts they are able and willing to make under strong immediate incentives, as in their capacity of present exertion for a distant object; and in the thoroughness of their application to work on ordinary occasions.
   - John Stuart Mill (1806-73)
     Principles of Political Economy, ed. Ashley, Bk. I, Ch. VII, 3, p. 105

4. The efficiency of industry may be expected to be great, in proportion as the fruits of industry are insured to the person exerting it.
   - John Stuart Mill (1806-73)
     Ibid., 6, p. 115

5. If a man is producing nothing,

nobody can be the worse for a reduction of his incentive to produce.
  - George Bernard Shaw (1856-1950) 'Socialism and Superior Brains', *The Fortnightly Review*, April 1894

63. INCOME

1. Income, *n*. The natural and rational gauge and measure of respectability.
   - Ambrose Bierce (1842-1914?) *The Devil's Dictionary*

2. Income is a series of events.
   - Irving Fisher (1867-1947) *The Theory of Interest*, 1930, Ch. I, p. 3

3. The purpose of income calculations in practical affairs is to give people an indication of the amount which they can consume without impoverishing themselves. Following out this idea, it would seem that we ought to define a man's income as the maximum value which he can consume during a week, and still expect to be as well off at the end of the week as he was at the beginning.
   - J.R.Hicks *Value and Capital*, 2nd ed., 1946, Pt. III, Ch. XIV, p. 172

4. Few people would assert that a man with fifty thousand a year is likely to have a very much happier life than if he had only a thousand.
   - Alfred Marshall (1842-1924) 'The Social Possibilities of Economic Chivalry', *Economic Journal*, March 1907, p. 8

5. Unearned increment.
   - John Stuart Mill (1806-73) 'The Right of Property in Land', *Dissertations and Discussions*, Vol. IV, p. 299

64. INDUSTRY

1. Industrial Relations are human relations.
   - Edward Heath Attributed

2. The economic case for the industrialisation of densely populated backward countries rests upon [the] mass phenomenon of disguised rural unemployment.
   - Kurt Mandelbaum *The Industrialisation of Backward Areas*, 1945, p. 2

3. Industry is limited by capital.
   - John Stuart Mill (1806-73) *Principles of Political Economy*, ed. Ashley, Bk. I, Ch. V, 1, p. 63

4. The real obstacle to successful democratisation can perhaps be summarised on the one hand as the ignorance of employees, and on the other as the ignorance of employers.
   - Sir Josiah Stamp (1880-1941) *Some Economic Factors in*

Modern Life, 1929, Ch. IV, p. 133

5. Industry does nothing but produce scarce things.
   - Léon Walras (1834-1910) *Elements of Pure Economics*, trans. W. Jaffé, Pt. I, Lesson 4, p. 73

65. INFLATION

1. Inflation means that your money won't buy as much today as it did when you didn't have any.
   - Anonymous Quoted by M.Z. Hepker, *A Modern Approach to Tax Law*, 1975

2. Inflation occurs when too much money is chasing too few goods.
   - Anonymous

3. QUESTION: What sex is to the novelist, inflation is to the economist. Discuss.

   ANSWER: I am not sure how I am supposed to answer this question but it may be said that both inflation and sex are characterised by a rising rate of interest.
   - Anonymous

4. There is no inherent mechanism in our present system, which can with certainty prevent competitive sectional bargaining for wages from setting up a vicious spiral of rising prices under full employment.
   - W.H. Beveridge (1879-1963)

Full Employment in a Free Society, 1944, p. 199

5. I find that the high prices we see today are due to some four or five causes. The principal and almost the only one (which no one has referred to until now) is the abundance of gold and silver.
   - Jean Bodin (1530-1596) *Réponse aux Paradoxes de Malestroit*, in A.E. Monroe, *Early Economic Thought*

6. I consider in general that an increase of actual money causes in a State a corresponding increase of consumption which gradually brings about increased prices.
   - Richard Cantillon (1680?-1734) *Essai sur la Nature du Commerce en Général*, 1755, trans. Henry Higgs, p. 163

7. By doubling the quantity of money in a State the prices of products and merchandise are not always doubled. A river which runs and winds about in its bed will not flow with double the speed when the amount of its water is doubled.
   - Richard Cantillon (1680?-1734) Ibid., p. 177

8. Inflation is repudiation.
   - Calvin Coolidge (1872-1933) Speech, 1922

9. Bolshevism was caused largely by the changes in the buying power of money.

- Lord d'Abernon
  (1857-1941)
  Quoted in Irving Fisher,
  The Money Illusion

10. If all prices and incomes rose
    equally, no harm would be done
    to anyone. But the rise is not
    equal. Many lose and some gain.
    – Irving Fisher (1867-1947)
      Stabilizing the Dollar, 1920,
      p. xxxiv

11. The attraction which inflation
    policies have for so many
    people grows, in part at least,
    out of what may be called the
    money illusions.
    – Irving Fisher (1867-1947)
      Ibid., Ch. II, p. 35

12. Inflation might almost be called
    legal counterfeiting.
    – Irving Fisher (1867-1947)
      Ibid., p. 36

13. To shake ourselves free of these
    illusions it would help greatly if,
    for the phrase 'a general rise in
    prices', we should substitute the
    phrase, 'a fall in the purchasing
    power of the dollar'. Our
    attention would then be focused
    on the money, which is the
    chief controller and disturber
    of prices.
    – Irving Fisher (1867-1947)
      Ibid.

14. Inflation is always and every-
    where a monetary phenomenon.
    – Milton Friedman
      Wincott Memorial Lecture,
      London, 16 Sept. 1970.
      Reprinted by the Institute of
      Economic Affairs.

15. Inflation does lubricate trade
    but by rescuing traders from
    their errors of optimism or
    stupidity.
    – J.K. Galbraith
      Money, 1975, Ch. II, p. 13

16. A fall in the value of gold must
    have . . . a most powerfully
    beneficial effect. It loosens the
    country, as nothing else could,
    from its old bonds of debt and
    habit. It throws increased
    rewards before all who are
    making and acquiring wealth. It
    excites the active and skilful
    classes of the community to
    new exertions, and is, to some
    extent, like a discharge from his
    debts is to the bankrupt long
    struggling against his burdens.
    All this is effected without a
    breach of national good faith,
    which nothing could
    compensate.
    – W. Stanley Jevons (1835-82)
      *Investigations in Currency
      and Finance*, 1884, II,
      Ch. V, pp. 96-7

17. The power of taxation by
    currency depreciation is one
    which has been inherent in the
    State since Rome discovered it.
    – John Maynard Keynes
      (1883-1946)
      'Social Consequences of
      Changes in the Value of
      Money', in *Essays in
      Persuasion*, 1933, Pt. II,
      pp. 86-7

18. It has long been recognised, by
    the business world and by
    economists alike, that a period
    of rising prices acts as a stimulus

to enterprise and is beneficial
to business men.
– John Maynard Keynes
  (1883-1946)
  *A Tract on Monetary
  Reform*, 1924, Ch. I, p. 18

19. Inflation is like sin; every
    government denounces it and
    every government practices it.
    – Sir Frederick Leith-Ross
      (1887-1968)
      Quoted in *The Observer*,
      30 June 1957

20. The issuers may have, and in the
    case of government paper,
    always have, a direct interest in
    lowering the value of the
    currency, because it is the
    medium in which their own
    debts are computed.
    – John Stuart Mill (1806-73)
      *Principles of Political
      Economy*, ed. Ashley,
      Bk. III, Ch. XIII, 1, p. 544

21. All holders of currency lose, by
    the depreciation of its value, the
    exact equivalent of what the
    issuer gains. A tax is virtually
    levied on them for his benefit.
    – John Stuart Mill (1806-73)
      Ibid., 5, p. 552

22. Inflation raises problems which
    give unusually wide scope to
    economic rationalisation of
    political prejudice.
    – E. Victor Morgan
      'Is Inflation Inevitable',
      Economic Journal, March
      1966, p. 2

23. Among the many disadvantages
    arising from alteration of the

coinage which affect the whole
community is . . . that the
prince could thus draw to
himself almost all the money of
the community and unduly
impoverish his subjects. And as
some chronic sicknesses are
more dangerous than others
because they are less perceptible,
so such an exaction is the more
dangerous the less obvious it is.
– Nicholas Oresme (1320?-82)
  *The Origin, Nature, Law and
  Alterations of Money*,
  trans. Johnson, p. 32

24. To take or augment profit by
    alteration of the coinage is
    fraudulent, tyrannical and
    unjust, and moreover it cannot
    be persisted in without the
    kingdom being, in many other
    respects also, changed to a
    tyranny . . . a tax levied by
    means of such changes is
    against the king's honour and
    injures his posterity.
    – Nicholas Oresme (1320?-82)
      Ibid., p. 47

25. Sometimes it hath hapned, that
    States (I know not by what raw
    advice) have raised or embased
    their money, hoping thereby, as
    it were, to multiply it, and make
    it pass for more than it did
    before; that is, to purchase more
    commodity or labour with it:
    all which indeed and in truth,
    amounts to no more than a tax,
    upon such people unto whom
    the state is indebted, or a
    defalkation of what is due; as
    also the like burthen upon all
    that live upon pensions,
    established rents, annuities, fees,

gratuities, etc.
- Sir William Petty (1623-87)
  'A Treatise of Taxes and
  Contributions', 1662, in
  *The Economic Writings of
  Sir William Petty*, ed. Hull,
  Vol. I, p. 84

26. Raising or embasing of moneys
    is a very pittiful and unequal
    way of taxing the people; and
    'tis a sign that the State sinketh,
    which catcheth hold on such
    weeds as are accompanied with
    the dishonour of impressing a
    princes effigies to justifie
    adulterate commodities, and the
    breach of publick faith, such as
    is the calling a thing what it
    really is not.
    - Sir William Petty (1623-87)
      Ibid., pp. 90-1

27. It may be laid down as a
    principle of universal applica-
    tion, that every man is injured
    or benefited by the variation of
    the value of the circulating
    medium in proportion as his
    property consists of money,
    or as the fixed demands on him
    in money exceed those fixed
    demands which he may have on
    others.
    - David Ricardo (1772-1823)
      Works, ed. Sraffa, Vol. III,
      p. 136

28. The Chancellor of the Exchequer
    has taken steps to stop the
    inflation before it runs away.
    - Student essay

66. *INHERITANCE*

1. Everyone knows that in all
   except the newest countries, the
   inequality in the amounts of
   property which individuals have
   received by way of bequest and
   inheritance is by far the most
   potent cause of inequality in
   the actual distribution of
   property.
   - Edwin Cannan (1861-1935)
     Quoted by A.B. Atkinson,
     Unequal Shares, 1974

2. The large inheritance of wealth
   probably has the effect of
   reducing the incentives to the
   heir to exercise his full
   capabilities – he has received
   the gold medal at the beginning
   of the race.
   - George J. Stigler
     'The Goals of Economic
     Policy', *Journal of Law and
     Economics*, October 1975,
     p. 292

67. *INNOVATION*

1. We ought not to be over anxious
   to encourage innovation, in
   cases of *doubtful* improvement,
   for an old system must ever
   have two advantages over a new
   one; it is established, and it is
   understood.
   - Reverend C.C. Colton
     (1780-1832)
     Lacon, 1845, Vol. I, DXXI

2. The full importance of an epoch-
   making idea is ofen not perceived
   in the generation in which it is
   made . . . The mechanical

100

inventions of every age are apt to be underrated relatively to those of earlier times. For a new discovery is seldom fully effective for practical purposes till many minor improvements and subsidiary discoveries have gathered themselves around it.
 — Alfred Marshall (1842-1924)
   Principles of Economics,
   8th ed., Bk. IV, Ch. VI,
   1, p. 205, footnote

3. Innovations are dangerous.
 — Proverb, in Thomas Fuller,
   Gnomologia, 1732, 3103

68. INSURANCE

1. Insurance, *n.* An ingenious modern game of chance in which the player is permitted to enjoy the comfortable conviction that he is beating the man who keeps the table.
 — Ambrose Bierce
   (1842-1914?)
   The Devil's Dictionary

69. INTEREST

1. How to have your cake and eat it too: lend it out at interest.
 — Anonymous

2. The most hated sort [of retail trade], and with the greatest reason, is usury, which makes a gain out of money itself, and not from the natural object of it.
 — Aristotle (384-322 B.C.)
   Politics, trans. B. Jowett,
   Bk. I, Ch. 10, 1258b

3. The usurer is the greatest Sabbath-breaker, because his plough goeth every Sunday.
 — Francis Bacon (1561-1626)
   Essays, XLI *of Usury*

4. Interest is the rent of stock, and is the same as the rent of land: the first, is the rent of the wrought or artificial stock; the latter, of the unwrought, or natural stock.
 — Nicholas Barbon (? -1698)
   A Discourse of Trade,
   1690, reprinted by the Johns
   Hopkins Press, 1903, p. 20

5. Interest works night and day, in fair weather and in foul. It gnaws at a man's substance with invisible teeth. It binds industry with its film, as a fly is bound upon a spider's web.
 — Henry Ward Beecher
   (1813-87)
   *Proverbs from Plymouth
   Pulpit*

6. No man of ripe years and of sound mind, acting freely, and with his eyes open, ought to be hindered, with a view to his advantage, from making such bargain, in the way of obtaining money, as he thinks fit: nor (what is a necessary consequence) any body hindered from supplying him, upon any terms he thinks proper to accede to.
 — Jeremy Bentham
   (1748-1832)
   Defence of Usury, Letter I

7. Present goods are, as a rule, worth more than future goods

of like kind and number. This proposition is the kernel and centre of the interest theory which I have to present.
- Eugen von Böhm-Bawerk (1851-1914)
The Positive Theory of Capital, trans. W. Smart, p. 237

8. Waiting necessarily commands a price.
- Gustav Cassel (1866-1945)
The Nature and Necessity of Interest, 1903, Ch. VII, p. 180

9. Usury is only one variety of the more general form of robbery which consists in taking advantage of the defects of the organisation of the market.
- Gustav Cassel (1866-1945)
Ibid., pp. 180-1

10. Some thousand years of practical experience have proved that the prosecution of the money lender only results in an extra, and usually very considerable charge being made, in order to cover the risk of breaking the law.
- Gustav Cassel (1866-1945)
Ibid., p. 182

11. Much of the antagonism to interest is in reality a disapproval, not of interest as a form of income, but of that distribution of property which makes so great a part of the interest income of the community flow into the pockets of some few privileged individuals.

- Gustav Castel (1866-1945)
Ibid., p. 183

12. The sweet simplicity of the three per cents.
- Benjamin Disraeli (1805-81)
Endymion, Ch. XCVI

13. The rate of interest acts as a link between income-value and capital-value.
- Irving Fisher (1867-1947)
The Nature of Capital and Income, 1923, Ch. XIII, 1, p. 202

14. The Theory of Interest, As Determined by IMPATIENCE to Spend Income and OPPORTUNITY to Invest It.
- Irving Fisher (1867-1947)
Title of Book, 1930

15. Rent and interest are merely two ways of measuring the same income; rent, as the yield per acre or other physical unit, and interest as the same yield expressed as a per cent of capital value.
- Irving Fisher (1867-1947)
The Theory of Interest, 1930, Ch. XV, p. 331

16. Interest springs from the power of increase which the reproductive forces of nature . . . give to capital. It is not an arbitrary, but a natural thing; it is not the result of a particular social organization, but of laws of the universe which underlie society. It is, therefore, just.
- Henry George (1839-97)
Progress and Poverty, Bk. III, Ch. III

17. High interest arises from *three* circumstances: a great demand for borrowing, little riches to supply that demand, and great profits arising from commerce.
    - David Hume (1711-76)
      Essays, Of Interest

18. Nothing is esteemed a more certain sign of the flourishing condition of any nation than the lowness of interest.
    - David Hume (1711-76)
      Ibid.

19. As labour must be supposed to be aided with some capital, the rate of interest is always determined by the *ratio which a new increment of produce bears to the increment of capital by which it was produced.*
    - W. Stanley Jevons (1835-82)
      Statistical Journal, 1866, p. 286

20. The interest of capital has no relation to the absolute returns to labour, but only to the increased return which the last increment of capital allows.
    - W. Stanley Jevons (1835-82)
      Ibid., p. 287

21. The rate of interest is the reward for parting with liquidity for a specified period.
    - John Maynard Keynes (1883-1946)
      The General Theory of Employment Interest and Money, Bk. IV, Ch. 13, p. 167

22. The habit of overlooking the relation of the rate of interest to hoarding may be a part of the explanation why interest has been usually regarded as the reward of not-spending, whereas in fact it is the reward of not-hoarding.
    - John Maynard Keynes (1883-1946)
      Ibid., p. 174

23. We have heard it said that five per cent is the natural interest of money.
    - Thomas Babington Macaulay (1800-59)
      Literary Essays Contributed to the 'Edinburgh Review', Southey's Colloquies, 1830

24. But though the greater or less quantity of money makes in itself no difference in the rate of interest, a change from a less quantity to a greater, or from a greater to a less, may and does make a difference in it.
    - John Stuart Mill (1806-73)
      Principles of Political Economy, ed. Ashley, Bk. III, Ch. XXIII, 4, p. 646

25. It is monstrous and unnatural that an unfruitful thing should bear, that a thing specifically sterile, such as money, should bear fruit and multiply of itself.
    - Nicholas Oresme (1320?-82)
      The Origin, Nature, Law and Alterations of Money, trans. Johnson, p. 25

26. Interest always carrieth with it an ensurance *praemium*.
    - Sir William Petty (1623-87)
      'Quantulumcunque concern-

ing money', 1682, in *The Economic Writings of Sir William Petty*, ed. Hull, Vol. II, p. 447

27. When a man giveth out his money upon condition that he may not demand it back until a certain time to come, whatsoever his own necessities shall be in the mean time, he certainly may take a compensation for this inconvenience which he admits against himself: and this allowance is that we commonly call usury.
    – Sir William Petty (1623-87) 'A Treatise of Taxes and Contributions', 1662, ibid., Vol. I, p. 47

28. Mediaeval theologians used to hold it sinful to pay or receive interest on capital. Surely St Thomas Aquinas enjoys a wry chuckle as he looks down on a world where nominal rates of interest are monstrously usurious, yet the real returns to lenders are more often than not negative.
    – A. Sibley 'Index-linked Securities', *Accountants' Magazine*, October 1974

29. The current rate of interest on money is the thermometer by which we can form an opinion as to the abundance or scarcity of capitals.
    – Anne Robert Jacques Turgot (1727-81) *Réflexions sur la Formation et la Distribution des Richesses*, 1766, Section 88

30. The rate of interest at which *the demand for loan capital and the supply of savings* exactly agree, and which more or less corresponds to the expected yield on the newly created capital, will then be the normal or natural real rate.
    – Knut Wicksell (1851-1926) *Lectures on Political Economy*, trans. E. Classen, Vol. II, p. 193

70. INVENTIONS

1. Inventions, and mechanical arts are not working half so much for the rich, the strong and the wise, as they are for the poor, the weak and the ignorant.
   – Henry Ward Beecher (1813-87) *Proverbs from Plymouth Pulpit*

2. Invention breeds invention.
   – Ralph Waldo Emerson (1803-82) 'Works and Days', *Society and Solitude*

3. Hitherto [1848] it is questionable if all the mechanical inventions yet made have lightened the day's toil of any human being. They have enabled a greater population to live the same life of drudgery and imprisonment, and an increased number of manufacturers and others to make fortunes ... they have not yet begun to effect those great changes in human destiny, which it is in their nature and in

their futurity to accomplish.
- John Stuart Mill (1806-73)
  *Principles of Political
  Economy*, ed. Ashley,
  Bk. IV, Ch. VI, 2, p. 751

4. Few new inventions were ever
   rewarded by a monopoly; for
   although the inventor often-
   times drunk with the opinion of
   his own merit, thinks all the
   world will invade and incroach
   upon him, yet I have observed,
   that the generality of men will
   scarce be hired to make use of
   new practices, which themselves
   have not throughly tried, and
   which length of time hath not
   vindicated from latent
   inconveniences.
   - Sir William Petty (1623-87)
     'A Treatise of Taxes and
     Contributions', 1662, in
     *The Economic Writings of
     Sir William Petty*, ed. Hull,
     Vol. I, pp. 74-5

5. Necessity is the mother of
   invention.
   - Proverb, 16th century

6. So far as I know, there is no
   definite reason why the
   inventions of the future should
   not be chiefly in the direction
   of simplifying and abbreviating
   industrial processes; so that at
   each step of improvement the
   demand for capital will be
   restricted instead of being
   enlarged.
   - Henry Sidgwick (1838-1900)
     *Principles of Political
     Economy*, 3rd ed., 1901,
     Bk. I, Ch. VI, p. 160

71. INVESTMENT

1. The best investments are often
   those that looked dead wrong
   when they were made.
   - Anonymous
     Stock Market Maxim

2. It is highly doubtful whether
   the achievements of the
   Industrial Revolution would
   have been permitted if the
   franchise had been universal. It
   is very doubtful, because a great
   deal of the capital aggregations
   that we are at present enjoying
   are the results of the wages that
   our fathers went without.
   - Aneurin Bevan (1897-1960)
     Democratic Values, Fabian
     Tract No. 282, 1950, p. 12

3. The ... question arises as to
   which is the better British
   'patriot', the British capitalist
   who leaves British labour in the
   lurch so he can make bigger
   profits in backward countries,
   or the American 'invader' who
   provides capital to electrify
   British homes and industries.
   - Ludwell Denny
     America Conquers Britain,
     1930, p. 151

4. Spending and investing differ
   only in degree, depending on
   the length of time elapsing
   between the expenditure and
   the enjoyment.
   - Irving Fisher (1867-1947)
     The Theory of Interest,
     Ch. I, p. 9

5. Investment is not only produced
   but also producing.

- M. Kalecki (1899-1970)
  *Essays in the Theory of
  Economic Fluctuations,*
  1939, p. 148

6. There is no clear evidence from
   experience that the investment
   policy which is socially
   advantageous coincides with
   that which is most profitable.
   - John Maynard Keynes
     (1883-1946)
     *The General Theory of
     Employment Interest and
     Money,* Bk. IV, Ch. 12,
     p. 157

7. The fact that so many
   opportunities for the profitable
   investment of resources in the
   development of human
   potentialities are neglected, and
   so many wasteful investments of
   the same kind made, is perhaps
   one of the most serious
   criticisms of existing society.
   - Frank H. Knight
     Risk, Uncertainty and Profit,
     1921, pp. 158-9, footnote

8. Unexpected new investment . . .
   can simply mean that stocks at
   the end of the period are
   different from what the entrepreneur expected.
   - Bertil Ohlin
     'Some Notes on the
     Stockholm Theory of
     Savings and Investment I',
     Economic Journal, March
     1937, p. 65

9. Investment dollars are high-
   powered dollars. Consumption
   dollars are too.
   - Paul A. Samuelson

*Foundations of Economic
Analysis,* 1947, p. 137

72. IRELAND

1. I know of nothing better
   calculated to make the blood
   boil than the cold accounts of
   the grasping, grinding tyranny
   to which the Irish people have
   been subjected, and to which,
   and not to any inability of the
   land to support its population,
   Irish pauperism and Irish
   famine are to be attributed; and
   were it not for the enervating
   effect which the history of the
   world proves to be everywhere
   the result of abject poverty, it
   would be difficult to resist
   something like a feeling of
   contempt for a race who, stung
   by such wrongs, have only
   occasionally murdered a
   landlord!
   - Henry George (1839-97)
     Progress and Poverty, Bk. II,
     Ch. II

2. Between the condition of the
   rack-rented Irish peasant and
   the Russian serf, the advantage
   was in many things on the side
   of the serf. The serf did not
   starve.
   - Henry George (1839-97)
     Ibid., Bk. VII, Ch. II

3. As Ireland exporting more than
   it imports doth yet grow poorer
   to a paradox.
   - Sir William Petty (1623-87)
     'A Treatise of Taxes and
     Contributions', 1662, in
     The Economic Writings of

Sir William Petty, ed. Hull, Vol. I, p. 46

73. KEYNES, JOHN MAYNARD

1st BARON KEYNES 1883-1946

1. Whenever I ask England's six leading economists a question, I get seven answers – two from Mr Keynes.
   - Winston Churchill (1874-1965)
   Quoted by Benjamin Higgins, *What do Economists Know?*, 1951

2. We are all Keynesians now.
   - Milton Friedman
   Quoted in P.A. Samuelson, *Economics*, 8th ed.

3. Keynes had long been suspect among his colleagues for the clarity of his writing and thought, the two often going together. In *The General Theory* he redeemed his academic reputation. It is a work of profound obscurity, badly written and prematurely published.
   - J.K. Galbraith *Money*, 1975, Ch. 16, pp. 217-8

4. Many people like quoting Keynes's dictum that economics should be like dentistry. Few of them note the singular lack of dentists who have written 'General Theories'.
   - F.H. Hahn 'The Winter of our Discontent', *Economica*, August 1973, p. 323

See also 40.12

5. The General Theory of Employment is the Economics of Depression.
   - J.R. Hicks 'Mr Keynes and the "Classics"; A Suggested Interpretation', *Econometrica*, April 1937

6. I evidently knew more about Economics than my examiners.
   - John Maynard Keynes (1883-1946)
   Commenting on the results of his Civil Service examination. Quoted in R.F. Harrod, *The Life of John Maynard Keynes*, Ch. 3

7. I believe myself to be writing a book on economic theory which will largely revolutionize – not, I suppose, at once but in the course of the next ten years – the way the world thinks about economic problems.
   - John Maynard Keynes (1883-1946)
   Letter to George Bernard Shaw, 1 Jan. 1935, ibid., Ch. 11

8. We are suffering just now from a bad attack of economic pessimism.
   - John Maynard Keynes (1883-1946)
   'Economic Possibilities for our Grandchildren', in *Essays in Persuasion*, 1933, Pt. V, p. 358

9. He [Keynes] brought the argument down from timeless

stationary states into the present, here and now, when the past cannot be changed and the future cannot be known.
 – Joan Robinson
    Economic Heresies, 1971,
    p. ix

74. KNOWLEDGE

1. Grace is given of God, but knowledge is bought in the market.
   – Arthur Hugh Clough
     (1819-61)
     The Bothie of Tober-na-Vuolich, IV

2. In a world where attention is a major scarce resource, information may be an expensive luxury, for it may turn our attention from what is important to what is unimportant.
   – Herbert A. Simon
     'Rationality as Process and as Product of Thought',
     American Economic Review,
     May 1978, p. 13

75. LABOUR

1. Labour gives a new creation for one extinguished.
   – Anonymous
     An Essay on the Political Economy of Nations,
     1821, p. 13

2. Human labour is not an *end* but a *means*.
   – Frédéric Bastiat (1801-50)
     Sophismes Economiques,

trans. G.R. Porter, Ch. II,
p. 21

3. Labour, *n.* One of the processes by which A acquires property for B.
   – Ambrose Bierce
     (1842-1914?)
     The Devil's Dictionary

4. Labour is the capital of our working men.
   – Stephen Grover Cleveland
     (1837-1908)
     Attributed

5. It is not the possession of land or money, but the command of labour that distinguishes the opulent from the labouring part of the community.
   – Sir Frederic Morton Eden
     (1766-1809)
     The State of the Poor,
     ed. A.G.L. Rogers, p. 1

6. Is a man the natural proprietor of the produce of his own labour? If he is not, what foundation is there for property at all?
   – John Gray (1799-1883)
     Lecture on Human Happiness, 1825

7. Every thing in the world is purchased by labour.
   – David Hume (1711-76)
     Essays, Of Commerce

8. There is no such thing as absolute cost of labour; it is all a matter of comparison.
   – W. Stanley Jevons (1835-82)
     Theory of Political Economy,
     4th ed., Preface

9. But though labour is never the cause of value, it is in a large proportion of cases the determining circumstance, and in the following way: *Value depends solely on the final degree of utility. How can we vary this degree of utility?– By having more or less of the commodity to consume. And how shall we get more or less of it? – By spending more or less labour in obtaining a supply.*
   – W. Stanley Jevons (1835-82)
   Ibid., Ch. IV, p. 165

10. Labour . . . is any painful exertion of mind or body undergone partly or wholly with a view to future good.
    – W. Stanley Jevons (1835-82)
    Ibid., Ch. V, p. 168

11. No man loves labour for itself.
    – Samuel Johnson (1709-84)
    Boswell's Life of Johnson,
    26 Oct. 1769

12. Labour is prior to, and independent of capital. Capital is only the fruit of labour, and would never have existed if labour had not first existed. Labour is the superior to capital, and deserves much higher consideration.
    – Abraham Lincoln (1809-65)
    Message to Congress, 3 Dec. 1861

13. Labour makes the far greatest part of the value of things.
    – John Locke (1632-1704)
    Two Treatises of Government, Bk. II, Ch. V, p. 42

14. The price of the necessaries of life is, in fact, the cost of producing labour.
    – Thomas Robert Malthus (1766-1834)
    Inquiry into the Nature and Progress of Rent, 1815, p. 48

15. We may define *labour* as any exertion of mind or body undergone partly or wholly with a view to some good other than the pleasure derived directly from the work.
    – Alfred Marshall (1842-1924)
    Principles of Economics,
    8th ed., Bk. II, Ch. III, 2, p. 65

16. Skilled labour counts only as simple labour intensified, or rather, as multiplied simple labour being considered equal to a greater quantity of simple labour.
    – Karl Marx (1818-83)
    Capital, Vol. I, Pt. I, Ch. I, 2

17. All their devices for cheapening labour simply resulted in increasing the burden of labour.
    – William Morris (1834-96)
    News from Nowhere

18. For the person engaged in it, labour is an evil.
    – Maffeo Pantaleoni (1857-1924)
    Pure Economics, trans. Bruce, Pt. III, Ch. V, p. 284

19. Labour . . . is the real measure of the exchangeable value of all commodities.

— Adam Smith (1723-90)
Wealth of Nations, ed.
Cannan, Vol. I, Bk. I,
Ch. V, p. 32

20. There may be more labour
in an hour's hard work than in
two hours easy business; or in
an hour's application to a trade
which it cost ten years labour to
learn, than in a month's
industry at an ordinary and
obvious employment.
— Adam Smith (1723-90)
Ibid., p. 33

21. During the predatory culture
labour comes to be associated
in men's habits of thought with
weakness and subjection to a
master. It is therefore a mark of
inferiority, and, therefore,
comes to be accounted
unworthy of man in his best
estate.
— Thorstein Veblen
(1857-1929)
*The Theory of the Leisure
Class*, Ch. III

76. LAISSEZ-FAIRE

1. Let us remember, that it [laissez-
faire] is a *practical rule*, and
not a doctrine of science, a rule
in the main sound, but like most
other sound practical rules,
liable to numerous exceptions;
above all, a rule which must
never for a moment be allowed
to stand in the way of the
candid consideration of any
promising proposal of social or
industrial reform.
— J.E. Cairnes (1824-75)

Essays in Political Economy,
1873, 'Political Economy and
Laissez-faire', p. 251

2. Laissez-faire, Supply-and-
demand, — one begins to be
weary of all that. Leave all to
egoism, to ravenous greed of
money, of pleasure, of
applause: — it is the Gospel of
Despair!
— Thomas Carlyle (1795-1881)
Past and Present, 1843,
Bk. III, Ch. IX

3. Laissez-faire, laissez passer.
— Vincent de Gournay
(1712-59)
Attributed

4. A considerable departure from
laissez-faire is necessary in order
to realise the theoretical results
of laissez-faire.
— Sir Hubert Henderson
(1890-1952)
Attributed

5. The principle of *laissez-faire*
may be safely trusted to in some
things but in many more it is
wholly inapplicable; and to
appeal to it on all occasions
savours more of the policy of
a parrot than of a statesman or
a philosopher.
— J.R. McCulloch (1789-1864)
*Treatise on the Succession to
Property Vacant by Death*,
1848

6. The man who accepts the
laissez-faire doctrine would
allow his garden to run wild so
that the roses might fight it out
with the weeds and the fittest

might survive.
— John Ruskin (1819-1900)
Attributed

77. LAND

1. The land is the source or matter
   from whence all wealth is
   produced. The labour of man is
   the form which produces it: and
   wealth in itself is nothing but
   the maintenance, conveniences
   and superfluities of life.
   — Richard Cantillon
     (1680?-1734)
     *Essai sur la Nature du
     Commerce en Générale*,
     1755, trans. Henry Higgs,
     p. 3

2. All classes and individuals in a
   State subsist or are enriched at
   the expense of the proprietors
   of land.
   — Richard Cantillon
     (1680?-1734)
     Ibid., p. 43

3. No land is bad, but land is
   worse. If a man owns land, the
   land owns him. Now let him
   leave home, if he dare.
   — Ralph Waldo Emerson
     (1803-82)
     'Wealth', *The Conduct of
     Life*, 1860

4. To permit one man to monopolise the land from which the
   support of others is to be
   drawn, is to permit him to
   appropriate their labour, and, in
   so far as he is permitted to do
   this, to appropriate them. It is
   to institute slavery.
   — Henry George (1839-97)
     Our Land and Land Policy,
     1871, in *Works*, 1904,
     Vol. VIII, p. 86

5. As labour cannot produce
   without the use of land, the
   denial of the equal right to the
   use of land is necessarily the
   denial of the right of labour to
   its own produce. If one man
   can command the land upon
   which others must labour, he
   can appropriate the produce of
   their labour as the price of his
   permission to labour...The one
   receives without producing; the
   others produce without receiving.
   — Henry George (1839-97)
     Progress and Poverty,
     Bk. VII, Ch. I

6. What is necessary for the use of
   land is not its private ownership,
   but the security of improvements. It is not necessary to say
   to a man, 'this land is yours', in
   order to induce him to cultivate
   or improve it. It is only
   necessary to say to him,
   'whatever your labour or capital
   produces on this land shall be
   yours'. Give a man security that
   he may reap, and he will sow.
   — Henry George (1839-97)
     Ibid., Bk. VIII, Ch. I

7. Private property in land is an
   obstacle to the investment of
   capital on land . . . The
   possibilities of free investment
   of capital in land, free
   competition in agriculture, are
   much greater under the system
   of free renting than under the
   system of private property in

land. Nationalisation of the
land, is, as it were, landlordism
without the landlord.
- V.I. Lenin (1870-1924)
  Selected Works, Vol. 1,
  p. 211

8. Land is but a particular form of
capital from the point of view
of the individual producer.
- Alfred Marshall (1842-1924)
  Principles of Economics,
  8th ed., Bk. V, Ch. X,
  3, p. 430

9. The limitation to production
from the properties of the soil,
is not like the obstacle opposed
by a wall, which stands
immovable in one particular
spot, and offers no hindrance
to motion short of stopping it
entirely. We may rather
compare it to a highly elastic
and extensible band, which is
hardly ever so violently
stretched that it could not
possibly be stretched any more,
yet the pressure of which is felt
long before the final limit is
reached, and felt more severely
the nearer that limit is
approached.
- John Stuart Mill (1806-73)
  *Principles of Political
  Economy*, ed. Ashley,
  Bk. I, Ch. XII, 2, pp. 176-7

10. No man made the land. It is the
original inheritance of the whole
species. Its appropriation is
wholly a question of general
expediency. When private
property in land is not expedient,
it is unjust. It is no hardship to
any one to be excluded from

what others have produced:
they were not bound to produce
it for his use, and he loses
nothing by not sharing in what
otherwise would not have
existed at all. But it is some
hardship to be born into the
world and to find all nature's
gifts previously engrossed, and
no place left for the new-comer.
- John Stuart Mill (1806-73)
  Ibid., Bk. II, Ch. II, 6,
  p. 233

11. The qualities of the soil can do
nothing . . . without external
demand.
- David Ricardo (1772-1823)
  Notes on Malthus, in *Works*,
  ed. Sraffa, Vol. II, p. 114

12. No one supposes, that the
owner of urban land, performs
qua owner, any function. He has
a right of private taxation; that
is all.
- R.H. Tawney (1880-1962)
  The Acquisitive Society,
  1921, Ch. III

13. What we mean by land in
practical life is something
which . . . consists very largely
of the accumulated result of
human effort.
- Philip H. Wicksteed
  (1844-1927)
  Attributed

14. Between the duties expected of
one during one's lifetime, and
the duties exacted from one
after one's death, land has
ceased to be either a profit or a
pleasure. It gives one position,
and prevents one from keeping

it up.
- Oscar Wilde (1854-1900)
  The Importance of Being Earnest, Act I

78. LAW

1. Justice, *n.* A commodity which in a more or less adulterated condition the State sells to the citizen as a reward for his allegiance, taxes and personal service.
   - Ambrose Bierce (1842-1914?)
     The Devil's Dictionary

2. LL.D. Letters indicating the degree *Tegumptionorum Doctor* ... Some suspicion is cast upon this derivation by the fact that the title was formerly ££.d., and conferred only upon gentlemen distinguished for their wealth.
   - Ambrose Bierce (1842-1914?)
     Ibid.

3. The whole circle of economic life in civilised societies rests upon, and is powerfully modified by, the actual system of legal relations, or body of positive law, which forms the skeleton, so to speak, of the social organism.
   - H.S. Foxwell (1849-1936)
     Introduction to A. Menger,
     The Right to the Whole Produce of Labour

4. The law, in its majestic equality, forbids the rich as well as the poor to sleep under bridges.

- Anatole France (1844-1924)
  Quoted in M.Z. Hepker,
  A Modern Approach to Tax Law, 2nd ed., p. 10

5. Law grinds the poor, and rich men rule the law.
   - Oliver Goldsmith (1728-74)
     The Traveller

6. Unnecessary laws are not good laws, but traps for money.
   - Thomas Hobbes (1588-1679)
     Leviathan, 1651, Pt. II, Ch.XXX

7. No arbitrary regulation, no act of the legislature, can add anything to the capital of the country; it can only force it into artificial channels.
   - J.R. McCulloch (1789-1864)
     Principles of Political Economy, new ed., Pt. I, Ch. VII, p. 219

8. To judge whether [a workman] is fit to be employed, may surely be trusted to the discretion of the employers whose interest it so much concerns. The affected anxiety of the law-giver lest they should employ an improper person, is evidently as impertinent as it is oppressive.
   - Adam Smith (1723-90)
     Wealth of Nations, ed. Cannan, Vol. I, Bk. I, Ch. X, p. 123

79. LENDING

1. Lend money to an enemy, and thou'lt gain him; to a friend, and thou'lt lose him.

- Benjamin Franklin
(1706-90)
Poor Richard's Almanac,
1740

2. Better give a shilling, than lend and lose half a crown.
   - Proverb, in Thomas Fuller, *Gnomologia*, 1732, 895

3. He that lends, gives.
   - Proverb, in George Herbert, *Outlandish Proverbs*, 1640

80. MACHINERY

1. Improvements in machinery are always more advantageous to the labourers, regarded as a class, than to capitalists.
   - J.R. McCulloch (1789-1864) *Principles of Political Economy*, new ed., Pt. I, Ch. VII, p. 205

2. Without doubt, machinery has greatly increased the number of well-to-do idlers.
   - Karl Marx (1818-83) *Capital*, Vol. I, Pt. IV, Ch. XV, 1

3. Machinery, like every other component of constant capital creates no new value, but yields up its own value to the product it serves to beget.
   - Karl Marx (1818-83) Ibid., 2

4. The instrument of labour, when it takes the form of a machine immediately becomes a competitor of the workman himself.

- Karl Marx (1818-83)
Ibid., 5

81. MACROECONOMICS

1. MACRO-ECONOMICS: a laudable attempt to explain how large parts (or the whole) of an economy work, without pretending to know how the component parts work.
   - Ralph Harris 'Everyman's Guide to Contemporary Economic Jargon', *Growth, Advertising and the Consumer*, 1964, p. 23

2. Macroeconomics is an outgrowth from the main stream of classical monetary theory following Keynes.
   - Harry G. Johnson (1923-77) *Macroeconomics and Monetary Theory*, 1971, Ch. 1, p. 1

3. The division of Economics between the Theory of Value and Distribution on the one hand and the Theory of Money on the other hand, is, I think, a false division. The right dichotomy is, I suggest, between the Theory of the Individual Industry or Firm and of the rewards and the distribution between the different uses of a *given* quantity of resources on the one hand, and the Theory of Output and Employment *as a whole* on the other hand.
   - John Maynard Keynes (1883-1946)

The General Theory of Employment Interest and Money, Bk. V, Ch. 21, p. 293

4. If our central controls succeed in establishing an aggregate volume of output corresponding to full employment as nearly as is practicable, the classical theory comes into its own again from this point onwards.
   — John Maynard Keynes
      (1883-1946)
      Ibid., Bk. VI, Ch. 24, p. 378

5. It was recognizing the difference between the future and the past that caused Hicks to become disillusioned with the IS/LM model with which generations of students have been taught to misinterpret the *General Theory*.
   — Joan Robinson
      'What Are the Questions?',
      Journal of Economic Literature, 1977, p. 1323

82. *MALTHUS, THOMAS ROBERT*

1766-1834

1. To get land's fruit in quantity takes jolts of labour even more, hence food will grow like one, two, three . . . while numbers grow like one, two, four . . .
   — Anonymous
      Song of Malthus: A Ballad on Diminishing Returns, quoted in Paul A. Samuelson, *Economics*, 8th ed.
      See also 93.6

2. Malthusian, *adj*. Pertaining to

Malthus and his doctrines. Malthus believed in artificially limiting population, but found that it could not be done by talking.
   — Ambrose Bierce
      (1842-1914?)
      The Devil's Dictionary

3. Malthus, when he stated that the mouths went on multiplying geometrically, and the food only arithmetically, forgot to say that the human mind was also a factor in political economy.
   — Ralph Waldo Emerson
      (1803-82)
      'Works and Days', *Society and Solitude*

4. Imagine Adam . . . figured on the growth of his first baby from the rate of its early months. From the fact that at birth it weighed ten pounds and in eight months thereafter twenty pounds, he might, with the arithmetical knowledge which some sages have supposed him to possess, have cyphered out a result quite as striking as that of Mr Malthus; namely, that by the time it got to be ten years old it would be as heavy as an ox, at twelve as heavy as an elephant, and at thirty would weigh no less than 175,716,339,548 tons.
   — Henry George (1839-97)
      Progress and Poverty, Bk. II, Ch. III

5. The note of gloom and pessimism which distinguishes so much of the economic doctrine

of the nineteenth century is in no small measure the legacy of Malthus.
  — Alexander Gray (1882-1921)
    The Development of Economic Doctrine, 1931, p. 163

6. If only Malthus, instead of Ricardo, had been the parent stem from which nineteenth-century economics proceeded, what a much wiser and richer place the world would be today!
  — John Maynard Keynes (1883-1946)
    'Thomas Robert Malthus', in *Essays in Biography*

7. Metaphysics, and enquiries into moral and political science, have become little else than vain attempts to revive exploded superstitions, or sophisms like those of Mr Malthus, calculated to lull the oppressors of mankind into a security of everlasting triumph.
  — Percy Bysshe Shelley (1792-1822)
    The Revolt of Islam, Preface

8. Philosopher Malthus came here last week. I got an agreeable party for him of unmarried people. There was only one lady who had had a child; but he is a good-natured man, and, if there are no appearances of approaching fertility, is civil to every lady.
  — Sydney Smith (1771-1845)
    Letter to a friend, 1831

83. MARKET(S)

1. The market is totally impartial.
  — Anonymous

2. But the market is the best judge of value; for by the concourse of buyers and sellers, the quantity of wares, and the occasion for them are best known. Things are just worth so much, as they can be sold for, according to the old rule *Valet Quantum Vendi Potest.*
  — Nicholas Barbon (? - 1698)
    A Discourse of Trade, 1690, reprinted by the Johns Hopkins Press, 1903, p. 16

3. We can no longer ask the invisible hand to do our dirty work for us.
  — E.H. Carr
    The New Society, 1951

4. Economists understand by the term *Market*, not any particular market place in which things are bought and sold, but the whole of any region in which buyers and sellers are in such free intercourse with one another that the prices of the same goods tend to equality easily and quickly.
  — Augustin Cournot (1801-77)
    Recherches sur les Principes Mathématiques de la Théorie des Richesses, Ch. IV

5. Despite the important role of enterprises and of money in our actual economy, and despite the numerous and complex problems they raise, the central characteristic of the market technique of

achieving co-ordination is fully displayed in the simple exchange economy that contains neither enterprises nor money.
– Milton Friedman
Capitalism and Freedom, 1962, Ch. I, p. 14

6. Whether under monopoly or so-called competitive conditions, markets are intrinsically unfair models of distribution.
– J.A. Hobson (1858-1940)
Confessions of an Economic Heretic, 1938, Ch. XIV

7. By a market I shall mean two or more persons dealing in two or more commodities, whose stocks of those commodities and intentions of exchanging are known to all.
– W. Stanley Jevons (1835-82)
Theory of Political Economy, 4th ed., Ch. IV, p. 85

8. In the same open market, at any moment, there cannot be two prices for the same kind of article.
– W. Stanley Jevons (1835-82)
Ibid., p. 91

9. A friend in the market is better than money in the chest.
– Proverb, in Thomas Fuller, *Gnomologia*, 1732, 119

10. Game is cheaper in the market, than in the fields and woods.
– Proverb, ibid., 1641

11. There are two fools in every market; one asks too little, one asks too much.
– Russian proverb

12. [Value] is adjusted . . . not by any accurate measure, but by the higgling and bargaining of the market, according to that sort of rough equality which, though not exact, is sufficient for carrying on the business of common life.
– Adam Smith (1723-90)
Wealth of Nations, ed. Cannan, Vol. I, Bk. I, Ch. V, p. 33

13. The real and effectual discipline which is exercised over a work-man, is . . . that of his customers. It is the fear of losing their employment which restrains his frauds and corrects his negligence.
– Adam Smith (1723-90)
Ibid., Ch. X, p. 131

14. Every individual . . . generally, indeed, neither intends to promote the public interest, nor knows how much he is promoting it. By preferring the support of domestic to that of foreign industry he intends only his own security; and by directing that industry in such a manner as its produce may be of the greatest value, he intends only his own gain, and he is in this, as in many other cases, led by an invisible hand to promote an end which was no part of his intention.
– Adam Smith (1723-90)
Ibid., Bk. IV, Ch. II, p. 421

15. The innumerable living participants of economy, state as well as private, collective as well as individual, must give

notice of their needs and of their relative strength not only through the statistical determination of plan commissions but by the direct pressure of supply and demand. The plan is checked and to a considerable measure realised through the market.
  − Leon Trotsky (1879-1940)
    Soviet Economy in Danger, 1932

16. The whole world may be looked upon as a vast general market made up of diverse special markets where social wealth is bought and sold. Our task then is to discover the laws to which these purchases and sales tend to conform automatically. To this end, we shall suppose that the market is perfectly competitive, just as in pure mechanics we suppose, to start with, that machines are perfectly frictionless.
  − Léon Walras (1834-1910)
    Elements of Pure Economics, trans. W. Jaffé, Pt. II, Lesson 5, p. 85

17. The one thing that the market cannot measure is the satisfaction derived from its own use.
  − Barbara Wootton
    Lament for Economics, 1938, p. 187

84. MARXISM

1. Marxism differs from anarchism in that it recognises *the necessity for the State* and for state power in a period of revolution in general, and in the period of transition from capitalism to socialism in particular.
  − V.I. Lenin (1870-1924)
    Selected Works, Vol. 6, p. 56

2. Marxism flourishes but in countries where capitalism is least successful.
  − Joan Robinson
    Marx, Marshall and Keynes, 1955

3. The religious quality of Marxism also explains a characteristic attitude of the orthodox Marxist toward opponents. To him, as to any believer in a faith, the opponent is not merely in error but in sin. Dissent is disapproved of not only intellectually but also morally.
  − Joseph A. Schumpeter (1883-1950)
    Capitalism, Socialism and Democracy, Ch. I, p. 5, footnote

4. Leninism is Marxism in the epoch of imperialism and the proletarian revolution.
  − Joseph Stalin (1879-1953)
    Foundations of Leninism, 1924

5. Marxian economics is essentially the economics of capitalism, while 'capitalist' economics is in a very real sense the economics of socialism.
  − Paul M. Sweezy
    'Economics and the Crisis of Capitalism', *Economic*

Forum, Spring 1935, p. 79

85. MATHEMATICS

1. Mathematics has no symbols for confused ideas.
   − Anonymous

2. The ability to judge the relevance of an economic theory and its conclusions to the real world, is but rarely associated with the ability to understand advanced mathematics.
   − D.G. Champernowne
   'On the Use and Misuse of Mathematics in Presenting Economic Theory', *Review of Economics and Statistics*, Nov. 1954, p. 369

3. The employment of mathematical symbols is perfectly natural when the relations between magnitudes are under discussion; and even if they are not rigorously necessary, it would hardly be reasonable to reject them . . . if they are able to facilitate the exposition of problems, to render it more concise, to open the way to more extended developments, and to avoid the digressions of vague argumentation.
   − Augustin Cournot (1801-77)
   Researches into the Mathematical Principles of the Theory of Wealth, 1838, trans. N.T. Bacon, pp. 3-4

4. *The conception of Man as a pleasure machine* may justify and facilitate the employment of mechanical terms and mathematical reasoning in social science.
   − F.Y. Edgeworth
   (1845-1926)
   Mathematical Psychics, 1881, Pt. I, p. 15

5. To treat *variables* as *constants* is the characteristic vice of the unmathematical economist.
   − F.Y. Edgeworth
   (1845-1926)
   Ibid., p. 127, note

6. Mathematics is as it were the universal language of the physical sciences. It is for physicists what Latin used to be for scholars; but it is unfortunately Greek to many economists. Hence the writer who wishes to be widely read . . . will do well not to multiply mathematical technicalities beyond the indispensible minimum, which we have seen reason to suppose is not very large. The parsimony of symbols, which is often an elegance in the physicist, is a necessity for the economist.
   − F.Y. Edgeworth
   (1845-1926)
   Quoted by J.N. Keynes, *Scope and Method of Political Economy*, 4th ed., p. 266

7. Our science must be mathematical, simply because it deals with quantities.
   − W. Stanley Jevons (1835-82)
   Theory of Political Economy, 4th ed., Ch. I, p. 3

8. The chief use of pure

mathematics in economic questions seems to be in helping a person to write down quickly, shortly and exactly, some of his thoughts for his own use: and to make sure that he has enough, and only enough, premises for his conclusions (i.e. that his equations are neither more nor less in number than his unknowns).
— Alfred Marshall (1842-1924)
Principles of Economics,
Preface to 1st ed., 1980

9. In my view every economic fact, whether or not it is of such a nature as to be expressed in numbers, stands in relation as cause and effect to many other facts: and since it *never* happens that all of them can be expressed in numbers, the application of exact mathematical methods to those which can is nearly always a waste of time, while in the large majority of cases it is positively misleading; and the world would have been further on its way forward if the work had never been done at all.
— Alfred Marshall (1842-1924)
Letter to A.L. Bowley,
3 March 1901. Quoted in
A.C. Pigou, *Memorials of Alfred Marshall*, p. 422

10. Objections from people innocent of mathematics are like objections to Chinese literature by people who cannot read Chinese.
— A.C. Pigou (1877-1959)
Quoted by Seymour Harris,
Review of Economic Statistics, November 1954, p. 383

11. The jury may still be out on whether mathematics, an incomplete language, can convey the variety of economic life in symbolic terms.
— Sidney Weintraub
Modern Economic Thought, 1977, p. 105

86. MONEY

1. Money is the blood and soul of men and whosoever has none wanders dead among the living.
— Anonymous

2. If you imposed the decimal coinage in this country you would have a revolution within a week.
— Herbert Henry Asquith (1852-1928)
Imperial Conference 1911, Cd. 5745, pp. 165-70 and 367-72. Quoted in N.E.A. Moore, *The Decimalisation of Britain's Currency*, HMSO, 1973

3. Man should always divide his wealth into three parts; one-third in land, one-third in commerce and one-third in his own hands.
— Babylonian Talmud

4. Money is like muck, not good except it be spread.
— Francis Bacon (1561-1626)
Essays, XV, *of Seditions and Troubles*

5. Money is economical power.
   — Walter Bagehot (1826-77)
   Lombard Street, 14th ed.,
   p. 4

6. Money is the measure of
   commerce.
   — Nicholas Barbon (? -1698)
   *Discourse Concerning
   Coining the New Money
   Lighter*, 1696, p. 92

7. Man is not nourished by money.
   He does not clothe himself with
   gold, he does not warm himself
   with silver.
   — Frédéric Bastiat (1801-50)
   Sophismes Economiques,
   trans. G.R. Porter, Ch. I,
   p. 16

8. Money is like snow. If it is
   blown into drifts it blocks up
   the highway, and nobody can
   travel; but if it is diffused over
   all the ground it facilitates every
   man's travel.
   — Henry Ward Beecher
   (1813-87)
   *Proverbs from Plymouth
   Pulpit*

9. Money speaks sense in a
   Language all Nations understand.
   — Aphra Behn (1640-89)
   The Rover, Act III, Sc I.
   Works, ed. M. Summers,
   Vol. I, p. 166

10. Money . . . [is] a pledge.
    — John Bellers (1654-1725)
    Writings, by A. Ruth Fry,
    1935, p. 39

11. It is much easier to get goods
    than money.
    — Jeremy Bentham
    (1748-1832)
    Defence of Usury, Letter III

12. The effect of forced frugality is
    also produced by the creating of
    paper money by government, or
    the suffering of the creation of
    paper money on the part of
    individuals. In this case, the
    effect is produced by a species
    of indirect taxation, which has
    hitherto passed almost
    unnoticed.
    — Jeremy Bentham
    (1748-1832)
    *A Manual of Political
    Economy*, Ch. 3. In
    J. Bowring (ed.), *Works of
    Jeremy Bentham*, Vol. 3,
    pp. 44-5

13. Money *is* a defence.
    — *Bible*, Authorised Version
    Ecclesiastes, Ch. 7, v. 12

14. Money answereth all *things*.
    — *Bible*, Authorised Version
    Ibid., Ch. 10, v. 19

15. Filthy lucre.
    — *Bible*, Authorised Version
    1 *Timothy*, Ch. 3, v. 3

16. The love of money is the root of
    all evil.
    — *Bible*, Authorised Version
    Ibid., Ch. 6, v. 10

17. Money, *n.* A blessing that is of
    no advantage to us excepting
    when we part with it.
    — Ambrose Bierce
    (1842-1914?)
    The Devil's Dictionary

18. What makes all doctrines plain
    and clear? —
    About two hundred pounds a
    year.
    And that which was prov'd true
    before,
    Prove false again? — Two
    hundred more.
    — Samuel Butler (1612-80)
      Hudebras, Part III, Canto I,
      1.1277

19. Money is the last enemy that
    shall never be subdued. While
    there is flesh there is money —
    or the want of money; but
    money is always on the brain so
    long as there is a brain in
    reasonable order.
    — Samuel Butler (1835-1902)
      'Elementary Morality' in
      Notebooks, 1918, p. 36

20. It has been said that the love of
    money is the root of all evil.
    The want of money is so quite
    as truly.
    — Samuel Butler (1835-1902)
      Erewhon, Ch. 10

21. Ready money *is* Aladdin's lamp.
    — Lord Byron (1788-1824)
      Don Juan, 12

22. They say that 'Knowledge is
    Power:' — I used to think so;
    but I now know that they
    meant *'money:'* and when
    Socrates declared, 'that all he
    knew was, that he knew
    nothing,' he merely intended to
    declare, that he had not a
    drachm in the Athenian World.
    — Lord Byron (1788-1824)
      Letter to Douglas Kinnaird,
      6 February, 1822

23. Cash is virtue.
    — Lord Byron (1788-1824)
      Ibid.

24. An acceleration or greater
    rapidity in circulation of money
    in exchange, is equivalent to an
    increase of actual money up to
    a point.
    — Richard Cantillon
      (1680?-1734)
      *Essai sur la Nature du
      Commerce en Générale*,
      1755, trans. Henry Higgs,
      p. 161

25. [Money] is of very uncertain
    value, and sometimes has no
    value at all, and even less.
    — Thomas Carlyle (1795-1881)
      Frederick the Great, Bk. IV,
      Ch. III

26. Cash Payment is the only nexus
    between man and man.
    — Thomas Carlyle (1795-1881)
      Quoted by Frederick Engels
      *The Condition of the
      Working-Class in England in
      1844*, 1892, Ch. XI, p. 277

27. The only quality demanded of a
    monetary system which is of
    any importance for promoting
    the trade and general welfare of
    the world, is stability.
    — Gustav Cassel (1866-1945)
      *Money and Foreign
      Exchange After 1914*,
      1922, p. 254

28. MONEY, Cash. *Money* comes
    from the Latin *moneta*, a
    surname of Juno, in whose
    temple at Rome money was
    coined. *Cash* from the French

casse, a chest, signifies that
which is put in a chest.
- George Crabb (1778-1851)
  Crabb's English Synonymes

29. The more we use monetary
policy, the less satisfactory it
seems.
   - James S. Duesenberry
     'Monetary Policy and
     Sectoral Credit Flows',
     American Economic Review,
     May 1974, p. 105

30. The value of a dollar is social, as
it is created by society.
   - Ralph Waldo Emerson
     (1803-82)
     'Wealth', *The Conduct of
     Life*, 1860

31. Money is the sinews of love, as
of war.
   - George Farquhar
     (1678-1707)
     Love and a Bottle

32. Money is the fruit of evil as
often as the root of it.
   - Henry Fielding (1707-54)
     Quoted in Esar and Bentley,
     *The Treasury of Humorous
     Quotations*

33. Money never bears interest
except in the sense of creating
convenience in the process of
exchange.
   - Irving Fisher (1867-1947)
     *The Purchasing Power of
     Money*, 1920, Ch. II, 1, p. 9

34. The level of prices varies
directly with the quantity of
money in circulation, provided
the velocity of circulation of

that money and the volume of
trade which it is obliged to
perform are not changed.
   - Irving Fisher (1867-1947)
     Ibid., p. 14

35. The truth is, that the purchasing
power of money has always
been unstable.
   - Irving Fisher (1867-1947)
     Stabilizing the Dollar, 1920,
     p. xxvi

36. We now have a gold dollar of
constant weight and varying
purchasing power; we need a
dollar of constant purchasing
power and, therefore, of varying
weight.
   - Irving Fisher (1867-1947)
     Ibid., p. xxvii

37. The chief evil of an unstable
dollar is uncertainty.
   - Irving Fisher (1867-1947)
     Ibid., p. xxxv

38. Monetary policy had not been
tried and found wanting. It had
not been tried. [During the
Great Depression.]
   - Milton Friedman
     Wincott Memorial Lecture,
     London, 16 Sept. 1970.
     Reprinted by the Institute
     of Economic Affairs

39. What used to be called the
quantity theory of money . . .
is now called monetarism.
   - Milton Friedman
     'Introduction' to Beryl
     W. Sprinkel, *Money and
     Markets: A Monetarist
     View*, 1971, p. xx

40. The study of money, above all fields in economics, is the one in which complexity is used to disguise truth or to evade truth, not to reveal it.
    - J.K. Galbraith
      Money, 1975, Ch. 1, p. 5

41. Bad money drives out good money. ['Gresham's Law'.]
    - Sir Thomas Gresham (1519-79)
      The phrase occurs in a Royal Proclamation of 1590, when Gresham was a leading government adviser

42. It is self-contradictory to discuss a process which admittedly could not take place without money, and at the same time to assume that money is absent or has no effect.
    - F.A. Hayek
      The Pure Theory of Capital, 1941, Pt. I, Ch. III, p. 31

43. Put not your trust in money, but put your money in trust.
    - Oliver Wendell Holmes (1809-94)
      The Autocrat of the Breakfast Table, II

44. When a man says money can do anything, that settles it: he hasn't any.
    - E.W. Howe (1853-1937)
      Sinner Sermons, 1926, p. 41

45. The safest way to double your money is to fold it over once and put it in your pocket.
    - Frank McKinney Hubbard (1868-1930)
      Quoted in Esar and Bentley, *The Treasury of Humorous Quotations*

46. Money having chiefly a fictitious value, the greater or less plenty of it is of no consequence.
    - David Hume (1711-76)
      Essays, Of Interest

47. The want of money can never injure any state within itself: for men and commodities are the real strength of any community.
    - David Hume (1711-76)
      Ibid., *Of Money*

48. The good policy of the magistrate consists only in keeping it [money], if possible, still increasing; because by that means he keeps alive a spirit of industry in the nation, and increases the stock of labour, in which consists all real power and riches.
    - David Hume (1711-76)
      Ibid.

49. It is only in this interval or intermediate situation, between the acquisition of money and rise of prices, that the increasing quantity of gold and silver is favourable to industry.
    - David Hume (1711-76)
      Ibid.

50. Money . . . is none of the wheels of trade: it is the oil which renders the motion of the wheels more smooth and easy. If we consider any one kingdom by itself, it is evident that the greater or less plenty of money is of no consequence, since the

prices of commodities are always proportioned to the plenty of money.
– David Hume (1711-76)
  Ibid.

51. The Almighty Dollar, that great object of universal devotion throughout our land.
– Washington Irving (1783-1859)
  The Creole Village

52. The amount of money itself can be no more regulated than the amounts of corn, iron, cotton or other common commodities produced and consumed by a people.
– W. Stanley Jevons (1835-82)
  Money and the Mechanism of Exchange, 23rd ed., 1910, p. 340

53. In civilized society, personal merit will not serve you so much as money will sir, you may make the experiment. Go into the street, and give one man a lecture on morality, and another a shilling, and see which will respect you the most.
– Samuel Johnson (1709-84)
  Boswell's Life of Johnson, 20 July 1763

54. There are few ways in which a man can be more innocently employed than in getting money.
– Samuel Johnson (1709-84)
  Ibid., 27 March 1775

55. A man cannot make a bad use of his money, so far as regards society, if he does not hoard it;

if he either spends it or lends it out, society has the benefit.
– Samuel Johnson (1709-84)
  Ibid., 23 March 1783

56. The importance of money essentially flows from its being a link between the present and the future.
– John Maynard Keynes (1883-1946)
  The General Theory of Employment Interest and Money, Bk. V, Ch. 21, p. 293

57. Money is only important for what it will procure.
– John Maynard Keynes (1883-1946)
  A Tract on Monetary Reform, 1924, Ch. I, p. 1

58. When increased or decreased purchasing power in the form of money, seeking to realise itself in actual purchases, comes into, or is withdrawn from, the market, the increase or decrease . . . is not spread evenly and proportionately over the various buyers.
– John Maynard Keynes (1883-1946)
  A Treatise on Money, 1930, Vol. I, Bk. II, Ch. 7, p. 92

59. The fact that monetary changes do not affect all prices in the same way, in the same degree, or at the same time, is what makes them significant.
– John Maynard Keynes (1883-1946)
  Ibid., p. 94

60. Money, as it is the most usual means of exchange, is also the most useful and convenient measure of value.
    − Mountifort Longfield (1802-84)
    Lectures on Political Economy, 1834, II

61. Money . . . is the centre around which economic science clusters; this is so, not because money or material wealth is regarded as the main aim of human effort, nor even as affording the main subject-matter for the study of the economist, but because in this world of ours it is the one convenient means of measuring human motive on a large scale.
    − Alfred Marshall (1842-1924)
    Principles of Economics, 8th ed., Bk. I, Ch. II, 4, p. 22

62. Come back next Thursday with a specimen of your money.
    − Groucho Marx (1895-1977)
    Chapter heading in autobiography *Groucho and Me*

63. Money is the alienated essence of man's work existence; this essence dominates him and he worships it.
    − Karl Marx (1818-83)
    'On the Jewish Question', *Early Writings*, ed. Bottomore

64. Although gold and silver are not by nature money, money is by nature gold and silver.
    − Karl Marx (1818-83)
    Capital, Vol. I, Pt. I, Ch. II

65. One sum of money is distinguishable from another only by its amount.
    − Karl Marx (1818-83)
    Ibid., Pt. II, Ch. IV

66. Money is like a sixth sense without which you cannot make a complete use of the other five.
    − Somerset Maugham (1874-1965)
    Of Human Bondage, 51

67. The mere introduction of a particular mode of exchanging things for one another by first exchanging a thing for money, and then exchanging the money for something else, makes no difference in the essential character of transactions. It is not with money that things are really purchased.
    − John Stuart Mill (1806-73)
    Principles of Political Economy, ed. Ashley, Bk. III, Ch. VII, 3, p. 487

68. There cannot, in short, be intrinsically a more insignificant thing, in the economy of society, than money; except in the character of a contrivance for sparing time and labour. It is a machine for doing quickly and commodiously, what would be done, though less quickly and commodiously, without it: and like many other kinds of machinery, it only exerts a distinct and independent influence of its own when it gets out of order.
    − John Stuart Mill (1806-73)
    Ibid., p. 488

69. Money is a commodity, and its value is determined like that of other commodities, temporarily by demand and supply, permanently and on the average by cost of production.
    - John Stuart Mill (1806-73)
      Ibid.

70. The demand for money ... consists of all the goods offered for sale. Every seller of goods is a buyer of money, and the goods he brings with him constitute his demand.
    - John Stuart Mill (1806-73)
      Ibid., Ch. VIII, 2, p. 490

71. The value of money, other things being the same, varies inversely as its quantity; every increase of quantity lowering the value, and every diminution raising it, in a ratio exactly equivalent.
    - John Stuart Mill (1806-73)
      Ibid., p. 493

72. Money can't buy friends, but you can get a better class of enemy.
    - Spike Milligan
      Puckoon, 6

73. Money calculation does all that we are entitled to ask of it. It provides a guide amid the bewildering throng of economic possibilities.
    - Ludwig von Mises (1881-1973)
      Socialism, English ed., 1936, p. 117

74. The price of money, like other prices, is determined in the last resort by the subjective valuations of buyers and sellers.
    - Ludwig von Mises (1881-1973)
      The Theory of Money and Credit, trans. H.E. Batson, Part 2, Ch. II, Sec. 1 § 1

75. Because it thus rationalises economic life itself, the use of money lays the foundation for a rational theory of that life. Money may not be the root of *all* evil, but it is the root of economic science.
    - Wesley Clair Mitchell (1874-1948)
      The Backward Art of Spending Money, 1937, p. 171

76. It must, however, never be forgotten that this money system is only an elaborated barter system.
    - A.F. Mummery (1855-95) and J.A. Hobson (1858-1940)
      The Physiology of Industry, 1889, Ch. VII, p. 189

77. There is required for carrying on the trade of the nation, a determinate sum of specifick money, which varies, and is sometimes more, sometimes less as the circumstances we are in requires.
    - Sir Dudley North (1641-91)
      Discourses upon Trade, 1691, Postscript

78. Just as the community cannot grant to the prince authority to misuse the wives of any of its citizens he will, it cannot give

him such a privilege over the coinage as he can only misuse, by exacting a profit from changing it.
– Nicholas Oresme (1320?-82)
The Origin, Nature, Law and Alterations of Money, trans. Johnson, p. 40

79. But it is pretty to see what money can do.
– Samuel Pepys (1633-1703)
Diary, 21 March 1667

80. A hundred pound passing a hundred hands for wages, causes a 10,000 1. worth of commodities to be produced, which hands would have been idle and useless, had there not been this continual motive to their employment.
– Sir William Petty (1623-87)
'A Treatise of Taxes and Contributions', 1662, in *The Economic Writings of Sir William Petty*, ed. Hull, Vol. I, p. 36

81. Money is but the fat of the body-politick, whereof too much doth as often hinder its agility, as too little makes it sick.
– Sir William Petty (1623-87)
'Verbum Sapienti', 1691, ibid., p. 113

82. The one obvious instrument of measurement available in social life is money. Hence, the range of our inquiry becomes restricted to that part of social welfare that can be brought directly or indirectly into relation with the measuring-rod of money. This part of welfare may be called economic welfare.
– A.C. Pigou (1877-1959)
Economics of Welfare, 4th ed., Pt. I, Ch. I, p. 11

83. Be the business never so painful, you may have it done for money.
– Proverb, in Thomas Fuller, *Gnomologia*, 1732, 857

84. A fool and his money are soon parted.
– Proverb, ibid., 98

85. But help me to money, and I'll help myself to friends.
– Proverb, ibid., 1030

86. A man without money, is a bow without an arrow.
– Proverb, ibid., 316

87. Money is a good servant, but a bad master.
– Proverb, in H.G. Bohn, *A Handbook of Proverbs*, 1855

88. Money is barren.
– Proverb

89. Money is often lost for want of money.
– Proverb, 17th century

90. Money is round, and rolls away.
– Proverb, 17th century

91. Too much money makes one mad.
– Proverb, 17th century

92. Money makes the man.

– Proverb, 16th century

93. Money talks.
   – Proverb, 17th century

94. 'Tis money, that begets money.
   – Proverb, in Thomas Fuller,
   Gnomologia, 1732, 5091

95. If thou wouldest reap money,
   sow money.
   – Proverb, ibid., 2722

96. A heavy purse makes a light
   heart.
   – Irish proverb

97. Getting money is like digging
   with a needle; spending it is like
   water soaking into sand.
   – Japanese proverb

98. No man ever had enough money.
   – Gipsy proverb

99. When money speaks the truth
   keep silent.
   – Russian proverb

100. Money is flat and meant to be
   piled up.
   – Scottish proverb

101. In the use of money, every one
   is a trader.
   – David Ricardo (1772-1823)
   *Proposals for an Economical
   and Secure Currency*, 1816,
   Sec. IV

102. Nothing comes amiss, so money
   comes withal.
   – William Shakespeare
   (1564-1616)
   The Taming of the Shrew,
   Act I, Sc. II

103. Money . . . enables us to get
   what we want instead of what
   other people think we want.
   – George Bernard Shaw
   (1856-1950)
   *The Intelligent Woman's
   Guide to Socialism*

104. Money is indeed the most
   important thing in the world;
   and all sound and successful
   personal and national morality
   should have this fact for its
   basis.
   – George Bernard Shaw
   (1856-1950)
   The Irrational Knot,
   Preface

105. Money is the most important
   thing in the world. It represents
   health, strength, honour,
   generosity and beauty as con-
   spicuously and undeniably as
   the want of it represents illness,
   weakness, disgrace, meanness
   and ugliness.
   – George Bernard Shaw
   (1856-1950)
   Major Barbara, Preface

106. Money is the counter that
   enables life to be distributed
   socially: it *is* life as truly as
   sovereigns and banknotes are
   money.
   – George Bernard Shaw
   (1856-1950)
   Ibid.

107. What is the use of money if you
   have to work for it?
   – George Bernard Shaw
   (1856-1950)
   Man and Superman, Act IV

108. Money, by means of which the whole revenue of the society is regularly distributed among all its different members, makes itself no part of that revenue. The great wheel of circulation is altogether different from the goods which are circulated by means of it.
     — Adam Smith (1723-90)
       Wealth of Nations, ed.
       Cannan, Vol. I, Bk. II,
       Ch. II, pp. 272-3

109. The gold and silver money which circulates in any country may very properly be compared to a highway, which, while it circulates and carries to market all the grass and corn of the country, produces itself not a single pile of either.
     — Adam Smith (1723-90)
       Ibid., p. 304

110. The quantity of money . . . must in every country naturally increase as the value of the annual produce increases.
     — Adam Smith (1723-90)
       Ibid., Ch. III, p. 322

111. That wealth consists in money, or in gold and silver, is a popular notion, which naturally arises from the double function of money, as the instrument of commerce, and as the measure of value.
     — Adam Smith (1723-90)
       Ibid., Bk. IV, Ch. I, p. 396

112. No complaint . . . is more common than that of a scarcity of money.
     — Adam Smith (1723-90)

Ibid., p. 404

113. Goods can serve many other purposes besides purchasing money, but money can serve no other purpose besides purchasing goods . . . It is not for its own sake that men desire money, but for the sake of what they can purchase with it.
     — Adam Smith (1723-90)
       Ibid., p. 405

114. Money, as a physical medium of exchange made a diversified civilisation possible.
     — Sir Josiah Stamp
       (1880-1941)
       Foreward in Irving Fisher,
       The Money Illusion

115. No man will take counsel, but every man will take money: therefore money is better than counsel.
     — Jonathan Swift (1667-1745)
       Thoughts on Various Subjects, 1706

116. The prices of the produce or manufactures of every nation will be higher or lower, according as the quantity of cash circulating in such nation is greater or less.
     — Jacob Vanderlint (?-1740)
       Money Answers all Things, 1734, p. 3

117. Plenty of money never fails to make trade flourish.
     — Jacob Vanderlint (?-1740)
       Ibid., p. 7

87. MONOPOLY

1. When bad men combine, the good must associate.
   - Edmund Burke (1729-97)
   Thoughts on the Cause of the Present Discontents

2. A nearly ideal condition would be that in which, in every department of industry, there should be one great corporation, working without friction and with enormous economy, and compelled to give to the public the full benefit of that economy.
   - John Bates Clark (1847-1938)
   The Control of Trusts, 1901, p. 29

3. The solidarity of labour on the one hand, and of capital on the other, is the great economic fact of the present day; and this growing solidarity is carrying us rapidly towards a condition in which all the labourers in a particular trade and all capitalists in that trade, acting, in each case, as one man, will engage in a blind struggle which, without arbitration, can only be decided by the crudest force and endurance.
   - John Bates Clark (1847-1938)
   Philosophy of Wealth, 1887, Ch. IV, p. 66

4. If any producer can continually increase his supply at a constant or diminished cost, there appears no general reason why he should not, by cutting out his competitors, supply the entire market.
   - F.Y. Edgeworth (1845-1926)
   Papers Relating to Political Economy, 1925, Vol. II, p. 87

5. Anyone who has observed how aspiring monopolists regularly seek and frequently obtain the assistance of the state to make their control effective can have little doubt that there is nothing inevitable about this development [growth of monopoly].
   - F.A. Hayek
   The Road to Serfdom, 1944, Ch. IV

6. The best of all monopoly profits is a quiet life.
   - J.R. Hicks
   'The Theory of Monopoly', *Econometrica*, 1935, p. 8

7. A man who employs a thousand others, is in himself an absolutely rigid combination to the extent of one thousand units among buyers in the labour market.
   - Alfred Marshall (1842-1924)
   Principles of Economics, 8th ed., Bk. VI, Ch. IV, 6, p. 568

8. Monopoly, in all its forms, is the taxation of the industrious for the support of indolence, if not of plunder.
   - John Stuart Mill (1806-73)
   Principles of Political Economy, ed. Ashley, Bk. IV, Ch. VII, 7, p. 792

9. Monopoly (as the word signifies)

is the sole selling power, which whosoever hath can vend the commodity whereupon he hath this power, either qualified as himself pleases, or at what price he pleaseth, or both, within the limits of his commission.
- Sir William Petty (1623-87) 'A Treatise of Taxes and Contributions', 1662, in *The Economic Writings of Sir William Petty*, ed. Hull, Vol. I, p. 74

10. Like many businessmen of genius he learned that free competition was wasteful, monopoly efficient.
- Mario Puzo *The Godfather*, Bk. III, Ch. 14

11. We have much less reason to expect that monopolists will . . . charge an equilibrium price than we have in the case of perfect competition; for competing producers *must* charge it as a rule under penalty of economic death, whilst monopolists, although having a *motive* to charge the monopolistic equilibrium price, are not forced to do so, but may be prevented from doing so by other motives.
- J.A. Schumpeter (1883-1950) 'The Instability of Capitalism', *Economic Journal*, September 1928, p. 371

12. Not only does the monopolist's secure market position enable him to relax his efforts of maximising profit, but his very

position may prevent his aiming at maximum profit. He may regard his immunity from competition as precarious or be afraid of unfavourable publicity and public censure.
- Tibor Scitovsky *Welfare and Competition*, 1951, p. 377

13. The monopolists, by keeping the market constantly under-stocked, by never fully supply-ing the effectual demand, sell their commodities much above the natural price.
- Adam Smith (1723-90) *Wealth of Nations*, ed. Cannan, Vol. I, Bk. I, Ch. VII, p. 63

14. The price of monopoly is upon every occasion the highest which can be got.
- Adam Smith (1723-90) Ibid.

15. People of the same trade seldom meet together, even for merri-ment and diversion, but the conversation ends in a conspiracy against the public, or in some contrivance to raise prices.
- Adam Smith (1723-90) Ibid., Ch. X, p. 130

16. In a free trade an effectual combination cannot be established but by the unanimous consent of every single trader, and it cannot last longer than every single trader continues of the same mind.
- Adam Smith (1723-90) Ibid.

17. Monopoly . . . is a great enemy
    to good management.
    - Adam Smith (1723-90)
      Ibid., Ch. XI, Pt. I, p. 148

18. It is not enough to prove that a
    given industry is not
    competitive. The crucial
    question is: how far do
    conditions in the industry
    depart from competition? In
    many and perhaps most cases
    the answer is that the departures
    are not large.
    - George Stigler
      The Theory of Price, 1946,
      pp. 215-16

19. All forms of personal excellence,
    superiority, skill and
    distinguished attainment
    constitute natural monopolies
    and find their reward under
    applications of the monopoly
    principle.
    - William G. Sumner
      (1840-1910)
      *A Group of Natural
      Monopolies*, 1888

20. No one can argue that a
    monopolist is impelled by 'an
    invisible hand' to serve the
    public interest.
    - R.H. Tawney (1880-1962)
      The Acquisitive Society,
      1921, Ch. III

21. The sharp distinction between
    monopoly prices and com-
    petitive prices which we (in
    common with other economists)
    have drawn here scarcely ever
    exists in reality.
    - Knut Wicksell (1851-1926)
      *Lectures on Political

Economy, trans. E. Classen,
Vol. I, p. 96

88. NATIONAL DEBT

1. The public is a debtor, whom no
   man can oblige to pay.
   - David Hume (1711-76)
     Essays, Of Public Credit

2. Our modern expedient, which
   has become very general, is to
   mortgage the public revenues,
   and to trust that posterity will
   pay off the incumbrances
   contracted by their ancestors.
   - David Hume (1711-76)
     Ibid.

3. The National Debt represents
   the savings of the poorer classes,
   rather than the money-bags and
   coffers of the rich and
   luxurious.
   - W. Stanley Jevons (1835-82)
     *Investigations in Currency
     and Finance*, 1884, II,
     Ch. IV, p. 92

4. The only part of the so-called
   national wealth that actually
   enters into the collective
   possessions of modern peoples is
   their National Debt.
   - Karl Marx (1818-83)
     Capital, Vol. I, Pt. VIII,
     Ch. XXXI

5. No nation ought to be without a
   debt. A national debt is a
   national bond.
   - Thomas Paine (1737-1809)
     'Of the Present Ability of
     America', *Common Sense,*
     1776

6. The National Debt is a very Good Thing and it would be dangerous to pay it off, for fear of Political Economy.
   - W.C. Sellar (1898-1951) and R.J. Yeatman (1897-1968) *1066 and All That*, Ch. 38

7. Call our national debt, if you please, a *wen*. This wen is too intimately connected with the main blood vessels to admit of the surgeon's knife.
   - William Spence (1783-1860) *Tracts of Political Economy*, 1822, p. xix

8. As a very important source of strength and security, cherish public credit. One method of preserving it is to use it as sparingly as possible.
   - George Washington (1732-99) Speech, 1796

89. OLIGOPOLY

1. Duopoly is not one problem, but several.
   - E.H. Chamberlin (1867-1967) 'Duopoly: Value Where Sellers Are Few', *Quarterly Journal of Economics*, November 1929, p. 91

2. The typical relation of prices to costs under oligopolistic conditions is not very different from the relation that would exist under monopolistic conditions.
   - James S. Duesenberry *Business Cycles and Economic Growth*, 1958, p. 113

90. PAYMENT

1. 'Take what you want', said God, 'and pay for it'.
   - Anonymous, quoted by Arthur Seldon, *Charge*, 1977

2. It is an economic axiom as old as the hills that goods and services can be paid for only with goods and services.
   - Albert J. Nock (1873-1945) *Memoirs of a Superfluous Man*, III, Ch. 3

3. He who pays the piper may call the tune.
   - Proverb, 17th century

4. He that paieth aforehand, hath neuer his worke well done.
   - Proverb, 16th century

5. He that pays last never pays twice.
   - Proverb, 17th century

6. He who pays too late pays too little.
   - Proverb

7. He is well paid that is well satisfied.
   - William Shakespeare (1564-1616) *Merchant of Venice*, Act IV, Sc. I

91. PLANNING

1. Beware of the market; it is

Capitalism's secret weapon!
Comprehensive planning is the
heart and core of genuine
socialism. [With reference to
Yugoslavia.]
- Anonymous
  Editorial, *Monthly Review*,
  March 1964

2. In developing our industrial
   strategy for the period ahead,
   we have had the benefit of
   much experience. Almost
   everything has been tried at
   least once.
   - Tony Benn
     *Observer, Sayings of the
     Week*, 17 March 1974

3. It was not the possibility of
   planning as such which has been
   questioned . . . but the
   possibility of successful
   planning.
   - F.A. Hayek
     *Collectivist Economic
     Planning*, 1935, p. 203

4. Planning and competition can
   be combined only by planning
   for competition, but not by
   planning against competition.
   - F.A. Hayek
     The Road to Serfdom,
     1944, Ch. III

5. The clash between planning and
   democracy arises simply from
   the fact that the latter is an
   obstacle to the suppression of
   freedom which the direction of
   economic activity requires.
   - F.A. Hayek
     Ibid., Ch. V

6. No large organisation - least of

all a government - which has
to commit resources far into the
future can afford not to forecast
and to seek to develop a
strategy for the best use of its
resources.
- Michael Shanks
  Planning and Politics, 1977,
  p. 105

92. POLITICS

1. The only remedy they [the
   Tories] have for every social
   problem is to enable private
   enterprise to suck at the teats
   of the State.
   - Aneurin Bevan (1897-1960)
     Quoted in V. Brome,
     Aneurin Bevan, Ch. 12,
     p. 176

2. Politics, *n*. The conduct of
   public affairs for private
   advantage.
   - Ambrose Bierce
     (1842-1914?)
     The Devil's Dictionary

3. The Left favours coercion in
   economic policy, and the Right
   coercion in everything else.
   - Samuel Brittan
     Daily Telegraph, 22 September 1979

4. A mixed economy is essential to
   social democracy.
   - Anthony Crosland (1918-77)
     Quoted in the *Daily
     Telegraph*, 25 January 1979

5. The highest economic good
   consists in giving the consumer
   what he thinks he wants, as

135

political good consists in giving the people the government it thinks it deserves.
- Maurice Dobb
  'The Problems of a Socialist Economy', *Economic Journal*, December 1933, p. 591

6. I sometimes think that given half a chance politicians would like to give extra tax and social security concessions to marginal constituencies only.
   - William Keegan
     The Observer, 17 September 1978

7. The political problem of mankind is to combine three things: economic efficiency, social justice, and individual liberty.
   - John Maynard Keynes (1883-1946)
     Attributed

8. Political work is the life-blood of all economic work.
   - Mao Tse-tung (1893-1976)
     Quotations from Chairman Mao Tse-tung, 1976, p. 135

9. An economist's 'lag' may be a politician's catastrophe.
   - George P. Schultz
     'Reflections on Political Economy', *Journal of Finance*, 1974, p. 324

10. That insidious and crafty animal, vulgarly called a statesman or politician, whose councils are directed by the momentary fluctuations of affairs.
    - Adam Smith (1723-90)

Wealth of Nations, ed. Cannan, Vol. I, Bk. IV, Ch. II, pp. 432-3

11. And he gave it for his opinion, that whoever could make two ears of corn, or two blades of grass, to grow upon a spot of ground where only one grew before, would deserve better of mankind, and do more essential service to his country, than the whole race of politicians put together.
    - Jonathan Swift (1667-1745)
      Gulliver's Travels, Voyage to Brobdingnag, Ch. 7

12. We may lay it down, as a universal maxim in political science, that sudden change is evil.
    - Robert Torrens (1780-1864)
      Essay on the External Corn Trade, 4th ed., 1827, Pt. III, Ch. IV, 5, p. 429

93. POPULATION

1. As prosperity increases, so do the pleasures which compete with marriage, while the feeling towards children takes on a new character of refinement, and both these facts tend to diminish the desire to beget, and to bear children.
   - L. Brentano (1844-1931)
     'The Doctrine of Malthus . . . ', *Economic Journal*, 1910, p. 385

2. Men multiply like mice in a barn if they have unlimited means of subsistence.

    — Richard Cantillon
(1680?-1734)
Essai sur la Nature du Commerce en Générale,
1755, trans. Henry Higgs,
p. 83

3. Each successive addition to the population brings a consumer and a producer.
    — Henry Charles Carey
(1793-1879)
Harmony of Interests, p. 86

4. The optimum density of population.
    — A.M. Carr-Saunders
(1886-1966)
Population Problem, 1922,
p. 200

5. Misery, up to the extreme point of famine and pestilence, instead of checking, tends to increase population.
    — Samuel Laing (1812-97)
National Distress, 1844,
p. 69

6. The power of population is indefinitely greater than the power in the earth to produce subsistence for man. Population, when unchecked, increases in a geometrical ratio. Subsistence only increases in an arithmetical ratio. A slight acquaintance with numbers will show the immensity of the first power in comparison with the second.
    — Thomas Robert Malthus
(1766-1834)
An Essay on the Principle of Population, 1798, Ch. I
See also 82.4

7. A man who is born into a world already possessed, if he cannot get subsistence from his parents on whom he has a just demand, and if the society do not want his labour, has no claim of *right* to the smallest portion of food, and, in fact, has no business to be where he is. At Nature's mighty feast there is no vacant cover for him. She tells him to be gone.
    — Thomas Robert Malthus
(1766-1834)
Ibid., Ch. V

8. From high real wages, or the power of commanding a large portion of the necessaries of life, two very different results may follow; one, that of a rapid increase of population, in which case the high wages are chiefly spent in the maintenance of large and frequent families: and the other, that of a decided improvement in the modes of subsistence and the conveniences and comforts enjoyed, without a proportionate acceleration in the rate of increase.
    — Thomas Robert Malthus
(1766-1834)
Principles of Political Economy, 2nd ed., p. 226

9. Increasing population is the most certain possible sign of the happiness and prosperity of a state: but the actual population may be only a sign of the happiness that is past.
    — Thomas Robert Malthus
(1766-1834)
Quoted in Lord Robbins,
The Theory of Economic

93. *Population*

Development, p. 24

10. The limitation of the number of births, by raising wages, will accomplish every thing which we desire, without trouble and without interference.
    - James Mill (1773-1836) *Elements of Political Economy*, 3rd ed., Ch. II, Sec. II, 4

11. It is vain to say, that all mouths which the increase of mankind calls into existence, bring with them hands. The new mouths require as much food as the old ones, and the hands do not produce as much.
    - John Stuart Mill (1806-73) *Principles of Political Economy*, ed. Ashley, Bk. I, Ch. XIII, 2, p. 191

12. Fewness of people, is real poverty.
    - Sir William Petty (1623-87) 'A Treatise of Taxes and Contributions', 1662, in *The Economic Writings of Sir William Petty*, ed. Hull, Vol. I, p. 34

13. The power of the labourer to support himself, and the family which may be necessary to keep up the number of labourers, does not depend on the quantity of money which he may receive for wages, but on the quantity of food, necessaries, and conveniences become essential to him from habit, which that money will purchase.
    - David Ricardo (1772-1823) *Principles of Political*

Economy and Taxation, ed. Sraffa, Ch. V, p. 93

14. With a population pressing against the means of subsistence, the only remedies are either a reduction of people, or a more rapid accumulation of capital.
    - David Ricardo (1772-1823) Ibid., p. 99

15. The friends of humanity cannot but wish that in all countries the labouring classes should have a taste for comforts and enjoyments, and that they should be stimulated by all legal means in their exertions to procure them. There cannot be a better security against a superabundant population.
    - David Ricardo (1772-1823) Ibid., p. 100

16. The most decisive mark of the prosperity of any country is the increase in the number of inhabitants.
    - Adam Smith (1723-90) *Wealth of Nations*, ed. Cannan, Vol. I, Bk. I, Ch. VIII, p. 72

17. [Poverty] . . . seems even to be favourable to generation.
    - Adam Smith (1723-90) Ibid., p. 80

18. The demand for men, like that for any other commodity, necessarily regulates the production of men; quickens it when it goes on too slowly, and stops it when it advances too fast.

– Adam Smith (1723-90)
Ibid., p. 82

94. POVERTY

1. God loves the poor, and that is why he made so many of them.
   – Anonymous

2. Poverty is the parent of revolution and crime.
   – Aristotle (384-322 B.C.)
   Politics, trans. B. Jowett, Bk. II, Ch. 6, 1265b

3. Poverty runs down hill and settles in the low places, while wealth can go up to the hill top and select its own position.
   – Henry Ward Beecher (1813-87)
   Proverbs from Plymouth Pulpit

4. You cannot sift out the poor from the community. The poor are indispensable to the rich.
   – Henry Ward Beecher (1813-87)
   Ibid.

5. Beggar, *n.* One who has relied on the assistance of his friends.
   – Ambrose Bierce (1842-1914?)
   The Devil's Dictionary

6. If we wish to protect the poor we shall be in favour of fixed rules and clear dogma. The *rules* of a club are occasionally in favour of the poor member. The drift of a club is always in favour of the rich one.
   – G.K. Chesterton

(1874-1936)
Orthodoxy, Ch. IX

7. To be poor and independent is very nearly an impossibility.
   – William Cobbett (1762-1835)
   Advice to Young Men

8. If rich, it is easy enough to conceal our wealth but, if poor, it is not quite so easy to conceal our poverty. We shall find it is less difficult to hide a thousand guineas, than one hole in our coat.
   – Reverend C.C. Colton (1780-1832)
   Lacon, 1845, Vol. I, CCXXXIII

9. Poverty consists in feeling poor.
   – Ralph Waldo Emerson (1803-82)
   'Domestic Life', *Society and Solitude*

10. There is no scandal like rags, nor any crime so shameful as poverty.
    – George Farquhar (1678-1707)
    The Beaux-Stratagem, Act I, Sc. 1

11. While it is true that *waste begets poverty*, it is equally true that *poverty begets waste*.
    – Irving Fisher (1867-1947)
    The Theory of Interest, 1930, Ch. XV, p. 338

12. Poverty is a culture.
    – Michael Harrington
    The Other America,

13. People who are much too
    sensitive to demand of cripples
    that they run races ask of the
    poor that they get up and act
    just like everyone else in society.
    - Michael Harrington
      Ibid., Ch. 7

14. The poor are the only consistent
    altruists; they sell all that they
    have and give to the rich.
    - Holbrook Jackson
      (1874-1948)
      Quoted in Esar and Bentley,
      *The Treasury of Humorous
      Quotations*

15. All the arguments which are
    brought to represent poverty as
    no evil, shew it to be evidently a
    great evil. You never find people
    labouring to convince you that
    you may live very happily upon
    a plentiful fortune.
    - Samuel Johnson (1709-84)
      Boswell's Life of Johnson,
      20 July 1763

16. Poverty is a great enemy to
    human happiness; it certainly
    destroys liberty, and it makes
    some virtues impracticable, and
    others extremely difficult.
    - Samuel Johnson (1709-84)
      Ibid., 7 December 1782

17. If a free society cannot help the
    many who are poor, it cannot
    save the few who are rich.
    - John F. Kennedy (1917-63)
      Speech, 1961

18. The people must comprehend
    that they are themselves the
    cause of their own poverty.
    - Thomas Robert Malthus

(1766-1834)
Attributed

19. The poverty of the poor is the
    chief cause of that weakness and
    inefficiency which are the cause
    of their poverty.
    - Alfred Marshall (1842-1924)
      *The Present Position of
      Economics*, 1885, p. 17

20. The study of the causes of
    poverty is the study of the
    causes of the degradation of
    a large part of mankind.
    - Alfred Marshall (1842-1924)
      Principles of Economics,
      8th ed., Bk. I, Ch. I, 1, p. 3

21. A poor man has not many
    marks for fortune to shoot at.
    - Proverb, in Thomas Fuller,
      Gnomologia, 1732, 354

22. A poor man's debt makes a
    great noise.
    - Proverb, ibid., 355

23. An empty purse frightens away
    friends.
    - Proverb, ibid., 597

24. Beggars can never be bankrupts.
    - Proverb, ibid., 963

25. Poor men's reasons are not heard.
    - Proverb, ibid., 3897

26. He that has nothing, is frightened
    at nothing.
    - Proverb, ibid., 2150

27. Poverty has no relatives.
    - Proverb

28. The filth and poverty permitted

or ignored in the midst of us are as dishonourable to the whole social body, as in the body natural it is to wash the face, but leave the hands and feet foul.
  — John Ruskin (1819-1900)
     Munera Pulveris, V

29. APOTHECARY: My poverty but not my will consents.
    ROMEO: I pay thy poverty and not thy will.
      — William Shakespeare (1564-1616)
         Romeo and Juliet, Act V, Sc. 1

30. The greatest of our evils and the worst of our crimes is poverty, and . . . our first duty, to which every other consideration should be sacrificed, is not to be poor.
      — George Bernard Shaw (1856-1950)
         Major Barbara, Preface

31. Those who minister to poverty and disease are accomplices in the two worst of all crimes.
      — George Bernard Shaw (1856-1950)
         Maxims for Revolutionists

32. An underdeveloped country is poor because it has no industry, and an underdeveloped country has no industry because it is poor.
      — H.W. Singer
         'Economic Progress in Underdeveloped Countries', *Social Research,* March 1949

33. What improves the circumstances of the greater part can never be regarded as an inconveniency to the whole. No society can surely be flourishing and happy, of which the far greater part of the members are poor and miserable.
      — Adam Smith (1723-90)
         Wealth of Nations, ed. Cannan, Vol. I, Bk. I, Ch. VIII, p. 80

34. In the advanced state of society . . . they are all very poor people who follow as a trade, what other people pursue as a pastime.
      — Adam Smith (1723-90)
         Ibid., Ch. X, pp. 102-3

35. Poverty is no disgrace to a man, but it is confoundedly inconvenient.
      — Reverend Sydney Smith (1771-1845)
         His Wit and Wisdom

36. When the poor feel as poor as the rich do, there will be bloody revolution.
      — Dame Rebecca West
         The Thinking Reed

37. As for the virtuous poor, one can pity them, of course, but one cannot possibly admire them.
      — Oscar Wilde (1854-1900)
         The Soul of Man under Socialism

38. To recommend thrift to the poor is both grotesque and insulting. It is like advising a man who is starving to eat less.
      — Oscar Wilde (1854-1900)
         Ibid.

39. It is plain poverty, no doubt, to need a thing and not to have

the use of it.
- Xenophon
  (c. 440 - c. 355 B.C.)
  The Economist, trans.
  Dakyns, Ch. VIII

95. PRICES

1. Prices have work to do. Prices
   are to guide and direct the
   economic activities of the
   people. Prices are to tell them
   what to do. Prices must be free
   to tell the truth.
   - Benjamin M. Anderson
     *Economics and the Public
     Welfare*, 1949, p. 550

2. Regulating the prices of goods
   in general would be an endless
   task, and no legislator has ever
   been weak enough to think of
   attempting it.
   - Jeremy Bentham
     (1748-1832)
     Defence of Usury, Letter V

3. Price, *n*. Value, plus a reasonable
   sum for the wear and tear of
   conscience in demanding it.
   - Ambrose Bierce
     (1842-1914?)
     The Devil's Dictionary

4. The price or intrinsic value of
   a thing is the measure of the
   quantity of land and of labour
   entering into its production,
   having regard to the fertility
   or produce of the land and to
   the quality of the labour.
   - Richard Cantillon
     (1680?-1734)
     *Essai sur la Nature du
     Commerce en Générale*,

1755, trans. Henry Higgs,
p. 29

5. Both monopolistic and competitive forces combine in the
   determination of most prices.
   - Edward H. Chamberlin
     (1867-1967)
     Quoted by Paul A. Samuel-
     son, *Economics*, 8th ed.

6. One person's price is another
   person's income.
   - Walter W. Heller
     'What's Right With
     Economics?', *American
     Economic Review*, March
     1975, p. 21

7. It seems a maxim almost self-
   evident, that the prices of
   every thing depend on the
   proportion between
   commodities and money, and
   that any considerable alteration
   on either has the same effect,
   either of heightening or
   lowering price.
   - David Hume (1711-76)
     Essays, Of Money

8. The highest price we can pay for
   anything is to ask it.
   - Walter Savage Landor
     (1775-1864)
     'Aeschines and Phocion',
     Imaginary Conversations

9. Market prices reflect the
   economic situation as it is, and
   not as it will be, and are
   therefore ineffective in co-
   ordinating investment decisions
   that come to fruition only over
   a long period.
   - Edward Joshua Mishan

'Reflections on Recent Developments in the Concept of External Effects', *Essays in Welfare Economics*, 2nd ed., p. 195

10. The system of constant prices, which is generally used in our society, does not yield maximum ophelimity [economic utility].
    - Vilfredo Pareto (1848-1923) *Manual of Political Economy*, trans. Schwier, Ch. VI, p. 265

11. If a man can bring to London an ounce of silver out of the earth in Peru, in the same time that he can produce a bushel of corn, then one is the natural price of the other; now if by reason of new and more easie mines a man can get two ounces of silver as easily as formerly he did one, then corn will be as cheap at ten shillings the bushel, as it was before at five shillings *caeteris paribus*.
    - Sir William Petty (1623-87) 'A Treatise of Taxes and Contributions', 1662, in *The Economic Writings of Sir William Petty*, ed. Hull, Vol. I, pp. 50-1

12. Natural price is only another name for cost of production.
    - David Ricardo (1772-1823) *Notes on Malthus*, in *Works*, ed. Sraffa, Vol. II, p. 46 and p. 224

13. The real price of every thing, what every thing really costs to the man who wants to acquire it, is the toil and trouble of acquiring it. What every thing is really worth to the man who has acquired it, and who wants to dispose of it or exchange it for something else, is the toil and trouble which it can save to himself, and which it can impose on other people.
    - Adam Smith (1723-90) *Wealth of Nations*, ed. Cannan, Vol. I, Bk. I, Ch. V, p. 32

14. At all times and places that is dear which is difficult to come at, or which it costs much labour to acquire; and that cheap which is to be had easily, or with very little labour.
    - Adam Smith (1723-90) Ibid., p. 35

15. When the price of any commodity is neither more nor less than what is sufficient to pay the rent of the land, the wages of labour, and the profits of the stock employed in raising, preparing, and bringing it to market, according to their natural rates, the commodity is then sold for what may be called its natural price.
    - Adam Smith (1723-90) Ibid., Ch. VII, p. 57

16. The actual price at which any commodity is commonly sold is called its market price. It may either be above or below, or exactly the same with its natural price.
    - Adam Smith (1723-90) Ibid., p. 58

17. The natural price ... is as it were, the central price, to which the prices of all commodities are continually gravitating.
    - Adam Smith (1723-90)
      Ibid., p. 60

18. Other things being equal, old well-established concerns tend to be more hostile to price cutting than younger concerns.
    - G. Stocking and M. Watkins
      Monopoly and Free Enterprise, 1951, p. 117

19. The price of commodities in the market is formed by means of a certain struggle which takes place between the buyers and the sellers.
    - Henry Thornton (1760-1815)
      An Enquiry into the Nature and Effects of the Paper Credit of Great Britain, 1802, Ch. VIII, p. 193

20. When there is a real scarcity, it is in the interest of the great body of consumers that the price of corn should be raised sufficiently high, to cause such a degree of economy in consumption as may enable the supply to last throughout the year.
    - Robert Torrens (1780-1864)
      An Essay on the External Corn Trade, 4th ed., 1827, Ch. 1, p. 7

21. The prices of things will certainly rise in every nation, as the gold and silver increase amongst the people; and, consequently, ... where the gold and silver decrease in any nation, the prices of all things must fall proportionably to such decrease of money, or the people must be distress'd; unless the number of people decrease in as great proportion as the cash decreaseth in any such nation.
    - Jacob Vanderlint (?-1740)
      Money Answers all Things, 1734, p. 5

22. The plenty or scarcity of any particular thing, is the sole cause whence any commodity or thing can become higher or lower in price; or, in other words, as the demand is greater or less in proportion to the quantity of any thing, so will such thing, whatsoever it is, be cheaper or dearer.
    - Jacob Vanderlint (?-1740)
      Ibid., p. 6

23. It is not that pearls fetch a high price *because* men have dived for them; but on the contrary, men dive for them because they fetch a high price.
    - Richard Whately (1787-1863)
      Introductory Lectures on Political Economy, 1832, p. 253

24. What is a cynic? ... A man who knows the price of everything and the value of nothing ... And a sentimentalist ... is a man who sees an absurd value in everything, and doesn't know the market price of any single thing.
    - Oscar Wilde (1854-1900)

Lady Windermere's Fan,
Act III

96. PRODUCTION

1. Man produces in order to
consume.
   – Frédéric Bastiat (1801-50)
   Sophismes Economiques,
   trans. G.R. Porter, Ch. I, p. 8

2. To consult exclusively the
immediate interest of
production, is to consult an
anti-social interest.
   – Frédéric Bastiat (1801-50)
   Ibid., p. 14

3. The control of the production
of wealth is the control of
human life itself.
   – Hilaire Belloc (1870-1953)
   Quoted in F.A. Hayek,
   The Road to Serfdom

4. Overproduction is practically
misdirected production.
   – John Bates Clark
   (1847-1938)
   'Introduction' to K. Rodbertus, *Overproduction and
   Crises*, 1898, p. 3

5. There is a perverse failure to
make the actual demand of
yesterday a basis for the
production of today, or to make
the demand of last year a basis
for the production of this year.
   – John Bates Clark
   (1847-1938)
   Ibid., p. 7

6. Production only fills a void that
it has itself created.

   – J.K. Galbraith
   The Affluent Society, 1958,
   Ch. 11, I

7. Production is 'exchange' with
Nature.
   – J. Hirshleifer
   *Investment, Interest and
   Capital*, 1970, p. 12

8. Production not being the sole
end of human existence, the
term unproductive does not
necessarily imply any stigma.
   – John Stuart Mill (1806-73)
   *Principles of Political
   Economy*, ed. Ashley, Bk. I,
   Ch. III, 1, p. 44

9. The essential requisites of
production are three – labour,
capital, and natural agents; the
term capital including all
external and physical requisites
which are products of labour,
the term natural agents all those
which are not.
   – John Stuart Mill (1806-73)
   Ibid., Ch. X, 1, p. 155

10. Some authors assume that if all
the factors of production are
doubled, the product will also
double. This may be
approximately true in certain
cases, but not rigorously or in
general . . . If, for example, one
were to engage in the
transportation business in Paris,
it would be necessary to assume
another business and another
Paris.
   – Vilfredo Pareto (1848-1923)
   Cours, 1879, § 714

11. A glut is an evil. It generally

implies production without profit, and sometimes without even the return of the capital employed.
— David Ricardo (1772-1823) *Notes on Malthus*, in *Works*, ed. Sraffa, Vol. II, p. 413

12. Maximum economic production does not lead necessarily to maximum economic satisfaction.
— Sir Josiah Stamp (1880-1941) *Some Economic Factors in Modern Life*, 1929, Ch. I, p. 14

97. PROFIT

1. If you mean to profit, learn to please.
— Charles Churchill (1731-64) *Gotham*, Bk. II, ℓ 8

2. It is a socialist idea that making profits is a vice; I consider the real vice is making losses.
— Winston Churchill (1874-1965) Quoted in Esar and Bentley, *The Treasury of Humorous Quotations*

3. Profits are due not to risks, but to superior skill in taking risks. They are not subtracted from the gains of labour but are earned, in the same sense in which the wages of skilled labour are earned.
— Frank A Fetter (1863-1949) *The Principles of Economics*, 1904, p. 291

4. Profit is the result of risks

wisely selected.
— Frederick Barnard Hawley (1843-1929) *Enterprise and the Productive Process*, 1907, Ch. VI, p. 108

5. Men must have profits proportionable to their expense and hazard.
— David Hume (1711-76) *Essays, Of Commerce*

6. Profits, as a source of capital increment for entrepreneurs, are a widow's cruse which remains undepleted however much of them may be devoted to riotous living. When, on the other hand, entrepreneurs are making losses, and seek to recoup these losses by curtailing their normal expenditure on consumption *i.e.* by saving more, the cruse becomes a Danaid jar which can never be filled up; for the effect of this reduced expenditure is to inflict on the producers of consumption-goods a loss of equal amount.
[A cruse is a small earthen vessel.]
— John Maynard Keynes (1883-1946) *A Treatise on Money*, 1930, Vol. I, Bk. III, Ch. 10, p. 139

7. Profit, in some cases, may be more properly said to be acquired than produced.
— James Maitland (1759-1839) *An Inquiry Into the Nature and Origin of Public Wealth*, 1804, Ch. II, p. 161

8. It must not . . . be forgotten, that even in the countries of most active competition, custom also has a considerable share in determining the profits of trade.
    — John Stuart Mill (1806-73)
      Principles of Political Economy, ed. Ashley, Bk. II, Ch. XV, 4, p. 415

9. The cause of profit is, that labour produces more than is required for its support.
    — John Stuart Mill (1806-73)
      Ibid., 5, p. 416

10. No profit whatever can possibly be made but at the expense of another . . . The merchant only thrives, and grows rich, by the pride, wantonness, and debauchery of youth; the husbandman by the price and scarcity of grain, the architect by the ruin of buildings; lawyers, and officers of Justice, by the suits and contentions of men; nay even the honour and office of Divines are derived from our death and vices. A physician takes no pleasure in the health even of his friends . . . nor a soldier in the peace of his country and so of the rest.
    — Michael de Montaigne (1533-92)
      'That the Profit of One man is the inconvenience of another', *Essays*, 1685 trans., Bk. I, Ch. 21, pp. 156-7

11. In all countries, and at all times, profits depend on the quantity of labour requisite to provide the necessaries for the labourers, on that land, or with that capital which yields no rent.
    — David Ricardo (1772-1823)
      Principles of Political Economy and Taxation, ed. Sraffa, Ch. VI, p. 126

12. Nothing contributes so much to the prosperity and happiness of a country as high profits.
    — David Ricardo (1772-1823)
      On Protection to Agriculture, 1822, Sec. V

13. There is no other way of keeping profits up but by keeping wages down.
    — David Ricardo (1772-1823)
      Ibid., Sec. VI

14. Normal profits are simply the supply price of entrepreneurship to a particular industry.
    — Joan Robinson
      'What is Perfect Competition?', *Quarterly Journal of Economics*, Nov. 1934, p. 106

15. The earnings of an entrepreneur sometimes represent nothing but the spoiliation of the workmen. A profit is made not because the industry produces much more than it costs, but because it fails to give to the workman sufficient compensation for his toil. Such an industry is a social evil.
    — Simonde de Sismondi (1773-1842)
      Nouveaux Principes d'Economie politique, 2nd ed., 1827, Vol. I, p. 92
      Quoted in Gide and Rist,

A History of Economic Doctrines

16. In exchanging the complete manufacture . . . something must be given for the profits of the undertaker who hazards his stock in this adventure.
    — Adam Smith (1723-90)
    Wealth of Nations, ed. Cannan, Vol. I, Bk. I, Ch. VI, p. 50

17. The profits of stock, it may perhaps be thought, are only a different name for the wages of a particular sort of labour, the labour of inspection and direction . . . [but] they are regulated . . . by the value of the stock employed, and are greater or smaller in proportion to the extent of this stock.
    — Adam Smith (1723-90)
    Ibid.

18. The whole produce of labour does not always belong to the labourer. He must in most cases share it with the owner of the stock which employs him.
    — Adam Smith (1723-90)
    Ibid., p. 51

98. PROGRESS

1. Progress is
   The law of life; man is not man as yet.
   — Robert Browning (1812-89)
   Paracelsus, Pt. 5

2. What we call 'progress' is the exchange of one nuisance for another nuisance.
   — Henry Havelock Ellis (1859-1939)
   Attributed

3. So long as all the increased wealth which modern progress brings goes but to build up great fortunes, to increase luxury and make sharper the contrast between the House of Have and the House of Want, progress is not real and cannot be permanent.
   — Henry George (1839-97)
   Progress and Poverty, 'Introductory — The Problem'

4. Compare society to a boat. Her progress through the water will not depend upon the exertion of her crew, but upon the exertion devoted to propelling her. This will be lessened by any expenditure of force required for bailing, or any expenditure of force in fighting among themselves, or in pulling in different directions.
   — Henry George (1839-97)
   Ibid., Bk. X, Ch. III

5. I confess I am not charmed with the ideal of life held out by those who think that the normal state of human beings is that of struggling to get on; that the trampling, crushing, elbowing, and treading on each other's heels, which form the existing type of social life, are the most desirable lot of human kind, or anything but the disagreeable symptoms of one of the phases of industrial progress.

— John Stuart Mill (1806-73)
*Principles of Political
Economy*, ed. Ashley,
Bk. IV, Ch. VI, 2, p. 748

6. Economic progress, in capitalist
society, means turmoil.
— Joseph A. Schumpeter
(1883-1950)
*Capitalism, Socialism and
Democracy*, Ch. III, p. 32

7. Discontent is the first step in
the progress of a man or a
nation.
— Oscar Wilde (1854-1900)
A Woman of No Importance,
Act II

99. PROPERTY

1. Property is a trust.
— Anonymous

2. The right of property enables an
industrious man to reap where
he has sown.
— Anonymous

3. If all property were to be
equally divided, the certain and
immediate consequence would
be, that there would soon be
nothing more to divide . . . if
the condition of the industrious
were not better than the
condition of the idle, there
would be no reason for being
industrious.
— Jeremy Bentham
(1748-1832)
Principles of the Civil Code,
Part I, Ch. 3. In J. Bowring
(ed.), *Works of Jeremy
Bentham*, Vol. 1, p. 303

4. A society in which every
member holds an equal quantity
of property needs no special
justification; only a society in
which property is unequal
needs it.
— Sir Isaiah Berlin
Quoted by A.B. Atkinson in
Unequal Shares, 1974, p. 77

5. In a free and just commonwealth, property rushes from
the idle and imbecile, to the
industrious, brave, and
persevering.
— Ralph Waldo Emerson
(1803-82)
'Wealth', *The Conduct of
Life*, 1860

6. Mine is better than ours.
— Benjamin Franklin
(1706-90)
Poor Richard's Almanac,
1756

7. Property is necessary, but it is
not necessary that it should
remain forever in the same
hands.
— Remy de Gourmont
(1858-1915)
Quoted in Esar and Bentley,
*The Treasury of Humorous
Quotations*

8. The assertion that the property
of every man ought in justice to
be equal to that of every other
is false, since justice demands
merely that every one should
have property. Indeed, amongst
persons variously endowed
inequality must occur, and
equality would be wrong.
— Georg Wilhelm Friedrich

99. Property

Hegel (1770-1831)
Philosophy of Right, trans.
Dyde, p. 56

9. Where there is no property,
there is no injustice.
 — John Locke (1632-1704)
 *An Essay Concerning Human
 Understanding*, Bk. IV,
 Ch. III, Sec. 18

10. The right of property has not
made poverty, but it has power-
fully contributed to make
wealth.
 — J.R. McCulloch (1789-1864)
 *Principles of Political
 Economy*, new ed., Pt. I,
 Ch. II, p. 87

11. Those who have little or no
property of their own to
protect, and little or no
prospect of acquiring any, will
never entertain any real respect
for that of others.
 — J.R. McCulloch (1789-1864)
 Ibid., Pt. III, Ch. II, p. 402

12. [Property] A patent entitling
one man to dispose of another
man's labour.
 — Thomas Robert Malthus
 (1766-1834)
 Attributed

13. Political Economy confuses on
principle two very different
kinds of private property, of
which one rests on the
producers' own labour, the
other on the employment of the
labour of others.
 — Karl Marx (1818-83)
 Capital, Vol. I, Pt. VIII,
 Ch. XXXIII

14. The laws of property have never
yet conformed to the principles
on which the justification of
private property rests. They
have made property of things
which never ought to be
property, and absolute property
where only a qualified property
ought to exist.
 — John Stuart Mill (1806-73)
 *Principles of Political
 Economy*, ed. Ashley, Bk. II,
 Ch. I, 3, pp. 208-9

15. The institution of property,
when limited to its essential
elements, consists in the
recognition, in each person, of
a right to the exclusive disposal
of what he or she have produced
by their own exertions, or
received either by gifts or fair
agreement, without force or
fraud, from those who produce
it.
 — John Stuart Mill (1806-73)
 Ibid., Ch. II, 1, p. 218

16. The essential principle of
property being to assure to all
persons what they have
produced by their labour and
accumulated by their
abstinence, this principle cannot
apply to what is not the
produce of labour, the raw
material of the earth.
 — John Stuart Mill (1806-73)
 Ibid., 5, pp. 229-30

17. Property is theft.
 — Pierre-Joseph Proudhon
 (1809-65)
 Qu'est-ce que la Propriété?,
 Ch. I

18. Without that sense of security
    which property gives, the land
    would still be uncultivated.
    - François Quesnay
      (1694-1774)
      Maximes, iv, Quoted in Gide
      and Rist, *A History of
      Economic Doctrines*, 1913,
      p. 24

19. It is clear enough that income
    from property is not the reward
    of waiting but the reward of
    employing a good stockbroker.
    - Joan Robinson
      'The Second Crisis of
      Economic Theory',
      American Economic Review,
      May 1972, p. 9

20. Present-day society may,
    indeed, be well compared to a
    band of travellers in the desert.
    Suffering with thirst, they find
    a spring which would suffice to
    refresh and strengthen them all;
    but a small number constitute
    themselves masters of the
    spring; they grudge giving the
    majority more than a few drops
    to quench their thirst; they
    themselves take long draughts,
    but the stream flows faster than
    they are able to drink, and so
    from satiety and want of
    goodwill they let half of the
    gushing stream waste itself in
    the sand.
    - Karl Rodbertus (1805-75)
      Overproduction and Crises,
      trans. Franklin, 1898,
      pp. 57-8

21. For it so falls out
    That what we have we prize not
      to the worth

Whiles we enjoy it, but being
  lack'd and lost,
Why, then we rack the value,
  then we find
The virtue that possession
  would not show us
Whiles it was ours.
- William Shakespeare
  (1564-1616)
  Much Ado About Nothing,
  Act IV, Sc. I

22. The property which every man
    has is his own labour, as it is the
    original foundation of all
    other property, so it is the most
    sacred and inviolable.
    - Adam Smith (1723-90)
      Wealth of Nations, ed.
      Cannan, Vol. I, Bk. I,
      Ch. X, p. 123

23. Property is the most ambiguous
    of categories. It covers a
    multitude of rights which have
    nothing in common except that
    they are exercised by persons
    and enforced by the State.
    - R.H. Tawney (1880-1962)
      The Acquisitive Society,
      1921, Ch. V

24. It is foolish . . . to maintain
    property rights for which no
    service is performed, for
    payment without service is
    waste.
    - R.H. Tawney (1880-1962)
      Ibid., Ch. VI

25. That low, bestial instinct which
    men call the right of property.
    - Leo Tolstoy (1828-1910)
      Story of a Horse, in *First
      Stories*

26. Property . . . becomes the most easily recognised evidence of a reputable degree of success as distinguished from heroic or signal achievement. It therefore becomes the conventional basis of esteem.
    - Thorstein Veblen (1857-1929) *The Theory of the Leisure Class*, Ch. II

27. If property had simply pleasures, we could stand it; but its duties make it unbearable. In the interest of the rich we must get rid of it.
    - Oscar Wilde (1854-1900) *The Soul of Man Under Socialism*, 1912, p. 9

100. PROSPERITY

1. Prosperity doth best discover vice; but adversity doth best discover virtue.
   - Francis Bacon (1561-1626) *Essays*, V, *of Adversity*

2. Can anybody remember when the times were not hard, and money not scarce.
   - Ralph Waldo Emerson (1803-82) 'Works and Days', *Society and Solitude*

3. Let's be frank about it – most people have never had it so good.
   - Harold Macmillan Speech, 20 July 1957. From the American vernacular – 'You never had it so good'. Also used by the Democratic Party in the Presidential elections, 1952

4. If a nation could not prosper without the enjoyment of perfect liberty and perfect justice, there is not in the world a nation which could ever have prospered.
   - Adam Smith (1723-90) *Wealth of Nations*, ed. Cannan, Vol. II, Bk. IV, Ch. IX, p. 172

5. Prosperity is the best protector of principle.
   - Mark Twain (1835-1910) 'Pudd'nhead Wilson's New Calendar', *Following the Equator*, Vol. II, Ch. II

6. Few of us can stand prosperity. Another man's I mean.
   - Mark Twain (1835-1910) Ibid., Ch. IV

7. There is an old time toast which is golden for its beauty. 'When you ascend the hill of prosperity may you not meet a friend'.
   - Mark Twain (1835-1910) Ibid., Ch. V

101. PROTECTIONISM

1. [Protectionism] is . . . the sacrifice of the consumer to the producer – of the end to the means.
   - Frédéric Bastiat (1801-50) *Sophismes Economiques*, trans. G.R. Porter, Ch. XVII, p. 126

2. A country which prohibits some

foreign commodities, does, *ceteris paribus*, obtain those which it does not prohibit at a less price than it would otherwise have to pay.
— John Stuart Mill (1806-73) *Principles of Political Economy*, ed. Ashley, Bk. V, Ch. X, 1, p. 919

3. By means of glasses, hotbeds, and hotwalls, very good grapes can be raised in Scotland, and very good wine too can be made of them at about thirty times the expence for which at least equally good can be brought from foreign countries. Would it be a reasonable law to prohibit the importation of all foreign wines, merely to encourage the making of claret and burgundy in Scotland.
— Adam Smith (1723-90) *Wealth of Nations*, ed. Cannan, Vol. I, Bk. IV, Ch. II, p. 423

102. PUBLIC EXPENDITURE

1. The inherent tendency will always be for public services to fall behind private production.
— J.K. Galbraith *The Affluent Society*, 1958, Ch. 18, III

2. Public works even of doubtful utility may pay for themselves over and over again at a time of severe unemployment, if only from the diminished cost of relief expenditure, provided that we can assume that a smaller

proportion of income is saved when unemployment is greater.
— John Maynard Keynes (1883-1946) *The General Theory of Employment Interest and Money*, Bk. III, Ch. 10, p. 127

3. Thrift should be the guiding principle in our government expenditure.
— Mao Tse-tung (1893-1976) *Quotations from Chairman Mao Tse-tung*, 1976, p. 189

4. Public money is like holy water; everyone helps himself to it.
— Italian proverb

5. Great nations are never impoverished by private, though they sometimes are by public prodigality and misconduct. The whole, or almost the whole public revenue, is in most countries employed in maintaining unproductive hands.
— Adam Smith (1723-90) *Wealth of Nations*, ed. Cannan, Vol. I, Bk. II, Ch. III, p. 324

103. PUBLIC GOODS

1. The duty of erecting and maintaining certain public works and certain public institutions, which it can never be for the interest of any individual or small number of individuals, to erect and maintain; because the profit could never repay the expence to any individual or small number of

153

individuals, though it may frequently do much more than repay it to a great society.
- Adam Smith (1723-90)
  Wealth of Nations, ed. Cannan, Vol. II, Bk. IV, Ch. IX, p. 185

2. Good men are a publick good.
   - Proverb, in Thomas Fuller, *Gnomologia*, 1732, 1718

3. That which is every bodies business, is no bodies business.
   - Izaak Walton (1593-1683) *The Compleat Angler*, 1653, Ch. II

104. RATIONING

1. Bare-shelf rationing.
   - Anonymous
     Quoted in Howard S. Ellis (ed.), *A Survey of Contemporary Economics*, 1948, p. 344

2. The proportions in which families of equal means need the different 'necessaries of life' are very different. In ordinary times they distribute their expenditure among the different necessaries in a way which seems best, some getting more bread, some more meat or milk, and so on. By equal rationing all this variety is done away with, ... allowances for age, sex, occupation, and other things can only be introduced with difficulty.
   - Edwin Cannan (1861-1935) 'Industrial Unrest', *Economic Journal*,

December 1917, p. 468

105. RENT

1. The extraordinary profit out of which rent arises is analogous to the extraordinary remuneration which an artizan of more than common dexterity obtains beyond the wages given to the workman of ordinary skill. In the one case the monopoly is bounded by the existence of inferior soils, in the other of inferior degrees of dexterity.
   - Samuel Bailey (1791-1870) *A Critical Dissertation on the Nature, Measures and Causes of Value*, 1825, pp. 196-7

2. The widow is gathering nettles for her children's dinner; a perfumed seigneur, delicately lounging in the Œil de Boeuf, hath an alchemy whereby he will extract from her the third nettle, and call it rent.
   - Thomas Carlyle (1795-1881) Quoted in Henry George, *Progress and Poverty*, Bk. V

3. Rent, in short, is the price of monopoly.
   - Henry George (1839-97) *Progress and Poverty*, Bk. III, Ch. II

4. It is not necessary to confiscate land; it is only necessary to confiscate rent.
   - Henry George (1839-97) Ibid., Bk. VIII, Ch. II

5. The historical foundation of

capitalism is rent, the product of labour upon land over and above what is requisite to maintain the labourers.
 — J.A. Hobson (1858-1940)
 The Evolution of Modern Capitalism, revised ed., 1926, Ch. I, p. 4

6. That which is rightly regarded as interest on 'free' or 'floating' capital, or on new investments of capital, is more properly treated as a sort of rent — a *Quasi-rent* — on old investments of capital . . . And thus even the rent of land is seen, not as a thing by itself, but as the leading species of a large genus.
 — Alfred Marshall (1842-1924)
 Principles of Economics, 8th ed., Bk. V, Ch. VIII, 6, p. 412

7. The rent of a house (or other building) is a composite rent, of which one part belongs to the site and the other to the buildings themselves.
 — Alfred Marshall (1842-1924)
 Ibid., Ch. XI, 7, p. 453

8. Rent is the effect of a monopoly.
 — John Stuart Mill (1806-73)
 Principles of Political Economy, ed. Ashley, Bk. II, Ch. XVI, 1, p. 422

9. Rent . . . forms no part of the cost of production which determines the value of agricultural produce.
 — John Stuart Mill (1806-73)
 Ibid., Bk. III, Ch. V, 2, p. 472

10. Rent . . . merely equalizes the profits of different farming capitals, by enabling the landlord to appropriate all extra gains occasioned by superioity of natural advantages.
 — John Stuart Mill (1806-73)
 Ibid., p. 473

11. Wages and profits represent the universal elements in production, while rent may be taken to represent the differential and peculiar.
 — John Stuart Mill (1806-73)
 Ibid., 4, p. 477

12. Compensation for improvements will not benefit the tenant so much as is generally supposed, because the privilege itself will have a pecuniary value; that is to say, a landlord will demand, and the tenant can afford to give, a higher rent in proportion.
 — J. Shield Nicholson (1850-1927)
 Principles of Political Economy, 2nd ed., 1902, Vol. II, Bk. II, Ch. IX, p. 322

13. Neither a landlord nor a tenant be.
 — R.H. Parker
 Attributed

14. When [a] man hath subducted his seed out of the proceed of his harvest, and also, what himself hath both eaten and given to others in exchange for clothes, and other natural necessaries; that the remainder of corn is the natural and true rent of the land for that year.

  – Sir William Petty (1623-87)
  'A Treatise of Taxes and
  Contributions', 1662, in
  *The Economic Writings of
  Sir William Petty*, ed. Hull,
  Vol. I, p. 43

15. Who is entitled to the rent of
the land? The producer of the
land, without doubt. Who made
the land? God. Then, proprietor,
retire!
  – Pierre-Joseph Proudhon
  (1809-65)
  What is Property?, trans.
  Tucker, Ch. III

16. I think rent, and the increase of
rent, the necessary and
unavoidable condition of an
increased supply of corn for an
increasing population.
  – David Ricardo (1772-1823)
  Notes on Malthus, in *Works*,
  ed. Sraffa, Vol. II, p. 117

17. Profits are the fund from which
all rent is derived. There is no
rent which did not at one time
constitute profits.
  – David Ricardo (1772-1823)
  Ibid., p. 157

18. Rent is that portion of the
produce of the earth, which is
paid to the landlord for the use
of the original and indestructible
powers of the soil.
  – David Ricardo (1772-1823)
  *Principles of Political
  Economy and Taxation*, ed.
  Sraffa, Ch. II, p. 67

19. Rent is always the difference
between the produce obtained
by the employment of two
equal quantities of capital and
labour.
  – David Ricardo (1772-1823)
  Ibid., p. 71

20. The labour of nature is paid, not
because she does much, but
because she does little. In
proportion as she becomes
niggardly in her gifts, she
exacts a greater price for her
gifts. Where she is munificent-
ly beneficent, she always
works gratis.
  – David Ricardo (1772-1823)
  Ibid., p. 76

21. Rent . . . is a symptom, but it is
never a cause of wealth.
  – David Ricardo (1772-1823)
  Ibid., p. 77

22. Corn which is produced by the
greatest quantity of labour is
the regulator of the price of
corn; and rent does not and
cannot enter in the least degree
as a component part of its
price.
  – David Ricardo (1772-1823)
  Ibid.

23. Whatever diminishes the
inequality in the produce
obtained from successive
portions of capital employed on
the same or on new land, tends
to lower rent; and that whatever
increases that inequality,
necessarily produces an opposite
effect, and tends to raise it.
  – David Ricardo (1772-1823)
  Ibid., p. 83

24. The interest of the landlord is
always opposed to that of the

consumer and manufacturer.
- David Ricardo (1772-1823)
  Ibid., Ch. XXIV, p. 335

25. [Rent] . . . all income secured
without personal exertion solely
in virtue of possession.
- Karl Rodbertus (1805-75)
  Quoted by C. Gide,
  *Principles of Political
  Economy*, trans. Vediz,
  p. 636

26. Economic rent, arising as it does
from variations of fertility or
advantages of situation, must
always be held as common or
social wealth, and used, as the
revenues raised by taxation are
now used, for public purposes.
- George Bernard Shaw
  (1856-1950)
  'The Economic Basis of
  Socialism', in *Fabian Essays*,
  1889

27. As soon as the land of any
country has all become private
property, the landlords, like all
other men, love to reap where
they never sowed, and demand
a rent even for its natural
produce.
- Adam Smith (1723-90)
  Wealth of Nations, ed.
  Cannan, Vol. I, Bk. I,
  Ch. VI, p. 51

28. The rent of land . . . considered
as the price paid for the use of
the land, is naturally a
monopoly price. It is not at all
proportioned to what the landlord may have laid out upon the
improvement of the land, or to
what he can afford to take; but

to what the farmer can afford
to give.
- Adam Smith (1723-90)
  Ibid., Ch. XI, p. 146

29. High or low wages and profit,
are the causes of high or low
price; high or low rent is the
effect of it.
- Adam Smith (1723-90)
  Ibid., p. 147

30. Rent may be considered as the
produce of those powers of
nature, the use of which the
landlord lends to the farmer.
- Adam Smith (1723-90)
  Ibid., Bk. II, Ch. V, p. 344

106. RISK

1. Risk varies inversely with
knowledge.
- Irving Fisher (1867-1947)
  The Theory of Interest,
  1930, Ch. IX, p. 221

2. Many of the greatest economic
evils of our time are the fruits of
risk, uncertainty, and ignorance.
It is because particular
individuals, fortunate in
situation or in abilities, are able
to take advantage of uncertainty
and ignorance, and also because
for the same reason big business
is often a lottery, that great
inequalities of wealth come
about; and these same factors
are also the cause of the
Unemployment of Labour, or
the disappointment of reasonable business expectations, and
of the impairment of efficiency
and production.

— John Maynard Keynes
(1883-1946)
The End of Laissez-Faire,
1926, Pt. IV, p. 47

3. Behold, the fool saith, 'Put not
all thine eggs in the one
basket' — which is but a manner
of saying, 'Scatter your money
and your attention', but the
wise man saith, 'Put all your
eggs in the one basket and —
WATCH THAT BASKET'.
— Mark Twain (1835-1910)
Pudd'nhead Wilson, Ch. 15

4. The contempt of risk and the
presumptuous hope of success,
are in no period of life more
active than at the age at which
young people choose their
professions.
— Adam Smith (1723-90)
Wealth of Nations, ed.
Cannan, Vol. I, Bk. I,
Ch. X, p. 110

107. SAVING

1. The last dime that is earned is
the first one that is saved.
— John Bates Clark
(1847-1938)
'Distribution as Determined
by a Law of Rent', *Quarterly
Journal of Economics*,
April 1891, p. 297

2. Saving is in reality demanding
and getting productive
instruments as a part of an
income.
— John Bates Clark
(1847-1938)
'Introduction' to

K. Rodbertus, *Overproduction and Crises*, 1898, p. 14

3. Over-production or a general
glut is only an external phase or
symptom of the real malady. The
disease in under-consumption or
over-saving.
— J.A. Hobson (1858-1940)
*The Evolution of Modern
Capitalism*, revised ed.,
1926, Ch. XI, p. 314

4. Whenever you save five shillings,
you put a man out of work for
a day.
— John Maynard Keynes
(1883-1946)
'Inflation and Deflation',
in *Essays in Persuasion*,
1933, Pt. II, p. 152

5. We shall mean by Savings the
sum of the differences between
the money-incomes of
individuals and their money-
expenditure on current
consumption.
— John Maynard Keynes
(1883-1946)
A Treatise on Money, 1930,
Vol. I, Bk. III, Ch. 9, p. 126

6. The principles of saving, pushed
to excess, would destroy the
motive to production. If every
person were satisfied with the
simplest food, the poorest
clothing, and the meanest
houses, it is certain that no
other sort of food, clothing,
and lodging would be in
existence.
— Thomas Robert Malthus
(1766-1834)
Principles of Political

Economy, 2nd ed.,
Introduction

7. The power to save depends on
an excess of income over
necessary expenditure.
   – Alfred Marshall (1842-1924)
   Principles of Economics,
   8th ed., Bk. IV, Ch. VII,
   7, p. 229

8. The person who saves his
income is no less a consumer
than he who spends it: he
consumes it in a different way;
it supplies food and clothing
to be consumed, tools and
materials to be used, by
productive labourers.
   – John Stuart Mill (1806-73)
   *Essays on some Unsettled
   Questions of Political
   Economy*, 1844, p. 48

9. What is saved is consumed.
   – John Stuart Mill (1806-73)
   *Principles of Political
   Economy*, ed. Ashley,
   Bk. I, Ch. V, 5, p. 71

10. Saving, in short, enriches, and
spending impoverishes, the
community along with the
individual.
   – John Stuart Mill (1806-73)
   Ibid., pp. 72-3

11. We are thus brought to the conclusion that the basis on which all
economic teaching since Adam
Smith has stood, viz., that the
quantity annually produced is
determined by the aggregate
of Natural Agents, Capital, and
Labour available is erroneous,
and that, on the contrary, the
quantity produced, while it can
never exceed the limits imposed
by these aggregates, may be, and
actually is, reduced far below
this maximum by the check that
undue saving and the consequent
accumulation of over-supply
exerts on production.
   – A.F. Mummery (1855-95)
   and J.A. Hobson
   (1858-1940)
   The Physiology of Industry,
   1889, Preface

12. Saving is getting.
   – Proverb, in Thomas Fuller,
   Gnomologia, 1732, 4069

13. Unequal distribution of income
is an excessively uneconomic
method of getting the necessary
saving done.
   – Joan Robinson
   *An Essay on Marxian
   Economics*, 1947, Ch. VIII,
   p. 65

14. Practically all business savings
which, in turn, constitute the
greater part of total saving – is
done with a specific investment
purpose in view.
   – Joseph A. Schumpeter
   (1883-1950)
   *Capitalism, Socialism and
   Democracy*, Ch. XXVIII,
   p. 395

15. What is annually saved is as
regularly consumed as what is
annually spent, and nearly in
the same time, too; but it is
consumed by a different set
of people.
   – Adam Smith (1723-90)
   Wealth of Nations, ed.

Cannan, Vol. I, Bk. II,
Ch. III, p. 320

16. Though the principle of expense ... prevails in almost all men upon some occasions, and in some men upon almost all occasions, yet in the greater part of men, taking the whole course of their life at an average, the principle of frugality seems not only to predominate, but to predominate very greatly.
    – Adam Smith (1723-90)
      Ibid., p. 324

108. SAY'S LAW

– 'Supply creates its own demand'

1. We see in almost every part of the world vast powers of production which are not put into action ... I don't at all wish to deny that some persons or others are entitled to consume all that is produced but the grand question is whether it is distributed in such a manner between the different parties concerned as to occasion the most effective demand for future produce ...
   – Thomas Robert Malthus (1766-1834)
     Letter to Ricardo, 7 July 1821, See *Works of David Ricardo*, ed. Sraffa, vol. IX, p. 10

2. But though men have the power to purchase they may not choose to use it.
   – Alfred Marshall (1842-1924)
     Principles of Economics,

8th ed., Bk. VI, Ch. XIII, 10, p. 710

3. When two persons perform an act of barter, each of them is at once a seller and a buyer. He cannot sell without buying ... If however we suppose that money is used, these propositions cease to be exactly true ... the effect of the employment of money ... is that it enables this one act of interchange to be divided into two separate operations ... Although he who sells, really sells only to buy, he need not buy at the same moment when he sells.
   – John Stuart Mill (1806-73)
     Essays on some Unsettled Questions of Political Economy, 1844, pp. 69-70
     See also 23.9

4. There is no amount of capital which may not be employed in a country, because demand is only limited by production. No man produces, but with a view to consume or sell, and he never sells, but with an intention to purchase some other commodity.
   – David Ricardo (1772-1823)
     Principles of Political Economy and Taxation, ed. Sraffa, Ch. XXI, p. 290

5. No act of saving subtracts in the least from consumption, provided the thing saved be reinvested or restored to productive employment. On the contrary, it gives rise to a consumption perpetually renovated and recurring; whereas

there is no repetition of an
unproductive consumption.
– Jean-Baptiste Say
(1767-1832)
*A Treatise on Political
Economy*, trans. Prinsep,
Vol. I, Bk. I, Ch. XI, p. 115

6. It is production which opens a
demand for production . . . a
product is no sooner created,
than it, from that instant,
affords a market for other
products to the full extent of its
own value . . . the only way of
getting rid of money is in the
purchase of some product or
other.
– Jean-Baptiste Say
(1767-1832)
Ibid., Ch. XV, pp. 163-5

109 SECOND-BEST, Theory of

1. The fundamental problem is
that, as with all second-best
arguments, determination of the
conditions under which a
second-best policy actually leads
to an improvement of social
welfare require detailed
theoretical and empirical
investigation by a first-best
economist. Unfortunately,
policy is generally formulated
by fourth-best economists and
administered by third-best
economists; it is therefore very
unlikely that a second-best
welfare optimum will result
from policies based on second-
best arguments.
– Harry G. Johnson (1923-77)
*The Efficiency and Welfare
Implications of the*

International Corporation, in
C.P. Kindleberger (ed.), *The
International Corporation*,
1970

2. It is *not* true that a situation in
which more, but not all, of the
optimum conditions are fulfilled
is necessarily, or is even likely
to be, superior to a situation in
which fewer are fulfilled.
– R.G. Lipsey and
Kelvin Lancaster
'The General Theory of
Second Best', *Review of
Economic Studies*, 1956/57,
p. 12

110. SELF-INTEREST

1. That which is common to the
greatest number has the least
care bestowed upon it. Every
one thinks chiefly of his own,
hardly at all of the common
interest; and only when he is
himself concerned as an
individual.
– Aristotle (384-322 B.C.)
Politics, trans. B. Jowett,
Bk. II, Ch. 3, 1261b

2. Generally speaking, there is no
one who knows what is for your
interest, so well as yourself – no
one who is disposed with so
much ardour and constancy to
pursue it.
– Jeremy Bentham
(1748-1832)
*A Manual of Political
Economy*, Ch. 1. In
J. Bowring (ed.), *Works of
Jeremy Bentham*, Vol. 3,
p. 33

3. I am a selfish man, as selfish as any man can be. But in me, somehow or other, so it happens, selfishness has taken the form of benevolence.
   - Jeremy Bentham (1748-1832) Quoted by J. Maccun, *Six Radical Thinkers*, 1907, p. 18

4. The world will always be governed by self-interest. We should not try to stop this, we should try to make the self-interest of cads a little more coincident with that of decent people.
   - Samuel Butler (1835-1902) Quoted in P.A. Samuelson, *Economics*, 8th ed.

5. He who works for his own interests will arouse much animosity.
   - Confucius (c. 551 - c. 479 B.C.) *The Analects*, IV, Ch. XII

6. It is *not* a correct deduction from the Principles of Economics that enlightened self-interest always operates in the public interest. Nor is it true that self-interest generally *is* enlightened; more often individuals acting separately to promote their own ends are too ignorant or too weak to attain even these.
   - John Maynard Keynes (1883-1946) *The End of Laissez-Faire*, 1926, Pt. IV, p. 39

7. It is only in a very imperfect state of the world's arrangements that any one can best serve the happiness of others by the absolute sacrifice of his own.
   - John Stuart Mill (1806-73) *Utilitarianism*, Ch. 2

8. It is in the interest of each to do what is good for all, but only if others will do likewise.
   - John Stuart Mill (1806-73) Attributed

9. Whenever men consult for the publick good, as for the advancement of trade, wherein all are concerned, they usually esteem the immediate interest of their own to be the common measure of good and evil.
   - Sir Dudley North (1641-91) *Discourses upon Trade*, 1691, Preface

10. The efforts of men are utilized in two different ways: they are directed to the production or transformation of economic goods, or else to the appropriation of goods produced by others.
    - Vilfredo Pareto (1848-1923) *Manual of Political Economy*, trans. Schwier, Ch. IX, p. 341

11. I know on which side my bread is buttered.
    - Proverb, in John Heywood, *Proverbs*, 1546

12. The ass that is common property is always the worst saddled.
    - English proverb

13. When two friends have a
common purse, one sings and
the other weeps.
    - Spanish proverb

14. We have always known that
heedless self-interest was bad
morals; we now know that it is
bad economics.
    - Franklin D. Roosevelt
      (1882-1945)
      Speech, 1937

15. That everyone understands his
own interest better than any
Government ever can is a maxim
that has been considerably
emphasised by economists. But
they have too lightly affirmed
that the interest of each to
avoid the greatest evil coincides
with the general interest. It is to
the interest of the man who
wishes to impoverish his
neighbour to rob him, and it
may be the latter's interest to
let him do it provided he can
escape with his life.
    - Simonde de Sismondi
      (1773-1842)
      *Nouveaux Principes
      d'Economique politique*,
      2nd ed., 1827, Vol. I,
      pp. 200-1, quoted in Gide
      and Rist, *A History of
      Economic Doctrines*

16. Everyone's interest if checked
by everbody else's would in
reality represent the common
interest. But when everyone is
seeking his own interest at the
expense of others as well as
developing his own means, it
does not always happen that he
is opposed by equally powerful
forces. The strong thus find it in
their interest to seize and the
weak to acquiesce, for the least
evil as well as the greatest good
is a part of the aim of human
policy.
    - Simonde de Sismondi
      (1773-1842)
      Ibid., p. 407

17. How selfish soever man may be
supposed, there are evidently
some principles in his nature,
which interest him in the
fortune of others, and render
their happiness necessary to
him, though he derives nothing
from it, except the pleasure of
seeing it.
    - Adam Smith (1723-90)
      *The Theory of Moral
      Sentiments*, 1759, Pt. I,
      Sec. I, Ch. I

18. It is not from the benevolence
of the butcher, the brewer, or
the baker, that we expect our
dinner, but from their regard to
their own interest. We address
ourselves, not to their humanity
but to their self-love, and never
talk to them of our necessities
but of their advantages.
    - Adam Smith (1723-90)
      Wealth of Nations, ed.
      Cannan, Vol. I, Bk. I,
      Ch. II, p. 16

19. The 'economic man' whose
only interest is the self-regarding
one and whose only human trait
is prudence, is useless for the
purposes of modern industry.
    - Thorstein Veblen
      (1857-1929)
      The Theory of the Leisure

163

Class, Ch. IX

111. SELLING

1. It is no sin to sell dear, but a sin to give ill measure.
   - Proverb, in James Kelly, *A Complete Collection of Scottish Proverbs*, 1721

2. To things of sale a seller's praise belongs.
   - William Shakespeare (1564-1616) *Love's Labour's Lost*, Act IV, Sc. III

3. All things are sold.
   - Percy Bysshe Shelley (1792-1822) *Queen Mab*, V

4. Every one lives by selling something.
   - Robert Louis Stevenson (1850-94) *Across the Plains*, Beggars

112. SHARES

1. Sell in May and go away.
   - Anonymous

2. Shares can seriously damage your wealth.
   - Anonymous

3. No grant of feudal privilege has ever equalled, for effortless return, that of the grandparent who bought and endowed his descendants with a thousand shares of General Motors or General Electric.

   - J.K. Galbraith *The New Industrial State*, 1967, Ch. 35, III

4. The shares are a penny, and ever so many are taken by Rothschild and Baring, And just as a few are allotted to you, you awake with a shudder despairing.
   - W.S. Gilbert (1836-1911) *Iolanthe*, 1882, II

5. October. This is one of the peculiarly dangerous months to speculate in stocks in. The others are July, January, September, April, November, May, March, June, December, August, and February.
   - Mark Twain (1835-1910) *Pudd'nhead Wilson*, Ch. 13

113. SLAVERY

1. The wear and tear of a slave is at the expence of his master; but that of a free servant is at his own expence.
   - Anonymous Quoted in Adam Smith, *Wealth of Nations*

2. Hunger was found to be a good substitute for the lash [on the transition from slavery to free labour].
   - Karl Rodbertus (1805-75) Attributed

3. The work done by freemen comes cheaper in the end than that performed by slaves.
   - Adam Smith (1723-90) *Wealth of Nations*, ed.

Cannan, Vol. I, Bk. I,
Ch. VIII, p. 83

114. SMITH, ADAM

1. To the practical politician and
   social reformer, Adam Smith
   ought to be a hero, no less than
   he is to the economist. To both
   he appears in the light of one of
   the greatest vanquishers of error
   on record, the literary Napoleon
   of his generation.
   − R.B. Haldane (1856-1928)
     The Life of Adam Smith,
     1887, Ch. I, p. 12

2. The fact is that the *Wealth of
   Nations* does not contain a
   single *analytic* idea, principle, or
   method that was entirely new
   in 1776.
   − Joseph A. Schumpeter
     (1883-1950)
     *History of Economic
     Analysis*, 1954, p. 184

3. To attribute to him [Adam
   Smith] a dogmatic theory of
   the natural right of the
   individual to absolute industrial
   independence . . . is to construct
   the history of economic
   doctrines from one's inner
   consciousness.
   − Henry Sidgwick (1838-1900)
     *Scope and Method of
     Economic Science*, 1885,
     p. 7

4. The *Wealth of Nations* is a
   stupendous palace erected upon
   the granite of self-interest.
   − George J. Stigler
     'Smith's Travels on the Ship

of State' in *Essays on Adam
Smith*, ed. Skinner and
Wilson, p. 237

115. SOCIALISM

1. Under capitalism man exploits
   man, under socialism, it's just
   the opposite.
   − Anonymous

2. The language of priorities is the
   religion of Socialism.
   − Aneurin Bevan (1897-1960)
     Quoted in V. Brome,
     Aneurin Bevan, Ch. 1, p. 6

3. Never confuse socialism with
   trade unionism.
   − Aneurin Bevan (1897-1960)
     Quoted by Paul Johnson,
     The Observer, 11 September
     1977

4. Grapeshot, *n*. An argument
   which the future is preparing in
   answer to the demands of
   American Socialism.
   − Ambrose Bierce
     (1842-1914?)
     The Devil's Dictionary

5. Capitalists . . . would welcome
   any commercial reorganisation
   which would bring them a
   calmer life. It is, we believe, not
   as a remedy for the miseries of
   the poor, but rather as an
   alleviation of the cares of the
   rich, that Socialism is coming
   upon us.
   − Reverend William Cunning-
     ham (1849-1919)
     'The Progress of Socialism in
     England', *The Contemporary*

Review, January 1879,
p. 252

6. The approach to Socialism cannot fail, especially when the next crisis directs the working men by force of sheer want to social instead of political remedies.
   - Frederick Engels (1820-95)
   The Condition of the Working Class in England in 1844, 1892, Ch. VIII, p. 236

7. English Socialism, i.e. Communism, rests directly upon the irresponsibility of the Individual.
   - Frederick Engels (1820-95)
   Ibid., Ch. XI, p. 297

8. There is a popular cliche, deeply beloved by conservatives, that socialism and communism are the cause of a low standard of living. It is much more nearly accurate to say that a low and simple standard of living makes socialism and communism feasible.
   - J.K. Galbraith
   American Capitalism, 1957, Ch. 12

9. The socialists believe in two things which are absolutely different and perhaps even contradictory: freedom and organisation.
   - Élie Halévy (1870-1937)
   Quoted in F.A. Hayek,
   The Road to Serfdom

10. There is not the slightest reason why a trial and error procedure, similar to that in a competitive market, could not work in a socialist economy to determine the accounting prices of capital goods and of the productive resources in public ownership.
    - Oskar Lange (1904-65)
    On the Economic Theory of Socialism, 1938, p. 89

11. Socialism is not an economic policy for the timid.
    - Oskar Lange (1904-65)
    Ibid., p. 125

12. Socialism is the society which grows directly out of capitalism.
    - V.I. Lenin (1870-1924)
    Selected Works, Vol. 8, p. 239

13. If we so order the economic activity of the society that no commodity is produced unless its importance is greater than that of the alternative that is sacrificed, we shall have completely achieved the ideal that the economic calculus of a socialist state sets before itself.
    - A.P. Lerner
    'Statics and Dynamics in Socialist Economies',
    Economic Journal, June 1937, p. 253

14. Without socialization of agriculture, there can be no complete, consolidated socialism.
    - Mao Tse-tung (1893-1976)
    Quotations from Chairman Mao Tse-tung, 1976, p. 29

15. The masses have a potentially inexhaustible enthusiasm for socialism.

— Mao Tse-tung (1893-1976)
Ibid., p. 121

16. Socialism is the abolition of
rational economy.
  — Ludwig von Mises
  (1881-1973)
  'Economic Calculation in the
  Socialist Commonwealth' in
  F.A. Hayek, *Collectivist
  Economic Planning*, 1935,
  p. 110

17. Without calculation, economic
activity is impossible. Since
under Socialism calculation is
impossible, under Socialism
there can be no economic
activity in our sense of the
word. In small and insignificant
things, rational action might still
persist. But, for the most part, it
would no longer be possible to
speak of rational production.
  — Ludwig von Mises
  (1881-1973)
  Socialism, English ed.,
  1936, p. 119

18. Socialism is what a Labour
government does.
  — Herbert Morrison
  (1888-1965)
  Quoted by Anthony Howard,
  The Times, 31 August 1978

19. The underlying motive of many
Socialists, I believe, is simply a
hypertrophied sense of order.
The present state of affairs
offends them not because it
causes misery, still less because
it makes freedom impossible,
but because it is untidy; what
they desire, basically, is to
reduce the world to something

resembling a chessboard.
  — George Orwell (1903-50)
  The Road to Wigan Pier,
  Ch. 11

20. Current experience suggests that
socialism is not a stage beyond
capitalism but a substitute for
it — a means by which the
nations which did not share in
the Industrial Revolution can
imitate its technical achievements; a means to achieve
rapid accumulation under a
different set of rules of the
game.
  — Joan Robinson
  Marx, Marshall and Keynes,
  1955

21. Socialism might be the only
means of restoring social
discipline.
  — Joseph A. Schumpeter
  (1883-1950)
  *Capitalism, Socialism and
  Democracy*, Ch. XVIII,
  p. 215

22. Socialism in being might be the
very ideal of democracy. But
socialists are not always so
particular about the way in
which it is to be brought into
being.
  — Joseph A. Schumpeter
  (1883-1950)
  Ibid., Ch. XX, p. 236

23. I object to socialism not because
it would divide the produce of
industry badly, but because it
would have so much less to
divide.
  — Henry Sidgwick (1838-1900)
  Principles of Political

167

Economy, 3rd ed., 1901,
Bk. III, Ch. VI, p. 516

24. [Socialism] is the younger brother of almost absolute despotism, having aspirations that are reactionary in the deepest sense, and striving for the downright destruction of the individual, who is regarded as an unjustifiable luxury of nature, to be improved so as to become a serviceable organ of the collectivity.
    — Herbert Spencer (1820-1903)
    Quoted in W.R. Inge, *The End of an Age*, 1948

25. The chief advantage that would result from the establishment of Socialism is, undoubtedly, the fact that Socialism would relieve us from that sordid necessity of living for others which, in the present condition of things, presses so hardly upon almost everybody.
    — Oscar Wilde (1854-1900)
    The Soul of Man Under Socialism, 1912, p. 1

26. Marx did not design his economics to assist in the planning of a socialist society.
    — P.J.D. Wiles
    The Political Economy of Communism, 1962

116. SPECULATION

1. Speculation regulates but seldom successfully manipulates price movements.
    — Irving Fisher (1867-1947)

Stabilizing the Dollar, 1920, p. xxx

2. The great danger is that the excess of speculation may bring its usual punishment.
    — W. Stanley Jevons (1835-82)
    Investigations in Currency and Finance, 1884, II, Ch. II, p. 49

3. Speculators may do no harm as bubbles on a steady stream of enterprise. But the position is serious when enterprise becomes the bubble on a whirlpool of speculation. When the capital development of a country becomes a by-product of the activities of a casino, the job is likely to be ill-done.
    — John Maynard Keynes (1883-1946)
    The General Theory of Employment Interest and Money, Bk. IV, Ch. 12, p. 159

4. Every transaction in which an individual buys produce in order to sell it again, is, in fact, a speculation.
    — J.R. McCulloch (1789-1864)
    Principles of Political Economy, new ed., Pt. II, Ch. III, p. 319

5. Speculation is . . . really only another name for foresight.
    — J.R. McCulloch (1789-1864)
    Ibid., p. 320

6. The prices of things are neither so much depressed at one time, nor so much raised at another, as they would be if speculative

dealers did not exist.
- John Stuart Mill (1806-73)
*Principles of Political
Economy*, ed. Ashley,
Bk. IV, Ch. II, 4, p. 705

7. No price is too low for a bear or too high for a bull.
- Proverb

8. There are two times in a man's life when he should not speculate: when he can't afford it, and when he can.
- Mark Twain (1835-1910)
'Pudd'nhead Wilson's New Calendar', *Following the Equator*, Vol. II, Ch. XX

117. SPENDING

1. He who spends too much is a robber.
- St Ambrose (340-97)
Quoted in *The' Summa Theologica' of St Thomas Aquinas*, Q. 66, Art. 2

2. Annual income twenty pounds, annual expenditure nineteen, nineteen and six, result happiness. Annual income twenty pounds, annual expenditure twenty pounds nought and six, result misery.
- Charles Dickens (1812-70)
David Copperfield, Ch. 12 (Mr Micawber)

3. It is better to *live* rich than to *die* rich.
- Samuel Johnson (1709-84)
Boswell's Life of Johnson, 17 April 1778

4. It is in general better to spend money than to give it away; for industry is more promoted by spending money than by giving it away.
- Samuel Johnson (1709-84)
Ibid., 23 March 1783

5. The workers spend what they get and the capitalists get what they spend.
- M. Kalecki (1899-1970)
Attributed - situation described in *Essays in the Theory of Economic Fluctuations*, 1939, p. 76

6. What is . . . expended, for the sake of something to be produced, is said to be consumed productively.
- James Mill (1773-1836)
Elements of Political Economy, 3rd ed., Ch. IV, Sec. I

7. Better die a beggar, than live a beggar.
- Proverb, in Thomas Fuller, *Gnomologia*, 1732, 888

8. Penny-wise and pound-foolish.
- Proverb, ibid., 3866

9. The prodigal robs his heir, the miser himself.
- Proverb, ibid., 4722

10. I can get no remedy against this consumption of the purse; borrowing only lingers and lingers it out, but the disease is incurable.
- William Shakespeare (1564-1616)
King Henry IV, Pt. II,

Act I, Sc. II

11. It is clear . . . that expenditure,
     not parsimony, is the province
     of the class of land proprietors,
     and, that it is on the due
     performance of this duty, by
     the class in question, that the
     production of national wealth
     depends.
     — William Spence (1783-1860)
       Tracts on Political Economy,
       1822, p. 32

118. STATISTICS

1. We are employed in narrowing
    the circle within which the final
    truths must lie, rather than in an
    attempt at once to seize them.
    — 15th Annual report of the
      Statistical Society
      *Journal of the Statistical
      Society*, 1849, p. 97

2. Any figure that looks interesting
    is probably wrong.
    — Anonymous
      Motto at the Central
      Statistical Office, quoted by
      Sir Claus Moser, 'Statistics
      and Public Policy', *Journal
      of the Royal Statistical
      Society*, Series A, 1980,
      p. 12

3. Figures can't lie, but liars can
    figure.
    — Anonymous

4. The government are very keen
    on amassing statistics. They
    collect them, add them, raise
    them to the *n*th power, take the
    cube root and prepare wonderful

diagrams. But you must never
forget that every one of these
figures comes in the first
instance from the village watch-
man, who just puts down what
he damn well pleases.
— Anonymous
  Quoted in Sir Josiah Stamp,
  *Some Economic Factors in
  Modern Life*

5. Statistics does not talk with a
    sample of one.
    — Anonymous

6. There seem to be striking
    similarities between the role of
    economic statistics in our
    society and some of the
    functions which magic and
    divination play in primitive
    society.
    — Ely Devons (1913-67)
      'Statistics as a Basis for
      Policy', *Lloyds Bank Review*,
      July 1954, p. 41

7. Statisticians should give short,
    general, cookbook courses only
    if it is necessary to prevent
    nonstatisticians from giving
    them.
    — Robert Hooke
      'Getting People to Use
      Statistics Properly', *The
      American Statistician*,
      February 1980, p. 39

8. Boswell — Sir Alexander Dick
              tells me, that he
              remembers having
              a thousand people
              in a year to dine at
              his house . . .
    Johnson — That, Sir, is about
              three a day.

Boswell — How your statement lessens the idea.

Johnson — That, Sir, is the good of counting. It brings everything to a certainty, which before floated in the mind indefinitely.
— Samuel Johnson (1709-84)
Boswell's Life of Johnson,
18 April 1783

9. The inhabitants of Skye, and of the other islands which I have seen, are commonly of the middle stature, with fewer among them very tall or very short than are seen in England, or perhaps, as their numbers are small, the chances of any deviation from the common measure are necessarily few.
— Samuel Johnson (1709-84)
A Journey to the Western Islands of Scotland, 1775,
p. 190

10. To count is a modern practice, the ancient method was to guess; and when numbers are guessed they are always magnified.
— Samuel Johnson (1709-84)
Ibid., pp. 226-7

11. He uses statistics as a drunken man uses lamp-posts — for support rather than illumination.
— Andrew Lang (1844-1912)
Quoted in Esar and Bentley,
The Treasury of Humorous Quotations

12. No study is less alluring or more dry and tedious than statistics, unless the mind and imagination are set to work or that the person studying is particularly interested in the subject; which is seldom the case with young men in any rank in life.
— William Playfair (1759-1823)
The Statistical Breviary,
1801

13. The perversity of Sir Claus Moser knows no bounds. He will insist on publishing hard, relentless, statistics that make nonsense of what politicians, civil servants, and too many of the rest of us have to say.
— J. Rogaly
Quoted by Sir Claus Moser
'Statistics and Public Policy',
Journal of the Royal Statistical Association, Series A, 1980, Pt. I, p. 10

119. SUBSIDIES

1. As a means of encouraging domestic industry the bounty has over the protective system all the advantages that the system of paying public officers fixed salaries has over the system prevailing in some countries, and in some instances in our own, of letting them make what they can.
— Henry George (1839-97)
Protection or Free Trade,
Ch. IX

2. In general we must reduce and eventually remove subsidies of all kinds which distort the relative cost of different forms

of energy, and which stimulate wasteful consumption . . . But the best way to help pensioners is to increase pensions, not to sell fuel to everybody far below its cost.

— Denis Healey
    Budget Speech, House of
    Commons, 12 November
    1974

3. We are gradually moving towards a situation where everybody is subsidising everybody else.

    — H.S. Houthakker
        Joint Economic Committee,
        *The Economics of Federal
        Subsidy Programmes*, Pt. I,
        May 1972, p. 9

4. The bounty to the white-herring fishery is a tonnage bounty; and is proportioned to the burden of the ship, not to her diligence or success in the fishery; and it has, I am afraid, been too common for vessels to fit out for the sole purpose of catching, not the fish, but the bounty.

    — Adam Smith (1723-90)
        Wealth of Nations, ed.
        Cannan, Vol. II, Bk. IV,
        Ch. V, p. 21

120. SUPPLY AND DEMAND

1. Supply-and-demand is not the one law of Nature; cash-payment is not the sole nexus of man with man.

    — Thomas Carlyle (1795-1881)
        Past and Present, 1843,
        Bk. III, Ch. IX

2. The level of the sea is not more

surely kept, than is the equilibrium of value in society, by the demand and supply: and artifice or legislation punishes itself, by reactions, gluts, and bankruptcies.

— Ralph Waldo Emerson
    (1803-82)
    'Wealth', *The Conduct of
    Life*, 1860

3. Articles of immediate and personal use, speaking generally, are constant in demand, variable in supply.

    — W. Stanley Jevons (1835-82)
        *Investigations in Currency
        and Finance*, 1884, II,
        Ch. I, p. 27

4. While demand is based on the desire to obtain commodities, supply depends mainly on the overcoming of the unwillingness to undergo 'discommodities'.

    — Alfred Marshall (1842-1924)
        Principles of Economics,
        8th ed., Bk. IV, Ch. I, 2,
        p. 140

5. We might as reasonably dispute whether it is the upper or the under blade of a pair of scissors that cuts a piece of paper, as whether value is governed by utility or cost of production.

    — Alfred Marshall (1842-1924)
        Ibid., Bk. V, Ch. III, 7,
        p. 348

6. *As a general rule*, the shorter the period which we are considering, the greater must be the share of our attention which is given to the influence of demand on value; and the longer the period,

the more important will be the
influence of cost of production
on value.
  - Alfred Marshall (1842-1924)
    Ibid., p. 349

7. The general doctrine that a
position of (stable) equilibrium
of demand and supply is a
position also of *maximum
satisfaction*.
  - Alfred Marshall (1842-1924)
    Ibid., Ch. XIII, 4, p. 470

8. It is the artificial law of supply
and demand, arising from the
principle of individual gain in
opposition to the well-being of
society, which has hitherto
compelled population to press
upon subsistance.
  - Robert Owen (1771-1858)
    Quoted in G.D.H. Cole,
    Robert Owen

9. I do not dispute either the
influence of demand on the price
of corn and on the price of all
other things, but supply follows
close at its heels, and soon takes
the power of regulating price in
his own hands.
  - David Ricardo (1772-1823)
    Letter to Malthus,
    24 November 1820, in
    Works, ed. Sraffa, Vol. VIII,
    p. 302

10. The *force* of the causes which
give utility to a commodity is
generally indicated by the word
Demand; and the *weakness* of
the obstacles which limit the
quantity of a commodity by
the word *Supply*.
  - Nassau W. Senior

(1790-1864)
*Outline of the Science of
Political Economy*, 'Nature
of Wealth', p. 14

11. The price of ability does not
depend on merit, but on supply
and demand.
  - George Bernard Shaw
    (1856-1950)
    'Socialism and Superior
    Brains', in *The Fortnightly
    Review*, April 1894

12. The market price of every
particular commodity is
regulated by the proportion
between the quantity which is
actually brought to market and
the demand of those who are
willing to pay the natural price
of the commodity.
  - Adam Smith (1723-90)
    Wealth of Nations, ed.
    Cannan, Vol. I, Bk. I,
    Ch. VII, p. 58

13. What is usually called the supply
curve is in reality the demand
curve of those who possess the
commodity.
  - Philip H. Wicksteed
    (1844-1927)
    'The Scope and Method of
    Political Economy in the
    Light of the "Marginal"
    Theory of Value and
    Distribution', *Economic
    Journal*, March 1914

121. TARIFFS

1. Tariffs only raise the prices of
things because they diminish the
quantity offered in the market.

— Frédéric Bastiat (1801-50)
Sophismes Economiques,
trans. Porter, Ch. I, p. 7

2. For other countries to tax our
exports to them is an injury to
us and an obstacle to trade. For
us to tax their exports to us is
not a correction of that injury;
it is just a separate additional
obstacle to trade.
— Sir William Beveridge
(1879-1963) *et al.*
Tariffs: The Case Examined,
1931, p. 110

3. Tariff, *n.* A scale of taxes on
imports, designed to protect the
domestic producer against the
greed of his consumer.
— Ambrose Bierce
(1842-1914?)
The Devil's Dictionary

4. By taxing exports . . . we may,
under certain circumstances,
produce a division of the
advantage of the trade more
favourably to ourselves.
— John Stuart Mill (1806-73)
*Essays on some Unsettled
Questions of Political
Economy*, 1844, p. 21

5. A protecting duty can never be
a cause of gain, but always and
necessarily of loss, to the
country imposing it, just so far
as it is efficacious to its end.
— John Stuart Mill (1806-73)
Ibid., p. 28

6. A country cannot be expected
to renounce the power of
taxing foreigners, unless
foreigners will in return practice

towards itself the same for-
bearance. The only mode in
which a country can save itself
from being a loser by the duties
imposed by other countries on
its commodities, is to impose
corresponding duties on theirs.
— John Stuart Mill (1806-73)
Ibid., p. 29

7. Taxes on imports are partly paid
by foreigners.
— John Stuart Mill (1806-73)
*Principles of Political
Economy*, ed. Ashley, Bk. V,
Ch. IV, 6, p. 854

8. Though I still think that the
introduction of a foreign
industry is often worth a
sacrifice, and that a temporary
protecting duty, if it were sure
to remain temporary, would
probably be the best shape in
which that sacrifice can be
made, I am inclined to believe
that it is safer to make it by an
annual grant from the public
treasury, which is not nearly so
likely to be continued
indefinitely.
— John Stuart Mill (1806-73)
Letters, ed. Hugh Elliot,
1910, Vol. II, p. 149

9. The second case, in which it will
generally be advantageous to
lay some burden upon foreign
for the encouragement of
domestic industry, is, when
some tax is imposed at home
upon the produce of the latter.
In this case, it seems reasonable
that an equal tax should be
imposed upon the produce of
the former.

     — Adam Smith (1723-90)
     Wealth of Nations, ed.
     Cannan, Vol. I, Bk. IV,
     Ch. II, p. 429

122. TAXATION

1. Neither will it be that a people
   overlaid with taxes should ever
   become valiant and martial.
   — Francis Bacon (1561-1626)
   Essays, XXIX *of the True
   Greatness of Kingdoms and
   Estates*

2. Render therefore unto Caesar
   the things which are Caesar's.
   — *Bible*, Authorised Version
   St Matthew, Ch. 22, v. 21

3. And it came to pass in those
   days, that there went out a
   decree from Caesar Augustus,
   that all the world should be
   taxed.
   — *Bible*, Authorised Version
   St Luke, Ch. 2, v. 1

4. The relative stability of profits
   after taxes is evidence that the
   corporation profits tax is in
   effect almost entirely shifted;
   the government simply uses the
   corporation as a tax collector.
   — K.E. Boulding
   *The Organisational Revolu-
   tion*, 1953, p. 277

5. An economy breathes through
   its tax loopholes.
   — Barry Bracewell-Milnes
   'Tax Avoidance can be Good
   News for the Tax Collector',
   Daily Telegraph, 16 July
   1979

6. To tax and to please, no more
   than to love and be wise, is not
   given to men.
   — Edmund Burke (1729-97)
   Speech on American
   Taxation, 19 April 1774

7. Would twenty shillings have
   ruined Mr. Hampden's fortune?
   No! but the payment of half
   twenty shillings, on the
   principle it was demanded,
   would have made him a slave.
   — Edmund Burke (1729-97)
   Ibid.

8. Taxing is an easy business. Any
   projector can contrive new
   compositions; any bungler can
   add to the old.
   — Edmund Burke (1729-97)
   Speech in the House of
   Commons, 11 February
   1780

9. That a great reluctance to pay
   taxes existed in all the colonies,
   there can be no doubt. It was
   one of the marked character-
   istics of the American people
   long after their separation from
   England.
   — G.S. Callender (1865-1915)
   *Selections from the
   Economic History of the
   United States, 1765-1860*,
   1909, p. 123

10. There is no such thing as a good
    tax.
    — Winston Churchill
    (1874-1965)
    *Observer, Sayings of the
    Week*, 6 June 1937

11. The art of taxation consists in

so plucking the goose as to
obtain the largest possible
amount of feathers with the
smallest possible amount of
hissing.
— Jean Baptiste Colbert
(1619-83)
Attributed

12. 'It was as true', said Mr. Barkis,
'as taxes is. And nothing's truer
than them'.
— Charles Dickens (1812-70)
David Copperfield, Ch. 21

13. An Englishman's home is his
tax haven.
— *The Economist*,
17 November 1979, p. 78

14. The science of taxation
comprises two subjects to which
the character of pure theory
may be ascribed: the laws of
incidence, and the principle of
equal sacrifice.
— F.Y. Edgeworth
(1845-1926)
*Papers Relating to Political
Economy*, 1925, Vol. II,
p. 64

15. That taxation upon the profits
of a monopolist cannot be
shifted is universally
acknowledged.
— F.Y. Edgeworth
(1845-1926)
Ibid., p. 97

16. In this world nothing can be
said to be certain, except death
and taxes.
— Benjamin Franklin
(1706-90)
Letter to Jean Baptiste Le

Roy, 13 November 1789

17. There can be no taxation
without misrepresentation.
— J.B. Handelsman
Quoted by Y. Barzel 'An
Alternative Approach to the
Analysis of Taxation',
*Journal of Political
Economy*, 1976, p. 1177

18. Now it is notorious — and is,
indeed, a long-standing
injustice — that the scale of the
taxpayer's allowances under
Schedule E are on an altogether
more niggardly and restricted
scale than under Schedule D.
Indeed, it has been said that the
pleasure of life depends
nowadays upon the schedule
under which a man lives . . .
— Lord Justice Harman
(1894-1970)
Quoted in Gwyneth
McGreggor, *Employees'
Deductions under the
Income Tax*

19. It is the small owner who offers
the only really profitable and
reliable material for taxation:
. . . He is made for taxation . . .
He swarms; he is far more tied
to his place and his calling than
the big owner; he has less skill,
and ingenuity as regards escape;
and he still has a large supply of
'ignorant patience of taxation'.
— Auberon Herbert
(1838-1906)
Quoted in J. Coffield,
*A Popular History of
Taxation*

20. To equal justice, appertaineth

also the equal imposition of
taxes; the equality whereof
dependeth not on the equality
of riches, but on the equality
of the debt that every man
oweth to the commonwealth
for his defence.
- Thomas Hobbes
(1588-1679)
Leviathan, 1651, Pt. II,
Ch. XXX

21. The equality of imposition,
consisteth rather in the equality
of that which is consumed, than
of the riches of the persons that
consume the same. For what
reason is there, that he which
laboureth much, and sparing the
fruits of his labour, consumeth
little, should be more charged,
than he that living idly, getteth
little, and spendeth all he
gets . . . ?
- Thomas Hobbes
(1588-1679)
Ibid.

22. There is a prevailing maxim
among some reasoners, *That*
every new tax creates a new
ability in the subject to bear it,
and that each increase of
public burdens increases
proportionably the industry
of the people.
- David Hume (1711-76)
Essays, Of Taxes

23. The wisdom of man never yet
contrived a system of taxation
that would operate with perfect
equality.
- Andrew Jackson
(1767-1845)
Speech, 1832

24. Excise: A hateful tax levied
upon commodities.
- Samuel Johnson (1709-84)
Dictionary of the English
Language

25. To render an increase of
taxation productive of greater
exertion, economy, and
invention, it should be slowly
and gradually brought about;
and it should never be carried
to such a height as to incapaci-
tate individuals from meeting
the sacrifices it imposes, by such
an increase of industry and
economy as it may be in their
power to make without
requiring any very violent
change of their habits.
- J.R. McCulloch (1789-1864)
Principles of Political
Economy, new ed., Pt. I,
Ch. II, p. 112

26. What an increase of rent is to
the farmers, an increase of
taxation is to the public . . . so
long as it is confined within
moderate limits, it acts as a
powerful stimulus to industry
and economy, and most
commonly occasions the
production of more wealth
than it abstracts.
- J.R. McCulloch (1789-1864)
Ibid., p. 114

27. There is scarcely any economic
principle which cannot be aptly
illustrated by a discussion of the
shifting of the effects of some
tax.
- Alfred Marshall (1842-1924)
Principles of Economics,
8th ed., Bk. V, Ch. IX,

1, p. 413

Ibid., Ch. III, 1, p. 823

28. Experience has shown that a large proportion of the results of labour and abstinence may be taken away by fixed taxation, without impairing, and sometimes even with the effect of stimulating, the qualities from which a great production and an abundant capital rise.
   — John Stuart Mill (1806-73)
   Principles of Political Economy, ed. Ashley, Bk. IV, Ch. I, 2, p. 697

29. When it is said that a temporary income ought to be taxed less than a permanent one, the reply is irresistible, that it is taxed less; for the income which lasts only ten years pays the tax only ten years, while that which lasts for ever pays for ever.
   — John Stuart Mill (1806-73)
   Ibid., Bk. V, Ch. II, 4, p. 811

30. Unless . . . savings are exempted from income tax, the contributors are twice taxed on what they save, and only once on what they spend.
   — John Stuart Mill (1806-73)
   Ibid., p. 813

31. A direct tax is one which is demanded from the very persons who, it is intended or desired, should pay it. Indirect taxes are those which are demanded from one person in the expectation and intention that he shall indemnify himself at the expense of another.
   — John Stuart Mill (1806-73)

32. The very reason which makes direct taxation disagreeable, makes it preferable . . . If all taxes were direct, taxation would be much more perceived than at present; and there would be a security which now there is not, for economy in the public expenditure.
   — John Stuart Mill (1806-73)
   Ibid., Ch. VI, 1, p. 864

33. Taxation is a most flexible and effective but also a dangerous instrument of social reform. One has to know precisely what one is doing lest the results diverge greatly from one's intentions.
   — Gunnar Myrdal
   Political Element in the Development of Economic Theory, 1953, p. 188

34. Suppose that money by way of tax, be taken from one who spendeth the same in super-fluous eating and drinking; and delivered to another who employeth the same, in improving of land, in fishing, in working of mines, in manufacture, etc. It is manifest, that such tax is an advantage to the State whereof the said different persons are members.
   — Sir William Petty (1623-87)
   'Political Arithmetick', 1690, in *The Economic Writings of Sir William Petty*, ed. Hull, Vol. I, p. 269

35. That which angers men most is

to be taxed above their
neighbours.
- Sir William Petty (1623-87)
  'A Treatise of Taxes and
  Contributions', 1662, ibid.,
  p. 32

36. It is generally allowed by all,
    that men should contribute to
    the publick charge but
    according to the share and
    interest they have in the publick
    peace; that is, according to their
    estates or riches.
    - Sir William Petty (1623-87)
      Ibid., p. 91

37. A tax on rent would affect rent
    only; it would fall wholly on
    landlords, and could not be
    shifted to any class of
    consumers.
    - David Ricardo (1772-1823)
      *Principles of Political
      Economy and Taxation*, ed.
      Sraffa, Ch. X, p. 173

38. A taxed commodity will not rise
    in proportion to the tax, if the
    demand for it diminish, and if
    the quantity cannot be reduced.
    - David Ricardo (1772-1823)
      Ibid., Ch. XVI, p. 220

39. Taxation can never be so
    equally applied, as to operate in
    the same proportion on the
    value of all commodities, and
    still to preserve them at the
    same relative value. It
    frequently operates very
    differently from the intention
    of the legislature, by its indirect
    effects.
    - David Ricardo (1772-1823)
      Ibid., p. 239

40. Almost all taxes on production
    fall finally on the consumer.
    - David Ricardo (1772-1823)
      On Protection to Agriculture,
      1822, Sec. IX

41. Taxes, after all, are the dues
    that we pay for the privileges of
    membership in an organised
    society.
    - Franklin D. Roosevelt
      (1882-1945)
      Speech, 1936

42. The nation should have a tax
    system which looks like some-
    one designed it on purpose.
    - William E. Simon
      Quoted in US Treasury,
      *Blueprints for Basic Tax
      Reform*, 1977

43. The subjects of every state
    ought to contribute towards the
    support of government, as
    nearly as possible, in proportion
    to their respective abilities; that
    is, in proportion to the revenue
    which they respectively enjoy
    under the protection of the
    state.
    - Adam Smith (1723-90)
      Wealth of Nations, ed.
      Cannan, Vol. II, Bk. V,
      Ch. II, Pt. II, p. 310

44. Every tax ought to be so
    contrived as both to take out
    and to keep out of the pockets
    of the people as little as possible,
    over and above what it brings
    into the public treasury of the
    state.
    - Adam Smith (1723-90)
      Ibid., p. 311

45. It is not very unreasonable that the rich should contribute to the public expense, not only in proportion to their revenue, but something more than in that proportion.
    − Adam Smith (1723-90)
    Ibid., p. 327

46. The power to tax . . . is not only the power to destroy but also the power to keep alive.
    − United States Supreme Court,
    Quoted in P.A. Samuelson, *Economics*, 8th ed.

47. In such experience as I have had with taxation − and it has been considerable − there is only one tax that is popular, and that is the tax that is on the other fellow.
    − Sir Thomas White (1866-1955)
    Debate in the Canadian Parliament, 1917

48. It would be strange if taxation by interest groups should not result in taxation according to interest.
    − Knut Wicksell (1851-1926)
    Quoted by R.A. Musgrave, *Theory of Public Finance*, 1959, p. 59

123. TIME

1. Remember that time is money.
   − Benjamin Franklin (1706-90)
   Advice to Young Tradesmen

2. Time . . . is the centre of the chief difficulty of almost every economic problem.
   − Alfred Marshall (1842-1924)
   Principles of Economics,
   Preface to the first edition, 1890

124. TRADE

1. If there could be an account taken of the balance of trade, I can't see where the advantage of it could be. For the reason that's given for it, that the overplus is paid in bullion, and the nation grow so much the richer, because the balance is made up in bullion, is altogether a mistake: for gold and silver are but commodities; and one sort of commodity is as good as another, so it be of the same value.
   − Nicholas Barbon (?-1698)
   Discourse Concerning Coining the New Money Lighter, 1696, p. 40

2. TRADE, . . . The old Middle English sense of *trade* was *path*; the word is allied to tread.
   − George Crabb (1778-1851)
   Crabb's English Synonymes

3. Trade is in its nature free, finds its own channel, and best directeth its own course: and all laws to give it rules and directions, and to limit and circumscribe it, may serve the particular ends of private men, but are seldom advantageous to the public.
   − Charles d'Avenant (1656-1714)

*An Essay on the East India
Trade*, in *Works*, ed.
Whitworth, republished
1967, Vol. I, p. 98

4. The greatest meliorator of the
   world is selfish, huckstering
   trade.
   — Ralph Waldo Emerson
     (1803-82)
     'Works and Days', *Society
     and Solitude*

5. No nation was ever ruined by
   trade.
   — Benjamin Franklin
     (1706-90)
     *Thoughts on Commercial
     Subjects*

6. No man is any the worse off
   because another acquires
   wealth by trade, or by the
   exercise of a profession; on the
   contrary, he cannot have
   acquired his wealth except by
   benefiting others to the full
   extent of what they considered
   to be its value.
   — Thomas Henry Huxley
     (1825-95)
     Administrative Nihilism,
     1871

7. You can no more define
   equilibrium in international
   trade than you can define a
   pretty girl, but you can
   recognise one if you meet one.
   — Per Jacobsson (1894-1963)
     Speech, 1949

8. A man who has never been
   engaged in trade himself may
   undoubtedly write well upon
   trade, and there is nothing

which requires more to be
illustrated by philosophy than
trade does.
— Samuel Johnson (1709-84)
  Boswell's Life of Johnson,
  16 March 1776

9. Nothing dejects a trader like the
   interruption of his profits.
   — Samuel Johnson (1709-84)
     Taxation No Tyranny,
     1775

10. Trade could not be managed by
    those who manage it, if it had
    much difficulty.
    — Samuel Johnson (1709-84)
      Letter to Mrs Thrale,
      16 November 1779

11. It is sometimes said that traders
    do not produce: that while the
    cabinet-maker produces
    furniture, the furniture-dealer
    merely sells what is already
    produced. But there is no
    scientific foundation for this
    distinction. They both produce
    utilities.
    — Alfred Marshall (1842-1924)
      Principles of Economics,
      8th ed., Bk. II, Ch. III,
      1, p. 63

12. Trade is a social act.
    — John Stuart Mill (1806-73)
      On Liberty, Ch. 5

13. The only direct advantage of
    foreign commerce consists in
    the imports.
    — John Stuart Mill (1806-73)
      *Principles of Political
      Economy*, ed. Ashley,
      Bk. III, Ch. XVII, 4, p. 578

14. The produce of a country exchanges for the produce of other countries, at such values as are required in order that the whole of her exports may exactly pay for the whole of her imports.
    — John Stuart Mill (1806-73)
    Ibid., Ch. XVIII, 4, p. 592

15. An honest man is not accountable for the vice and folly of his trade, and therefore ought not to refuse the exercise of it. It is the custom of his country, and there is profit in it. We must live by the world, and such as we find it, so make use of it.
    — Michael de Montaigne (1533-92)
    Attributed

16. England's Treasure by Forraign Trade, or The Ballance of Our Forraign Trade is the Rule of our Treasure.
    — Thomas Mun (1571-1641)
    Title of book

17. There can be no trade unprofitable to the publick; for if any prove so, men leave it off; and whenever the traders thrive, the publick, of which they are part, thrives also.
    — Sir Dudley North (1641-91)
    Discourses upon Trade, 1691, Preface

18. Trade is nothing else but a commutation of superfluities; for instance: I give of mine, what I can spare, for somewhat of yours, which I want, and you can spare.
    — Sir Dudley North (1641-91)
    Ibid., p. 2

19. Buy cheap, sell dear.
    — Proverb, 16th century

20. Buying and selling is but winning and losing.
    — Proverb, in Thomas Fuller, *Gnomologia*, 1732, 1036

21. The usual trade and commerce is cheating all round by consent.
    — Proverb, ibid., 4814

22. By means of [foreign trade], the narrowness of the home market does not hinder the division of labour in any particular branch of art or manufacture from being carried to the highest perfection.
    — Adam Smith (1723-90)
    Wealth of Nations, ed. Cannan, Vol. I, Bk. IV, Ch. I, p. 413

23. No inconvenience can arise by an unrestrained trade, but very great advantage; since if the cash of the nation be decreased by it, which prohibitions are designed to prevent, those nations that get the cash will certainly find everything advance in price, as the cash increases amongst them. And . . . our manufactures, and every thing else, will soon become so moderate as to turn the balance of trade in our favour, and thereby fetch the money back again.
    — Jacob Vanderlint (?-1740)
    Money Answers all Things, 1734, pp. 43-4

125. TRADE UNIONS

1. The methods by which a trade
   union can alone act, are
   necessarily destructive; its
   organization is necessarily
   tyrannical.
   - Henry George (1839-97)
     Progress and Poverty,
     Bk. VI, Ch. I

2. Monopolistic combination is
   common enough in all parts of
   the economic system; very
   much the same motives which
   drive business men to form rings
   and cartels drive their
   employees to form unions. The
   one, as much as the other, is a
   natural product of a gregarious
   animal.
   - J.R. Hicks
     The Theory of Wages, 1932,
     Pt. II, Ch. VII, p. 137

3. All classes of society are trades
   unionists at heart, and differ
   chiefly in the boldness, ability,
   and secrecy with which they
   pursue their respective interests.
   - W. Stanley Jevons (1835-82)
     *The State in Relation to
     Labour*, 1882, p. vi

4. As a matter of fact, . . . those
   who most need combination to
   better their fortunes are just
   those who are the least able to
   carry it out.
   - W. Stanley Jevons (1835-82)
     Ibid., p. 106

5. Most if not all of the gains of
   union labour [in the United
   States] are made at the expense
   of non-unionised workers and
   not at the expense of earnings
   on capital.
   - H.G. Johnson (1923-77) and
     P. Mieskowski
     'The Effects of Unionization
     on the Distribution of
     Income: A General Equili-
     brium Approach', *Quarterly
     Journal of Economics*,
     November 1970, p. 560

6. All of you who have read trade
   union literature know that there
   are not only trade unions in
   England, but also alliances
   between workers and capitalists
   in a particular industry for the
   purpose of raising prices and of
   robbing everybody else.
   - V.I. Lenin (1870-1924)
     Selected Works, Vol. 7,
     p. 419

7. Capacity to labour is to the
   poor man what stock is to the
   capitalist. But you would not
   prevent a hundred or a thousand
   capitalists from forming themselves into a company, or
   combination who should . . .
   dispose of their property as
   they might, in their collective
   capacity judge most
   advantageous for their
   interests: – so why then should
   not a hundred or a thousand
   labourers be allowed to do the
   same by *their stock*.
   - J.R. McCulloch
     (1789-1864)
     *Treatise on the Succession
     to Property Vacant by Death*,
     1848

8. Trade unionism has enabled
   skilled artisans, and even many

classes of unskilled workers, to enter into negotiations with their employers with the same gravity, self-restraint, dignity and forethought as are observed in the diplomacy of great nations. It has led them generally to recognise that a simply aggressive policy is a foolish policy, and that the chief use of military resources is to preserve an advantageous peace.
   – Alfred Marshall (1842-1924)
   Principles of Economics,
   8th ed., Bk. VI, Ch. XIII,
   7, p. 703

9. Unionism seldom, if ever, uses such power as it has to insure better work; almost always it devotes a large part of that power to safeguarding bad work.
   – H.L. Mencken (1880-1956)
   Prejudices: Third Series,
   1922, 4

10. There must be some better mode of sharing the fruits of human productive power than by diminishing their amount. Yet this is not only the effect, but the intention, of many of the conditions imposed by some Unions on workmen and on employers.
    – John Stuart Mill (1806-73)
    'Thornton on Labour and its Claims', *Dissertations and Discussions*, Vol. IV,
    pp. 80-1

11. I think it's ludicrous that it takes 17 unions to build a motor car in Britain.
    – Lord Scanlon

Observer, Sayings of the Week, 30 July 1979

126. UNEMPLOYMENT

1. The rate of unemployment is 100 per cent if it is you that is unemployed.
   – Anonymous

2. A man willing to work, and unable to find work, is perhaps the saddest sight that Fortune's inequality exhibits under this sun.
   – Thomas Carlyle (1795-1881)
   Chartism, Ch. IV

3. Both public and private investment should be carried out only to the extent to which they are considered useful. If the effective demand thus generated fails to provide full employment, the gap should be filled by increasing consumption and not piling up unwanted public or private capital equipment.
   – M. Kalecki (1899-1970)
   'Three Ways to Full Employment' in Oxford University, Institute of Statistics, *The Economics of Full Employment*, 1945, p. 53

4. We believe that if men have the talent to invent new machines that put men out of work, they have the talent to put those men back to work.
   – John F. Kennedy (1917-63)
   Speech, 1962

5. If the Treasury were to fill old bottles with banknotes, bury

them at suitable depths in disused coalmines which are then filled up to the surface with town rubbish, and leave it to private enterprise on well-tried principles of *laissez-faire* to dig the notes up again . . . there need be no more unemployment and, with the help of the repercussions, the real income of the community, and its capital wealth also, would probably become a good deal greater than it actually is.
- John Maynard Keynes (1883-1946) *The General Theory of Employment Interest and Money*, Bk. III, Ch. 10, p. 129

6. In a sense, unemployment is all frictional.
- Franco Modigliani 'The Monetarist Controversy', *American Economic Review*, March 1977, p. 3

7. Hitler had already found how to cure unemployment before Keynes had finished explaining why it occurred.
- Joan Robinson 'The Second Crisis of Economic Theory', *American Economic Review*, May 1972, p. 8

127. UTILITARIANISM

1. The greatest happiness of the greatest number is the foundation of morals and legislation.
- Jeremy Bentham (1748-1832) *The Commonplace Book*, in J. Bowring (ed.), *Works of Jeremy Bentham*, Vol. 10, p. 142

2. That action is best which procures the greatest happiness for the greatest numbers; and that worst, which in like manner, occasions misery.
- Francis Hutcheson (1694-1746) *Inquiry into the Original of our Ideas of Beauty and Virtue*, 1725, Treatise II, 3

3. In the golden rule of Jesus of Nazareth, we read the complete spirit of the ethics of utility. To do as you would be done by, and to love your neighbour as yourself, constitute the ideal perfection of utilitarian morality.
- John Stuart Mill (1806-73) *Utilitarianism*, Ch. 2

128. UTILITY

1. Of everything which we possess there are two uses; both belong to the thing as such, but not in the same manner, for one is the proper, and the other the improper or secondary use of it. For example, a shoe is used for wear, and is used for exchange; both are uses of the shoe.
- Aristotle (384-322 B.C.) *Politics*, trans. B. Jowett, Bk. I, Ch. 9, 1257a

2. By the principle of utility is

meant that principle which
approves or disapproves of every
action whatsoever, according to
the tendency which it appears
to have to augment or diminish
the happiness of the party
whose interest is in question.
- Jeremy Bentham
  (1748-1832)
  *Introduction to the Principles
  of Morals and Legislation*,
  Ch. 1, in J. Bowring (ed.),
  Works of Jeremy Bentham,
  Vol. 1, p. 1

3. The degree of utility varies with
   the quantity of commodity, and
   ultimately decreases as that
   quantity increases.
   - W. Stanley Jevons (1835-82)
     Theory of Political Economy,
     4th ed., Ch. III, p. 53

4. A person distributes his income
   in such a way as to equalise the
   utility of the final increments of
   all commodities consumed.
   - W. Stanley Jevons (1835-82)
     Ibid., Ch. IV, p. 140

5. We are not in a position to
   weigh the satisfactions for
   similar persons of Pharaoh's
   slaves against Fifth Avenue's
   motor cars, or dear fuel and
   cheap ice to Laplanders against
   cheap fuel and dear ice to
   Hottentots.
   - John Maynard Keynes
     (1883-1946)
     A Treatise on Money, 1930,
     Vol. I, Bk. II, Ch. 8, p. 104

6. A stronger incentive will be
   required to induce a person to
   pay a given price for anything if

he is poor than if he is rich. A
shilling is the measure of less
pleasure, or satisfaction of any
kind, to a rich man than to a
poor one.
- Alfred Marshall (1842-1924)
  Principles of Economics,
  8th ed., Bk. I, Ch. II, 2,
  p. 19

7. The members of a collectivity
   enjoy *maximum ophelimity*
   [economic utility] in a certain
   position when it is impossible
   to find a way of moving from
   that position very slightly in
   such a manner that the
   ophelimity enjoyed by each of
   the individuals of that
   collectivity increases or
   decreases.
   - Vilfredo Pareto (1848-1923)
     Manual of Political Economy,
     trans. Schwier

8. We never know the worth of
   water, till the well is dry.
   - Proverb, in Thomas Fuller,
     Gnomologia, 1732, 5451

129. VALUE

1. A thing cannot be valuable in
   itself without reference to
   another thing, any more than a
   thing can be distant in itself
   without reference to another
   thing.
   - Samuel Bailey (1791-1870)
     *A Critical Dissertation on
     the Nature, Measures and
     Causes of Value*, 1825, p. 5

2. The value of all wares arise from
   their use; things of no use, have

no value, as the *English* phrase
is, *they are good for nothing.*
- Nicholas Barbon (?-1698)
  A Discourse of Trade,
  1690, p. 13

3. The value of a thing is just as
   much as it will bring.
   - Samuel Butler (1612-80)
     Quoted by K. Marx, *Capital,*
     Everyman ed., p. 5

4. [Value is an] estimate of the
   resistance to be overcome
   before we can enter upon the
   possession of the thing desired.
   - Henry Charles Carey
     (1793-1879)
     *Principles of Political
     Economy,* Vol. I, Ch. 2

5. Value is a relation between
   persons.
   - Fernando Galliani (1728-87)
     Della Moneta, quoted in
     K. Marx, *Capital,* Ch. I, 4

6. Value is the most invisible and
   impalpable of ghosts, and comes
   and goes unthought of while
   the visible and dense matter
   remains as it was.
   - W. Stanley Jevons (1835-82)
     *Investigations in Currency
     and Finance,* 1884, II,
     Ch. IV, p. 80

7. Value depends entirely on
   utility.
   - W. Stanley Jevons (1835-82)
     Theory of Political Economy,
     4th ed., Ch. I, p. 1

8. Cost of production determines
   supply;
   Supply determines final degree

   of utility;
   Final degree of utility determines
   value.
   - W. Stanley Jevons (1835-82)
     Ibid., Ch. IV, p. 165

9. We cannot discuss the valuation
   of things without knowing what
   it is that is being evaluated.
   - Frank H. Knight
     Risk, Uncertainty and Profit,
     1921, p. 125

10. Goods have a value from the
    uses they are apply'd to; and
    their value is greater or lesser,
    not so much from their more or
    less valuable, or necessary uses:
    as from the greater or lesser
    quantity of them in proportion
    to the demand for them.
    Example water is of great use,
    yet of little value; because the
    quantity of water is much
    greater than the demand for it.
    Diamonds are of little use, yet
    are of great value, because the
    demand for diamonds is much
    greater, than the quantity of
    them.
    - John Law (1671-1729)
      *Money and Trade
      Considered,* 1705

11. As values, all commodities are
    only definite masses of
    congealed labour time.
    - Karl Marx (1818-83)
      Capital, Vol. I, Pt. I, Ch. I, 1

12. Nothing can have value, without
    being an object of utility. If
    the thing is useless, so is the
    labour contained in it.
    - Karl Marx (1818-83)
      Ibid.

13. The value of a commodity is expressed in its price before it goes into circulation, and is therefore a precedent condition of circulation, not its result.
    - Karl Marx (1818-83)
      Ibid., Pt. II, Ch. V

14. Value is . . . nothing inherent in goods, no property of them, but merely the importance that we first attribute to the satisfaction of our needs.
    - Carl Menger (1840-1921)
      Principles of Economics,
      trans. Dingwall and Hoselitz,
      Ch. III, 1, p. 116

15. The value which a commodity will bring in any market is no other than the value which, in that market, gives a demand just sufficient to carry off the existing or expected supply.
    - John Stuart Mill (1806-73)
      Principles of Political Economy, ed. Ashley,
      Bk. III, Ch. II, 4, p. 448

16. The value . . . of an article . . . is determined by the cost of that portion of the supply which is produced and brought to market at the greatest expense.
    - John Stuart Mill (1806-73)
      Ibid., Ch. V, 1, p. 471

17. Value is a relative term. The value of a thing means the quantity of some other thing, or of things in general, which it exchanges for.
    - John Stuart Mill (1806-73)
      Ibid., Ch. VI, 1, p. 478

18. Possessing utility, commodities derive their exchangeable value from two sources: from their scarcity, and from the quantity of labour required to obtain them.
    - David Ricardo (1772-1823)
      Principles of Political Economy and Taxation,
      ed. Sraffa, Ch. I, p. 12

19. The word VALUE . . . has two different meanings, and sometimes expresses the utility of some particular object, and sometimes the power of purchasing other goods which the possession of that object conveys. The one may be called 'value in use'; the other, 'value in exchange'.
    - Adam Smith (1723-90)
      Wealth of Nations, ed. Cannan, Vol. I, Bk. I,
      Ch. IV, p. 30

20. Nothing is more useful than water: but it will purchase scarce any thing . . . A diamond, on the contrary, has scarce any value in use; but a very great quantity of other goods may frequently be had in exchange for it.
    - Adam Smith (1723-90)
      Ibid.

21. The value of any commodity . . . to the person who possesses it, and who means not to use or consume it himself, but to exchange it for other commodities, is equal to the quantity of labour which it enables him to purchase or command.

— Adam Smith (1723-90)
Ibid., Ch. V. p. 32

22. If among a nation of hunters . . .
it usually costs twice the labour
to kill a beaver which it does to
kill a deer, one beaver should
naturally exchange for or be
worth two deer.
— Adam Smith (1723-90)
Ibid., Ch. VI, p. 49

23. In that early and rude state of
society which precedes both the
accumulation of stock and the
appropriation of land, the
proportion between the
quantities of labour necessary
for acquiring different objects
seems to be the only circumstance which can afford any rule
for exchanging them for one
another.
— Adam Smith (1723-90)
Ibid.

130. WAGES

1. Whether you work by the piece
or the day,
Decreasing the hours increases
the pay.
— Anonymous

2. To fix the *minimum* of wages, is
to exclude from labour many
workmen who would otherwise
have been employed; it is to
aggravate the distress you wish
to relieve.
— Jeremy Bentham
(1748-1832)
A Manual of Political
Economy, Ch. 3 in J. Bowring
(ed.), *Works of Jeremy*

Bentham, Vol. 3, p. 66

3. The labourer is worthy of his
hire.
— *Bible*, Authorised Version
St Luke, Ch. 10, v. 7

4. What we find, in effect, is, not a
whole population competing
indiscriminately for all occupations, but a series of industrial
layers, superposed on one
another, within each of which
the various candidates for
employment possess a real and
effective power of selection,
while those occupying the
several strata are, for all
purposes of effective competition, practically isolated from
each other.
— J.E. Cairnes (1824-75)
*Some Leading Principles of
Political Economy*, 1874,
Part I, Ch. III, p. 72

5. Non-competing groups.
— J.E. Cairnes (1824-75)
Ibid., p. 73

6. Everyone knows that the whole
or net advantageousness of
different employments is highly
unequal. If equality prevailed,
we should find well-to-do
parents in doubt whether to
make their sons civil engineers
or naval stokers, doctors or
road-sweepers.
— Edwin Cannan (1861-1935)
Wealth, 3rd ed., Ch. XII,
p. 207

7. A few men without employment, and a few employers
without souls, are the conditions

of a general reduction of wages below the point to which more legitimate causes would reduce them.
  – John Bates Clark
    (1847-1938)
    Philosophy of Wealth,
    1887, Ch. IX, p. 169

8. Real wages, and indeed real income in general, consist of those final physical events in the *outer* world which give us our *inner* enjoyments.
  – Irving Fisher (1867-1947)
    The Theory of Interest,
    1930, Ch. I, 3, pp. 5-6

9. It is but a truism that labour is most productive where its wages are largest. Poorly paid labour is inefficient labour, the world over.
  – Henry George (1839-97)
    Progress and Poverty,
    Bk. IX, Ch. II

10. The wages of labour are indeed equal to the product of the labourer, but of the labourer who finds employment under the least favourable conditions.
  – Charles Gide (1847-1932)
    Principles of Political Economy, trans. Vediz,
    Pt. II, Ch. III, p. 513

11. The theory of the determination of wages in a free market is simply a special case of the general theory of value. Wages are the price of labour.
  – J.R. Hicks
    The Theory of Wages, 1932,
    Pt. I, Ch. I, p. 1

12. If the labourers in a given trade are not of equal efficiency, then, strictly speaking, they have no marginal product. We cannot tell what would be the difference to the product if one man were removed from employment; for it all depends which man is removed.
  – J.R. Hicks
    Ibid., Ch. II, p. 28

13. As in other things, so in men, not the seller, but the buyer determines the price. For let a man, as most men do, rate themselves at the highest value they can; yet their true value is no more than it is esteemed by others.
  – Thomas Hobbes
    (1588-1679)
    Leviathan, 1651, Pt. I,
    Ch. X

14. The wages of a working man are ultimately coincident with what he produces, after the deduction of rent, taxes, and the interest of capital.
  – W. Stanley Jevons (1835-82)
    Theory of Political Economy,
    4th ed., Ch. VIII, p. 270

15. The true reward which an occupation offers to labour has to be calculated by deducting the money value of all its disadvantages from that of all its advantages; and we may describe this true reward as the *net advantages* of the occupation.
  – Alfred Marshall (1842-1924)
    Principles of Economics, 8th ed., Bk. II, Ch. IV, 2, p. 73

16. *Wages* are determined by the bitter struggle between capitalist and worker.
    - Karl Marx (1818-83) 'First Manuscript' in *Early Writings*, ed. Bottomore

17. If the ratio which capital bears to population increases, wages will rise; if the ratio which population bears to capital increases, wages will fall.
    - James Mill (1773-1836) *Elements of Political Economy*, 3rd ed., Ch. II, Sec. II, 1

18. When the labourers receive wages for their labour, without waiting to be paid by a share of the commodity produced, it is evident that they sell their title to that share. The capitalist is then the owner, not of the capital only, but of the labour also. If what is paid as wages is included, as it commonly is, in the term capital, it is absurd to talk of labour separately from capital.
    - James Mill (1773-1836) Ibid., Ch. III, Sec. II

19. The bad workmen who form the majority of the operatives in many branches of industry, are decidedly of opinion that bad workmen ought to receive the same wages as good.
    - John Stuart Mill (1806-73) *On Liberty*, Ch. 4

20. As a general rule, remuneration by fixed salaries does not in any class of functionaries produce the maximum of zeal.
    - John Stuart Mill (1806-73) *Principles of Political Economy*, ed. Ashley, Bk. II, Ch. I, 3, p. 206

21. The really exhausting and the really repulsive labours, instead of being better paid than others, are almost invariably paid the worst of all . . . The hardships and the earnings, instead of being directly proportional, as in any just arrangements of society they would be, are generally in an inverse ratio to one another.
    - John Stuart Mill (1806-73) Ibid., Ch. XIV, 1, p. 388

22. Management . . . by hired servants, who have no interest in the result but that of preserving their salaries, is proverbially inefficient, unless they act under the inspecting eye, if not the controlling hand, of the person chiefly interested: and prudence almost always recommends giving to a manager not thus controlled a remuneration partly dependent on the profits.
    - John Stuart Mill (1806-73) Ibid., Ch. XV, 1, p. 407

23. Wages . . . are independent of capital only when they are derived from the prodigality of nature; and the rule is that this prodigality does not exist, and that where it does exist, it soon disappears.
    - Maffeo Pantaleoni (1857-1924) *Pure Economics*, trans. Bruce, Pt. III, Ch. V, p. 299

24. The law that appoints such wages . . . should allow the labourer but just wherewithal to live; for if you allow double, then he works but half so much as he could have done, and otherwise would; which is a loss to the Publick of the fruit of so much labour.
    - Sir William Petty (1623-87) 'A Treatise of Taxes and Contributions', 1662, in *The Economic Writings of Sir William Petty*, ed. Hull, Vol. I, p. 87

25. When wages are low profits must be high.
    - David Ricardo (1772-1823) *Notes on Malthus*, in *Works*, ed. Sraffa, Vol. II, p. 393

26. The natural price of labour is that price which is necessary to enable the labourers, one with another, to subsist and to perpetuate their race, without either increase or diminution.
    - David Ricardo (1772-1823) *Principles of Political Economy and Taxation*, ed. Sraffa, Ch. V, p. 93

27. The produce of labour constitutes the natural recompense or wages of labour.
    - Adam Smith (1723-90) *Wealth of Nations*, ed. Cannan, Vol. I, Bk. I, Ch. VIII, p. 66

28. The workmen desire to get as much, the masters to give as little as possible. The former are disposed to combine in order to raise, the latter in order to lower

the wages of labour.
    - Adam Smith (1723-90) Ibid., p. 68

29. The masters, being fewer in number, can combine more easily; and the law, besides, authorises, or at least does not prohibit their combinations, while it prohibits those of the workmen.
    - Adam Smith (1723-90) Ibid.

30. In . . . disputes the masters can hold out much longer . . . In the long-run the workman may be as necessary to his master as his master is to him, but the necessity is not so immediate.
    - Adam Smith (1723-90) Ibid.

31. The demand for those who live by wages, it is evident, cannot increase but in proportion to the increase of the funds which are destined for the payment of wages.
    - Adam Smith (1723-90) Ibid., pp. 70-1

32. It is not the actual greatness of national wealth, but its continual increase, which occasions a rise in the wages of labour.
    - Adam Smith (1723-90) Ibid., p. 71

33. Though the wealth of a country should be very great, yet if it has long been stationary, we must not expect to find the wages of labour very high in it . . . The hands on the contrary, would, in this case, naturally

multiply beyond their
employment.
- Adam Smith (1723-90)
  Ibid., p. 73

34. A plentiful subsistence increases
the bodily strength of the
labourer, and the comfortable
hope of bettering his condition,
and of ending his days perhaps
in ease and plenty, animates him
to exert that strength to the
utmost. Where wages are high
accordingly, we shall always
find the workmen more active,
diligent, and expeditious, than
where they are low.
- Adam Smith (1723-90)
  Ibid., p. 83

35. Our merchants and master-
manufacturers complain much
of the bad effects of high wages
in raising the price, and thereby
lessening the sale of their goods
both at home and abroad. They
say nothing concerning the bad
effects of high profits.
- Adam Smith (1723-90)
  Ibid., Ch. IX, p. 100

36. The whole of the advantages
and disadvantages of the
different employments of
labour and stock must, in the
same neighbourhood, be either
perfectly equal or continually
tending to equality. If in the
same neighbourhood, there was
any employment evidently
either more or less advantageous
than the rest, so many people
would crowd into it in the one
case, and so many would desert
it in the other, that its
advantages would soon return to

the level of other employments.
- Adam Smith (1723-90)
  Ibid., Ch. X, p. 101

37. The pension system is only an
alternative to paying a higher
salary to those rendering
existing services and leaving
them subsequently to look after
their own superannuation
allowance.
- Sir Josiah Stamp
  (1880-1941)
  Wealth and Taxable Capacity,
  1922, Ch. II, p. 57

38. If a minimum wage is effective,
it must . . . have one of two
effects: first, workers whose
services are worth less than the
minimum wage are discharged
(and thus forced into
unregulated fields of employment or into unemployment . . .)
or, second, the productivity of
low-efficiency workers is
increased.
- George J. Stigler
  'The Economics of Minimum
  Wage Legislation', *American
  Economic Review*, June
  1946, p. 358

39. Were justice and benefice
consulted, instead of antipathy,
in awarding the rewards of
labour under the system of
unequal remuneration, the
largest shares of reward . . .
would be given as a compensation to those who underwent
the most severe or repulsive toil.
But to such labourers, simply
because they are the most
helpless, does competition with
its unequal remuneration,

uniformly afford the smallest
shares.
  - William Thompson
    (1775-1833)
    Labour Rewarded, 1827,
    p. 31

40. The wages of sin is alimony.
  - Carolyn Wells (187?-1942)
    Quoted in Esar and Bentley,
    *The Treasury of Humorous
    Quotations*

41. One man's wage rise is another
    man's price increase.
  - Sir Harold Wilson
    *Observer, Sayings of the
    Week*, 11 January 1970

131. WAR

1. Wars drive up riches in heaps, as
   winds drive up snows, making
   and concealing many abysses.
  - Walter Savage Landor
    (1775-1864)
    'Aristoteles and Callisthenes',
    Imaginary Conversations

2. There cannot be a greater
   security for the continuance of
   peace than the imposing on
   ministers the necessity of
   applying to the people for
   taxes to support a war.
  - David Ricardo (1772-1823)
    'Funding System', *Supple-
    ment to the Encyclopaedia
    Britannica*, 1820

3. In the midst of the most
   destructive foreign war . . . the
   greater part of manufacturers
   may frequently flourish greatly;
   and, on the contrary, they may

decline on the return to peace.
  - Adam Smith (1723-90)
    Wealth of Nations, ed.
    Cannan, Vol. I, Bk. IV,
    Ch. I, p. 411

4. 'In war', answered the weaver,
   'the strong make slaves of the
   weak, and in peace the rich
   make slaves of the poor.'
  - Oscar Wilde (1854-1900)
    The Young King

132. WEALTH

1. It is better to be miserable and
   rich than it is to be miserable
   and poor.
  - Anonymous

2. We have more reason to be
   proud of our ways of making
   wealth than of our ways of
   using it.
  - Anonymous

3. Riches are a good handmaiden
   but the worst mistress.
  - Francis Bacon (1561-1626)
    *De Dignitate et Augmentis
    Scientiarum*, Bk. VI, Ch. III,
    VI, *Riches*

4. Riches are for spending.
  - Frances Bacon (1561-1626)
    Essays, XXVIII, *Of Expense*

5. I cannot call riches better than
   the baggage of virtue.
  - Francis Bacon (1561-1626)
    Ibid., XXXIV, *Of Riches*

6. Of great riches there is no real
   use, except it be in the
   distribution.

— Francis Bacon (1561-1626)
Ibid.

7. Wealth is not such for economic
purposes, unless it is scarce and
transferable, and so desirable
that some one is anxious to give
something else for it.
— Walter Bagehot (1826-77)
Economic Studies, ed.
Hutton, III, p. 132

8. Wealth maketh many friends.
— *Bible*, Authorised Version
Proverbs, Ch. 19, v. 4

9. Lay not up for yourselves
treasures upon earth, where
moth and rust doth corrupt, and
where thieves break in and steal.
— *Bible*, Authorised Version
St Matthew, Ch. 6, v. 19

10. For where your treasure is,
there will your heart be also.
— *Bible*, Authorised Version
Ibid., v. 21

11. Ye cannot serve God and
mammon.
— *Bible*, Authorised Version
Ibid., v. 24

12. For what is a man profited, if he
shall gain the whole world, and
lose his own soul?
— *Bible*, Authorised Version
Ibid., Ch. 16, v. 26

13. It is easier for a camel to go
through the eye of a needle,
than for a rich man to enter into
the kingdom of God.
— *Bible*, Authorised Version
Ibid., Ch. 19, v. 24

14. If we command our wealth, we
shall be rich and free: if our
wealth commands us, we are
poor indeed.
— Edmund Burke (1729-97)
'Letters on a Regicide
Peace', 1. *Works of Edmund
Burke*, 1877, p. 159

15. For as wealth is power, so all
power will infallibly draw
wealth to itself by some means
or other.
— Edmund Burke (1729-97)
Speech in the House of
Commons, 11 February
1780

16. Wealth . . . per se, I never too
much valued, and my acquaintance with its possessors has by
no means increased my
veneration for it.
— Frances (Fanny) Burney
(1752-1840)
Diary, 8 December 1782,
Everyman ed., p. 86

17. There is but one right mode of
using enormous fortunes —
namely, that the possessors
from time to time during their
own lives should so administer
these as to promote the
permanent good of the
communities from which they
were gathered.
— Andrew Carnegie
(1835-1919)
'The Administration of
Wealth' in *The Gospel of
Wealth and Other Timely
Essays*, 1962, p. 30

18. [Wealth] . . . these sources of
human welfare which are

material, transferable and
limited in quantity.
- John Bates Clark
(1847-1938)
The Distribution of Wealth,
1899, Ch. I, p. 1

19. That mankind as a whole shall
become richer does not, of
necessity, involve an increase in
human welfare.
- John Bates Clark
(1847-1938)
The Philosophy of Wealth,
1886, Ch. VII, p. 107

20. The rich are more envied by
those who have a little, than by
those who have nothing.
- Reverend C.C. Colton
(1780-1832)
Lacon, 1845, Vol. I,
CLXXXI

21. The wealth of all nations arises
from the labour and industry of
the people.
- Charles d'Avenant
(1656-1714)
*Discourses on the Public
Revenues and on the Trade
of England*, 1698, in *Works*,
ed. Whitworth, republished
1967, Vol. I, p. 138

22. Riches, *n*. The savings of many
in the hands of one.
- Eugene V. Debs (1855-1926)
Quoted by Ambrose Bierce,
The Devil's Dictionary

23. The art of getting rich consists
not in industry, much less in
saving, but in a better order, in
timeliness, in being at the right
spot.

- Ralph Waldo Emerson
(1803-82)
'Wealth', *The Conduct of
Life*, 1860

24. No rich man is ugly.
- Zsa Zsa Gabor
Quoted by John Brain,
Sunday Times, 26 October
1975

25. Wealth is not without its
advantages and the case to the
contrary, although it has often
been made, has never proved
widely persuasive.
- J.K. Galbraith
The Affluent Society, 1958,
Ch. 1

26. Wealth can be accumulated but
to a slight degree, and . . .
communities really live, as the
vast majority of individuals live,
from hand to mouth.
- Henry George (1839-97)
Progress and Poverty, Bk. II,
Ch. IV

27. Ill fares the land, to hastening
ills a prey,
Where wealth accumulates, and
men decay.
- Oliver Goldsmith (1728-74)
The Deserted Village

28. His best riches, ignorance of
wealth.
- Oliver Goldsmith (1728-74)
Ibid.

29. Where wealth and freedom
reign, contentment fails,
And honour sinks where
commerce long prevails.
- Oliver Goldsmith (1728-74)

The Traveller

30. The persons who compose the
    Independent classes are
    Dependent upon two things:
    first, upon the *industry* of their
    fellow creatures; second, upon
    injustice which enables them
    to command it.
    — John Gray (1799-1883)
       *Lecture on Human
       Happiness*, 1825

31. *Caeteris paribus*, he who is rich
    in a civilised society, must be
    happier than he who is poor.
    — Samuel Johnson (1709-84)
       Boswell's Life of Johnson,
       20 July 1763

32. It is wonderful to think how
    men of very large estates not
    only spend their yearly income,
    but are often actually in want
    of money.
    — Samuel Johnson (1709-84)
       Ibid., 10 April 1778

33. The insolence of wealth will
    creep out.
    — Samuel Johnson (1709-84)
       Ibid., 18 April 1778

34. He who has money to spare, has
    it always in his power to benefit
    others; and of such power a
    good man must always be
    desirous.
    — Samuel Johnson (1709-84)
       Letter to Boswell, 3 June
       1782

35. It is better that a man should
    tyrannise over his bank balance
    than over his fellow-citizens.
    — John Maynard Keynes

(1883-1946)
*The General Theory of
Employment Interest and
Money*, Bk. VI, Ch. 24,
p. 374

36. Wealth may . . . be defined as
    consisting of all potentially
    exchangeable means of
    satisfying human needs.
    — John Neville Keynes
       (1852-1949)
       *The Scope and Method of
       Political Economy*, 4th ed.,
       1917, Ch. III, p. 95

37. Wherever there is excessive
    wealth, there is also in the train
    of it excessive poverty; as where
    the sun is brightest the shade is
    deepest.
    — Walter Savage Landor
       (1775-1864)
       'Aristoteles and Callisthenes',
       Imaginary Conversations

38. Hunger and thirst were the first
    forms of the desire of wealth.
    — Thomas Edward Cliffe
       Leslie (1826-82)
       *Essays in Political and Moral
       Philosophy*, 1879, XIV,
       p. 220

39. Affluence means influence.
    — Jack London (1876-1916)
       Attributed

40. Excess of wealth is the cause of
    covetousness.
    — Christopher Marlowe
       (1564-93)
       The Jew of Malta, Act I,
       Sc. 2

41. Wealth . . . includes all those

things, external to a man, which (i) belong to him, and do not belong equally to his neighbours, and therefore are distinctly his; and which (ii) are directly capable of a money measure, − a measure that represents on the one side the efforts and sacrifices by which they have been called into existence, and, on the other, the wants which they satisfy.
− Alfred Marshall (1842-1924)
  Principles of Economics,
  8th ed., Bk. II, Ch. II, 2,
  p. 57

42. The growth of wealth involves in general a deliberate waiting for a pleasure which a person has (rightly or wrongly) the power of commanding in the immediate present, and that his willingness so to wait depends on his habit of vividly realizing the future and providing for it.
    − Alfred Marshall (1842-1924)
      Ibid., Bk. IV, Ch. VII, 9,
      p. 234

43. Men do not desire to be *rich*, but to be richer than other men.
    − John Stuart Mill (1806-73)
      Posthumous Essay on Social Freedom, *Oxford and Cambridge Review*,
      January 1907

44. People do not grow rich by keeping their money unused . . . they must be willing to spend in order to gain.
    − John Stuart Mill (1806-73)
      Principles of Political Economy, ed. Ashley,

'Preliminary Remarks', p. 3

45. Wealth . . . may be defined, all useful or agreeable things which possess exchangeable value.
    − John Stuart Mill (1806-73)
      Ibid., p. 9

46. God shows his contempt for wealth by the kind of person he selects to receive it.
    − Austin O'Malley
      (1858-1932)
      Quoted in Esar and Bentley,
      The Treasury of Humorous Quotations

47. Millionaires are still alive and kicking, and it takes a good deal of ignorance to assert the opposite.
    − Jan Pen
      Income Distribution, 1971,
      Ch. I, 1

48. According to the Left, rich people are poor people with money.
    − Jan Pen
      Ibid., Ch. VII, 1

49. Labour is the father and active principle of wealth, as lands are the mother.
    − Sir William Petty (1623-87)
      'A Treatise of Taxes and Contributions', 1662, in
      The Economic Writings of Sir William Petty, ed. Hull,
      Vol. I, p. 68

50. A great fortune, in the hands of a fool is a great misfortune.
    − Proverb, in Thomas Fuller,
      Gnomologia, 1732, 194

51. God help the rich; the poor
    can beg.
    – Proverb, ibid., 1675

52. Moderate riches will carry you;
    if you have more, you must
    carry them.
    – Proverb, ibid., 3427

53. Not possession, but use is the
    only riches.
    – Proverb, ibid., 3681

54. Prosperity has everything
    cheap.
    – Proverb, ibid., 3964

55. Rich men have no faults.
    – Proverb, ibid., 4036

56. Rich men long to be richer.
    – Proverb, ibid., 4038

57. Riches are but the baggage of
    fortune.
    – Proverb, ibid., 4042

58. Riches serve a wise man, but
    command a fool.
    – Proverb, ibid., 4047

59. Riches rather enlarge than
    satisfy appetites.
    – Proverb, ibid., 4048

60. The rich follow wealth; and the
    poor the rich.
    – Proverb, ibid., 4733

61. A full cup must be carried
    steadily.
    – English proverb

62. As individuals seem generally to
    grow rich by grasping a larger
    and larger portion of the wealth
    already in existence, nations do
    so by the production of wealth
    that did not previously exist.
    The two processes differ in this,
    that the one is an *acquisition*,
    the other a *creation*.
    – John Rae (1796-1872)
      *The Sociological Theory of
      Capital*, Article VIII, p. 383

63. In reality the 'reward' of owning
    wealth is owning wealth.
    – Joan Robinson
      Economic Heresies, 1971,
      Ch. 3, p. 28, footnote

64. A growth in wealth is not at all
    the same thing as reducing
    poverty.
    – Joan Robinson
      'The Second Crisis of
      Economic Theory',
      American Economic Review,
      May 1972, p. 7

65. Be not concerned if thou findest
    thyself in possession of
    unexpected wealth; Allah will
    provide an unexpected use for it.
    – James Jeffrey Roche
      (1847-1908)
      Quoted in Esar and Bentley,
      *The Treasury of Humorous
      Quotations*

66. It is an unfortunate human
    failing that a full pocket book
    often groans more loudly than
    an empty stomach.
    – Franklin D. Roosevelt
      (1882-1945)
      Speech, 1940

67. A great fortune is a great slavery.
    – Seneca (4 B.C.-65 A.D.)
      Attributed

68. Have more than thou showest,
    Speak less than thou knowest,
    Lend less than thou owest.
    – William Shakespeare
      (1564-1616)
      King Lear, Act I, Sc. IV

69. There is some ill a-brewing
        towards my rest,
    For I did dream of money-bags
        tonight.
    – William Shakespeare
      (1564-1616)
      Merchant of Venice, Act II,
      Sc. V

70. I am a Millionaire. That is my
    religion.
    – George Bernard Shaw
      (1856-1950)
      Major Barbara, Act II

71. In an ugly and unhappy world
    the richest man can purchase
    nothing but ugliness and
    unhappiness.
    – George Bernard Shaw
      (1856-1950)
      Maxims for Revolutionists

72. The man with toothache thinks
    everyone happy whose teeth are
    sound. The poverty stricken
    man makes the same mistake
    about the rich man.
    – George Bernard Shaw
      (1856-1950)
      Ibid.

73. Money is worth nothing to the
    man who has more than enough.
    – George Bernard Shaw
      (1856-1950)
      'Socialism for Millionaires',
      Contemporary Review,
      February 1896

74. Wealth is a power usurped by
    the few, to compel the many to
    labour for their benefit.
    – Percy Bysshe Shelley
      (1792-1822)
      Attributed

75. Every man is rich or poor
    according to the degree in
    which he can afford to enjoy
    the necessaries, conveniences,
    and amusements of human life.
    – Adam Smith (1723-90)
      Wealth of Nations, ed.
      Cannan, Vol. I, Bk. I, Ch. V,
      p. 32

76. It would be too ridiculous to go
    about seriously to prove, that
    wealth does not consist in
    money, or in gold and silver;
    but in what money purchases,
    and is valuable only for
    purchasing.
    – Adam Smith (1723-90)
      Ibid., Bk. IV,
      Ch. I, p. 404

77. In all well-instituted common-
    wealths, care has been taken to
    limit men's possessions; which is
    done for many reasons, and,
    among the rest, for one which,
    perhaps, is not often considered,
    that when bounds are set to
    men's desires, after they have
    acquired as much as the laws
    will permit them, their private
    interest is at an end, and they
    have nothing to do but to take
    care of the public.
    – Jonathan Swift (1667-1745)
      *Thoughts on Various
      Subjects*, 1706

78. A society is rich when material

goods, including capital, are
cheap, and human beings dear.
- R.H. Tawney (1880-1962)
  The Acquisitive Society,
  1921

79. In order to stand well in the
    eyes of the community, it is
    necessary to come up to a
    certain, somewhat indefinite,
    conventional standard of
    wealth.
    - Thorstein Veblen
      (1857-1929)
      *The Theory of the Leisure
      Class*, Ch. II

80. In order to gain and to hold the
    esteem of men it is not
    sufficient merely to possess
    wealth or power. The wealth or
    power must be put in evidence,
    for esteem is awarded only on
    evidence.
    - Thorstein Veblen
      (1857-1929)
      Ibid., Ch. III

81. I don't 'old with Wealth. What is
    Wealth? Labour robbed out of
    the poor.
    - H.G. Wells (1866-1946)
      Kipps, Bk. II, Ch. 4

82. Wealth is that, and that only,
    whereby a man may be
    benefited.
    - Xenophon
      (c.440-c.355 B.C.)
      The Economist, trans.
      Dakyns, Ch. I

133. WORK

1. Work is the price you pay for

money.
- Anonymous

2. All true work is religion.
   - Thomas Carlyle (1795-1881)
     Past and Present, 1843,
     Bk. III, Ch. XII

3. Workers are distinct from work.
   For the purpose of a study of
   distribution they are related to
   it as capitalists are related to
   capital. They own it, and therefore they justly claim its
   products.
   - John Bates Clark
     (1847-1938)
     'Distribution as Determined
     by a Law of Rent', *Quarterly
     Journal of Economics*,
     April 1891, p. 302

4. Naturally, the workers are
   perfectly free; the manufacturer
   does not force them to take his
   materials and his cards, but he
   says to them . . . 'If you don't
   like to be frizzled in my frying-
   pan, you can take a walk into
   the fire'.
   - Frederick Engels (1820-95)
     *The Condition of the
     Working Class in England in
     1844*, 1892, Ch. VII,
     pp. 197-8

5. It was truly a splendid structure,
   and Yossarian throbbed with a
   mighty sense of accomplishment
   each time he gazed at it and
   reflected that none of the work
   that had gone into it was his.
   - Joseph Heller
     Catch-22, Ch. 2

6. Nobody works as hard for his

money as the man who marries it.

— Frank McKinney Hubbard
(1868-1930)
Quoted in Esar and Bentley,
The Treasury of Humorous Quotations

7. I like work: it fascinates me. I can sit and look at it for hours. I love to keep it by me: the idea of getting rid of it nearly breaks my heart.
— Jerome K. Jerome
(1859-1927)
Three Men in a Boat, 1899,
Ch. 15

8. It is not always possible to graduate work to the worker's liking; in some businesses a man who insisted on working only a few hours a day would soon have no work to do.
— W. Stanley Jevons (1835-82)
Theory of Political Economy,
4th ed., Ch. V, p. 180

9. Work is struggle.
— Mao Tse-tung (1893-1976)
Quotations from Chairman Mao Tse-tung, 1976, p. 200

10. The first effect of the shortening of the working day results from the self-evident law, that the efficiency of labour-power is in an inverse ratio to the duration of its expenditure.
— Karl Marx (1818-83)
Capital, Vol. I, Pt. IV,
Ch. XV, 3

11. When a potter grows rich, will he go on with his trade? Does he not become idle and careless,

and consequently a worse potter? And equally, if he is too poor to provide himself with tools and other things he needs for his craft, his work will be worse, and he will not make such good craftsmen of his sons and apprentices. So work and workmen suffer from both causes, poverty and riches as well.
— Plato (c.428-347 B.C.)
The Republic, trans.
Cornford, Bk. IV, Ch. XI

12. To work is not necessarily to produce anything.
— Pierre-Joseph Proudhon
(1809-65)
Attributed

13. I am persuaded that Britain's present economic difficulties have a great deal to do with work-motivation problems that lie outside the economics of rewards and punishments, and one reason why economists seem to have so little to contribute to this area is the neglect in traditional economic theory of this whole issue of commitment and the social revelations surrounding it.
— Amartya Sen
'Rational Fools: A Critique of the Behavioural Foundations of Economic Theory', in Hahn and Hollis (ed.), *Philosophy and Economic Theory*

14. Work banishes those three great evils, boredom, vice and poverty.
— Voltaire (1694-1778)
Candide, Ch. XXX

15. When a man says he wants to
     work, what he means is that he
     wants wages.
     — Richard Whately
        (1787-1863)
        Quoted by Henry Sidgewick,
        *Principles of Political
        Economy*

16. Work is the curse of the
     drinking classes.
     — Oscar Wilde (1854-1900)
        In H. Pearson, *Life of
        Oscar Wilde*, Ch. 12

INDEX OF KEY WORDS

This index is arranged alphabetically, both for the key words and for the entries following each key work. Each entry gives part of the quotation to indicate the context and the key word itself is then abbreviated. The reference consists of two numbers, the first of which indicates the topic and the second the quotation. For example, one entry under 'Parrot' reads 'You can make even a p. into a learned political economist 40.4'. This refers to the 4th quotation appearing under the 40th topic, which is 'Economists'. The numbers and titles of the topics appear at the top of the pages.

Employed: fit to be e. 78.8;
innocently e. . . . in getting
money. 86.54; whilst luxury e. a
million of the poor 4.8
Employer: where the sole e. is the
state 58.37
Employers: few e. without souls
130.7; trusted to the discretion
of e. 78.8
Employment: Capitalism with near-
full e. 14.28; continual motive to
their e. 86.80; fear of losing their
e. 83.13; few men without e.
130.7; spiral of rising prices under
full e. 65.4; various candidates for
e. 103.4
Employments: advantages and
disadvantages of the different e.
130.36; net advantageousness of
different e. 130.6
Emulation: propensity for e. 23.15
Encouragement: Consumption never
needs e. 23.8
End: If all economists were laid e. to
e. 40.32
Ends: Economics is not concerned at
all with any e. as such 39.76;
relationship between e. and scarce
means 39.75
Enlightened: e. self-interest 110.6
Enterprise: bubbles on a steady
stream of e. 116.3; railways are a
concern which should never be left
to private e. 25.5; rising prices
acts as a stimulus to e. 65.18; to
enable private e. to suck at the
teats of the state. 92.1
Enterprises: contains neither e. nor
money. 83.5
Entrepreneur: earnings of an e.
sometimes represent nothing but
the spoilation of the workmen.
97.15
Entrepreneurs: power which belongs
to e. 14.16; system of free
competition is . . . one of fooling
e. 20.15; to e. what the
co-ordinating function creates.
20.4
Entrepreneurship: Normal profits are
simply the supply price of e. 97.14

Envied: rich are more e. 132.20
Environment: excessive concern with
the e. 59.1; man is his own c.
39.40; reshaping our physical e.
59.6
Epochs: different economical e.
39.60
Equal: e. imposition of taxes 122.20;
e. quantity of property needs
no special justification 99.4; e.
rationing 104.2; principle of e.
sacrifice. 122.14
Equalise: to e. the utility of the final
increments 128.4
Equality: e. is most suitable to
human nature 34.5; e. would be
wrong. 99.8; In politics, e. 39.25;
law, in its majestic e. 78.4; more
nearly the actual proportion
approaches to e. 60.1; never yet
contrived a system of taxation
that would operate with perfect e.
122.23; sort of rough e. 83.12;
tending to e. 130.36; where goals
of efficiency, freedom of choice,
and e. conflict. 39.87
Equally: If all property were to be e.
divided 99.3
Equilibrium: can no more define e.
in international trade 124.7;
conformity with a moving e.
39.18; e. of value in society
120.2; position of stable e.
120.7
Esteem: e. is awarded only on
evidence. 132.80; Property . . .
becomes the conventional basis of
e. 99.26
Ethic: Protestant e. 14.24
Ethics: absence of the sunlight of e.
38.32
Europe: glory of E. is extinguished
for ever. 40.6
Events: Income is a series of e. 63.2
Everything: e. depends on e. else
39.2
Evil: Government . . . a necessary e.
58.25; labour is an e. 75.18; love
of money the root of all e.
86.16; Money is the fruit of e.
86.32; poverty . . . a great e.

Profits are due not to r. 97.3

Rival: intolerable competition of a foreign r. 53.2

Rivalry: competition is . . . r. in mutual service. 20.3

River: r. which runs and winds 65.7

Robbed: Wealth . . . Labour r. out of the poor. 132.81

Robber: He who spends too much is a r. 117.1

Robbery: fair exchange is no r. 49.6

Robbing: I live by r. the poor. 27.4; r. everybody else. 125.6

Rod: measuring r. of money. 39.68

Routine: agricultural class is . . . attached . . . to r. 2.1

Row: economics cannot be marked out by a r. of posts 39.14

Ruined: No nation was ever r. by trade 124.5

Rules: cannot be a collection of practical r. 39.63; r. of a club 94.6

Running: charged in accordance with r. costs 25.5

Rupee: chapter on the fall of the r. 39.92

Rural: disguised r. unemployment. 64.2

Russia: Communism will pass away from R. 19.2; in R. the coercive machinery 5.9

Sabotage: a sagacious use of s. 9.14

Sacrifice: Cost means s. 25.1; principle of equal s. 122.14

Salaried: who employ s. managers - 46.2

Salaries: remuneration by fixed s. 130.20

Sale: Advertising is a necessary consequence of s. by description. 1.1; in true commerce there is no s. 18.15

Same: ought to receive the s. wages 130.19; s. treatment of similar persons. 47.4.

Sample: s. of one 118.5

Satisfaction: Maximum economic production does not lead necessarily to maximum economic s. 96.12; position also of maximum s. 120.7

Satisfactions: economic and non-economic s. 39.14; not in a position to weigh the s. 128.5

Satisfied: He is well paid that is well s. 90.7

Satisfies: Nothing s. the man 4.2

Save: if parsimony did not s. and store up 13.19

Saved: Capital is s. from profits 13.13; Everything which is produced is consumed; both what is s. and what is said to be spent 23.9

Savings: National Debt represents the s. of the poorer classes 88.3; s. of many in the hands of one. 132.22; Unless . . . s. are exempted from income tax 122.30

Scarce: Industry does nothing but produce s. things 64.5; relationship between ends and s. means which have alternative uses. 39.75; Wealth . . . is s. 132.7

Scarcity: No complaint . . . is more common than that of a s. of money. 86.112; plenty or s. of any particular thing 95.22; When there is a real s. 95.20

Science: dismal s. 39.15; great tragedy of s. 38.11; In . . . s. authority has ever been the great opponent of truth. 38.13; maxim of s. 38.2; Not a gay s. 39.15; positive s. 38.15; s. of business 39.6

Sciolists: opportunity which it gave to s. 40.18

Scissors: upper or the under blade of a pair of s. 120.5

Scotland: grapes can be raised in S. 101.3

Security: give a man s. that he may reap 77.6; hurt your credit by offering too much s. 26.9; intends only his own s. 83.14; sense of s. which property gives 99.18; will prefer freedom to s. 8.6

Sedition: s. and even anarchy are beneficial 38.13

Self: every agent is actuated only by
s.-interest. 39.21; granite of s.
interest 114.4; mechanics of
utility and s.-interest 39.36

Selfish: I am a s. man 110.3; s.,
huckstering trade. 124.4; s.
spirit of commerce 18.8

Selfishness: used their power in the
interest of their own s. 17.14

Self-sufficing: no individual is s.
58.28

Seller: Every s. of goods is a buyer
of money 86.70

Sellers: price . . . is formed by means
of a certain struggle which takes
place between the buyers and the
s. 95.19

Selling: Unfair competition: s.
cheaper 20.12

Sense: Money is like a sixth s. 86.66;
Money speaks s. 86.9

Sentimentalist: s. . . . is a man who
sees an absurd value in everything
95.24

Serf: s. did not starve. 72.2

Servant: Money is a good s. 86.87

Sex: dummy for s. 36.5

Shakespeare: Government could
print a good edition of S.'s works
58.21

Share: contented with his s. 47.7

Shareholders: directors . . . are
always s. 58.24; mass of inert s.
46.2

Sharing: s. the fruits of human
productive power 125.10

Shelf: Bare s. rationing 104.1

Shilling: Better give a s. 79.2; s. is
worth more to a man when he is
poor 34.21; To fork out his
copper and pocket your s. 19.1

Shillings: Whenever you save five
s. 107.4

Shirt: from s.-sleeves to s.-sleeves.
17.4

Shoddy: Up goes the price of s. 57.4

Shortening: effect of the s. of the
working day 133.10

Silver: does not warm himself with s.
86.7; gold and s. are but
commodities 124.1

Similar: same treatment of s. persons.
47.4

Simple: doctrines of economics are
not s. 39.55

Simplify: knowing how to s. 38.5

Sin: inflation is like s. 65.19

Skill: forms of personal excellence,
superiority, s. . . . constitute
natural monopolies 87.19; greater
part of the s. 35.8

Skilled: S. labour 75.16

Slave: man in debt is so far a s.
29.4; would have made him a s.
122.7

Slavery: great fortune is a great s.
132.67; is to institute s. 77.4

Slaves: s. of some defunct economist.
40.13

Slum: nineteenth-century London s.
39.94

Slumps: Booms and s. 10.5

Small: infinitely s. amount of
commodity 48.1

Smith: depressing to go back to
Adam S. 39.11; genius of Adam
S. 38.32

Snow: Money is like s. 86.8

Social: dishonourable to the whole s.
body 94.28; For the s. sciences
man is his own environment.
39.40; general theory of s. affairs.
39.23; main motive of economic
study is to help s. improvement.
39.67; meeting s. objectives
39.19; phenomena of s. industry.
20.7; Political economy is
inseparably intertwined with
many of the branches of s.
philosophy. 39.64; s. hygiene of
full employment. 44.5; Trade is a
s. act. 124.12

Socialisation: s. of labour 14.14

Socialism: planning is the heart and
core of genuine s. 91.1; victory of
s. is possible 14.10

Socialist: Communist is a s. 19.3;
principle of economy is one of
the basic principles of s.
economies. 41.6; s. idea that
making profits is a vice. 97.2

Socialists: common error of s. 20.18

pressure of s. and demand 83.15; grand concern is to increase s. 23.7; S. determines final degree of utility 129.8; which finds the secret of the universe in s. and demand 39.15

Surplus: consumer's s. 23.6; definite 's.' problem 2.2; production of s.-value 14.13

Swerve: swore to move without a s. 36.7

Talent: do not have equal t. 47.9

Tariffs: working of t. 53.3

Tastes: Their t. may not be the same. 3.5

Tax: alteration of the coinage . . . a t. 65.24; lottery . . . is properly a t. 55.3

Taxation: creation of paper money . . . a species of indirect t. 86.12; Monopoly . . . is the t. of the industrious 87.8; necessity of t. 58.29; right of private t. 77.12

Taxes: best of all t. 58.30; t. to support a war. 131.2

Taxing: By t. exports 121.4

Taxpayers: members of a government are invariably t. 58.24

Teachers: almost complete absorption of the younger t. 40.7

Teaching: Economists . . . remain largely a t. order. 40.29

Technological: Economists are t. radicals. 40.1; usufruct of the community's t. knowledge 13.21

Telescopic: if their t. faculty were not perverted. 54.9

Tempestuous: if in t. seasons 54.6

Tenant: Compensation for improvements will not benefit the t. 105.12; Neither a landlord nor a t. be. 105.13

Tendencies: best statement of economic t. 39.50; Political economy does not deal with particular facts but with general t. 39.81; statement of economic t. 38.27

Terms: different meanings in which the same t. have been used 40.16

Testing: t. of hypotheses 36.3

Textbooks: Normality is a fiction of economic t. 39.78

Theft: Property is t. 99.17

Theorists: t. give the impression 48.8

Theory: believe myself to be writing a book on economic t. 73.7; communication between abstract t. and concrete application. 39.95; essence of progress in t. 21.2; t. . . . unification that constitutes econometrics. 36.1; to judge the relevance of an economic t. 85.2; What used to be called the quantity t. of money 86.39

Thermometer: interest on money is the t. 69.29

Thieves: t. break in and steal. 132.9

Thorns: crown of t. 57.1

Thought: origin of economic t. 39.29

Threadneedle Street: the Old Lady of T. 5.5

Three: simplicity of the t. per cents. 69.12

Thrift: recommend t. to the poor 94.38; T. should be the guiding principle 102.3; whatever may be happening to t. 45.3

Time: every business transaction into which t. enters. 9.6

Timeliness: art of getting rich consists . . . in t. 132.23

Times: Can anybody remember when the t. were not hard 100.2

Toil: lightened the day's t. 70.3; real price . . . is the t. and trouble 95.13; severe or repulsive t. 130.39

Tool: there are t.-makers and t.-users. 40.23

Tools: box of t. 40.27; engaged in forging t. 36.8

Toothache: a man with t. 132.72

Trade: all the labourers in a particular t. and all capitalists in that t. 87.3; custom also has a considerable share in determining the profits of t. 97.8; Every man to his t. 35.6; In a free t. an effectual combination cannot be established

whatever may be happening to thrift 45.3; impediment to the increase of public w. 47.11; natural progress of England towards w. 58.33; Nobody who has w. to distribute 34.19; opportunity of men of very large w. 34.7; property . . . has powerfully contributed to make w. 99.10; Rent . . . is never a cause of w. 105.21; shares can seriously damage your w. 112.2; should always divide his w. into three parts 86.3; So long as all the increased w. . . . goes but to build up great fortunes 98.3; That w. consists in money . . . is a popular notion 86.111; w. can go up to the hill top 94.3; W. depends upon commerce 18.10; w. . . . is nothing but the maintenance, conveniences and superfluities of life. 77.1; W. of Nations 114.2; w. that . . . enters into the collective possessions of modern peoples 88.4; What does bring happiness; poverty and w. have both failed 60.2

Welfare: attention to the aesthetic will increase economic w. 56.7; chief sources of social w. 59.6; Economic w. 39.68; leads to an improvement in social w. 109.1; paradox of the w. state 58.14 richer does not, of necessity, involve an increase in human w. 132.19; This part of w. may be called economic w. 86.82; very poor measure of w. 56.1

Wheel: great w. of circulation 86.108
Widow: w. is gathering nettles 105.2
Wines: law to prohibit the importation of all foreign w. 101.3
Work: put a man out of w. for a day 107.4; safeguarding bad w. 125.9;

same old hard w. 43.2; thoroughness of their application to w. 62.3; unable to find w. 126.2; w. expands so as to fill the time available 8.8; w. is accomplished by those employees 8.12; What is the use of money if you have to w. for it? 86.107
Worker: struggle between capitalist and w. 130.16
Workers: alliances between w. and capitalists 125.6; independence of the w. 39.71; W. are distinct from work 133.3; w. spend what they get 117.5
Working: Capitalists and proprietors do no more than give the w. man 15.1; every effort of the w. classes 39.27; necessity of w. 17.14; revolt of the w. class 14.14; W. men of all countries, unite! 17.13
Workman: competitor of the w. 80.4; discipline which is exercised over a w. 83.13; fails to give to the w. sufficient compensation for his toil. 97.15
Workmen: bad w. ought to receive the same wages 130.19; find the w. more active 130.34
Works: duty of erecting and maintaining certain public w. 103.1; Public w. even of doubtful utility 102.2; w. but half so much 130.24
World: have a w. to win 17.13
Worth: never know the w. of water, till the well is dry. 128.8

Young: seldom the case with y. men 118.12; y. people choose their professions 106.4
Youth: merchant only thrives . . . by the pride, wantonness and debauchery of y. 97.10

INDEX OF AUTHORS AND SOURCES

Like the key word index, the entries in this index refer not to pages but to individual quotations. Each reference contains two numbers, the first of which indicates the number of the topic and the second the actual quotation.

241

Index of Authors and Sources

North, Sir Dudley 4.9; 22.5; 86.77; 110.9; 124.17; 124.18

Ohlin, Bertil 71.8
O'Malley, Austin 132.46
Oresme, Nicholas 65.23; 65.24; 69.25; 86.78
Orwell, George. Pen name of Eric Arthur Blair 47.14; 115.19
Oscar II, King of Sweden 41.8
Owen, Robert 120.8

Paine, Thomas 58.25; 58.26; 88.5
Pantaleoni, Maffeo 49.5; 75.18; 130.23
Pareto, Vilfredo 38.30; 95.10; 96.10; 110.10; 128.7
Parker, R.H. 105.13
Parkinson, C. Northcote 8.8; 8.9; 8.10
Pen, Jan 34.12; 132.47; 132.48
Pepys, Samuel 86.79
Peter, Laurence J. 8.11; 8.12
Petty, Sir William 27.3; 35.2; 35.3; 44.7; 55.3; 65.25; 65.26; 69.26; 69.27; 70.4; 72.3; 86.80; 86.81; 87.9; 93.12; 95.11; 105.14; 122.34; 122.35; 122.36; 130.24; 132.49
Phelps Brown, E.H. 37.13; 39.66; 40.22
Pigou, A.C. 10.7; 39.67; 39.68; 39.69; 39.70; 40.23; 50.2; 54.9; 56.5; 58.27; 85.10; 86.82
Pinero, Sir Arthur Wing 51.5
Plato 35.4; 35.5; 58.28; 133.11
Playfair, William 118.12
Postan, M.M. 40.24
Pound, Ezra 37.14
Proudhon, Pierre-Joseph 19.13; 19.14; 19.15; 39.71; 47.15; 99.17; 105.15
Proverbs 6.5; 6.6. 9.9; 9.10; 9.11; 9.12; 12.3; 12.4; 12.5; 16.4; 16.5; 16.6; 17.16; 26.7; 26.8; 29.7; 29.8; 29.9; 35.6; 41.9; 42.3; 49.6; 67.3; 70.5; 79.2; 79.3; 83.9; 83.10; 83.11; 86.83; 86.84; 86.85; 86.86; 86.87; 86.88; 86.89; 86.90; 86.91; 86.92; 86.93; 86.94; 86.95; 86.96;

86.97; 86.98; 86.99; 86.100; 90.3; 90.4; 90.5; 90.6; 94.21; 94.22; 94.23; 94.24; 94.25; 94.26; 94.27; 102.4; 103.2; 107.12; 110.11; 110.12; 110.13; 111.1; 116.7; 117.7; 117.8; 117.9; 124.19; 124.20; 124.21; 128.8; 132.50; 132.51; 132.52; 132.53; 132.54; 132.55; 132.56; 132.57; 132.58; 132.59; 132.60; 132.61
Publilius, Syrus 4.10
Punch 16.7
Puzo, Mario 87.10

Quesnay, François 39.72; 99.18

Rae, John 132.62
Ricardo, David 2.3; 13.13; 13.14; 23.11; 28.3; 28.4; 28.5; 30.3; 34.13; 39.73; 39.74; 40.25; 57.7; 58.29; 65.27; 77.11; 86.101; 93.13; 93.14; 93.15; 95.12; 96.11; 97.11; 97.12; 97.13; 105.16; 105.17; 105.18; 105.19; 105.20; 105.21; 105.22; 105.23; 105.24; 108.4; 120.9; 122.37; 122.38; 122.39; 122.40; 129.18; 130.25; 130.26; 131.2
Robbins, Lord 34.14; 39.75; 39.76; 48.6
Robertson, Sir Dennis H. 36.7; 38.31
Robinson, Joan 13.15; 14.17; 14.18; 20.20; 20.21; 20.22; 34.15; 39.78; 39.79; 40.26; 40.27; 40.28; 45.8; 46.2; 73.9; 81.5; 84.2; 97.14; 99.19; 107.13; 115.20; 126.7; 132.63; 132.64
Roche, James Jeffrey 132.65
Rodbertus, Johann Karl 31.3; 35.7; 99.20; 105.25; 113.2
Rogaly, J. 118.13
Rogers, Will 5.8
Roosevelt, Franklin D. 110.14; 122.41; 132.66
Röpke, Wilhelm 5.9
Roscher, Wilhelm Georg Friedrich 38.33; 39.80
Routh, Guy 40.29
Ruskin, John 18.14; 18.15; 76.6; 94.28

242